# THE REGULAR

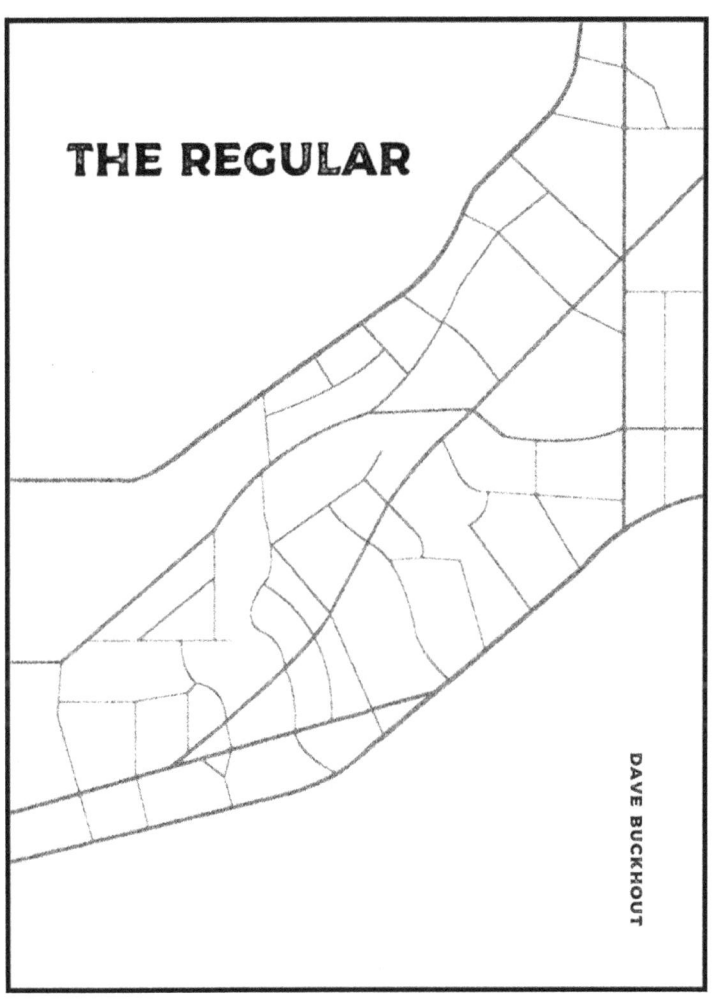

# THE REGULAR

DAVE BUCKHOUT

*atmosphere press*

A NEW DAWN BREAKS. *The haze is fine mesh gauze. Steam loiters as it would about a geyser field. It is felt, implied, seen. The magenta sphere labors as it lifts off the muddy horizon, a new day smoldering, belabored asphalt smoking like tarpits. Flaming, festering, the daylight draws a mute breath.... Eyes open on this morning, a day staunch in its mid-Summer promise; August arising, mercury aspiring, sucking mist through indolent filters of humidity. It hints at the broiler to come, the fight ahead.... Kudzu runners claim a copse of pine, curtained vines draped as organic gothic sculpture. Fields of the weed swallow parkway buffers. Once detailed in low arbor, bounded by flagstone, they have been rendered historical beneath rotting steppes of convenience-culture litter. Urban canyons fossilize the wrapper, the bottle and can. Vine fields swallow it all.... WPA era stonewalls border the nearby city avenue, mortar flaking to dust. A rain-sluiced knoll erodes fat red flats baked to cracking by the vengeful southern heat. The city sidewalks, once knit of precise hexagonal blocks—once solid, unquestioned—are now upturned by the steady ambition of a century-old catalpa, fire ants boiling up from the voids of sidewalk block.... It is here, within this roiling stew, where the city wreaths a homegrown prodigy—a wandering guru down in the haze, hunkered within its sweat-stained penumbra.*

*To one Marvin Goodspeed, this here is home.*

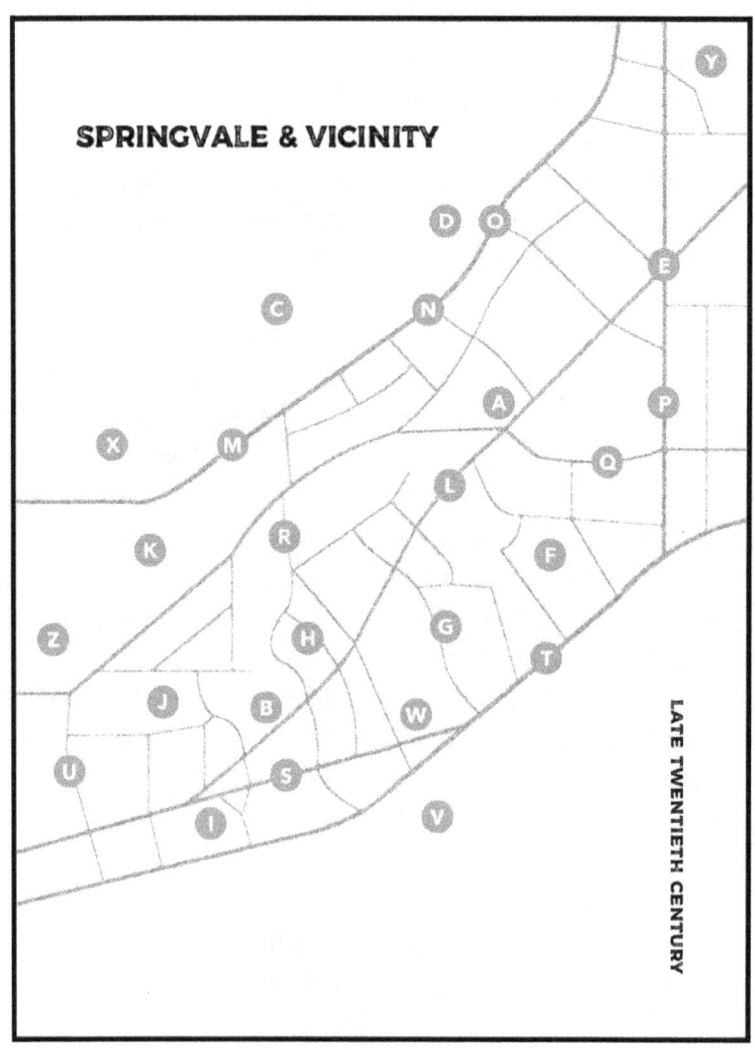

SPRINGVALE & VICINITY

LATE TWENTIETH CENTURY

A · The Asa Inman

B · The Woodruff House

C · The Parkway Connector

D · D.O.T. Land (formerly Auburn Hills)

E · The Points

F · The Field Parks

G · The Ashlands / Alta Terrace

H · Waverly Park

I · Delta Point Park

J · The Druid Heights

K · The Long Acres

L · Austin Avenue

M · Highland Avenue

N · Washita / Highland

O · Colquitt / Highland

P · DeKalb Avenue

Q · Euclid Avenue

R · Elizabeth Street

S · Edgewood Avenue

T · Memorial Avenue

U · Dixie Way

V · South Atlantic Railroad

W · The Carriage House

X · Bremen Steel Yards

Y · Candler Hills

Z · Old Fifth Ward

*What strange habitations does genius choose among men* . Walter Hines Page

NEW SOUTH SUBTERRANEAN

HE SHIFTS IN HIS seat atop bar stool, a lean-to-sinewy build weighed down by an *epic* hangover. He locks a gaze on his nemesis and stews. A nonchalant simmer boils up into something resembling a care, in the presence of one who has done him wrong.

"Damn you," he mutters, upgrading his stare to a glare in glowering at a fifth of bourbon, one splash above empty.

"Had you dead-to-rights, fucker. Dead. To. Rights."

He wants to pour its remains in a urinal and piss on it. It is a hate that runs deep, sinew-deep; but is in vain. There is no revenge to be had here, the beguiling spirit insured from retribution. It is the devil's own.

"You....have not conquered me," he stutters, despite proof to the contrary. For our man ain't lookin' so hot. And yet beneath the pallid guise, he is flush with a smoldering inner resolve, is somehow strengthened by the futility of this fight. It is strange, dutiful. His stare projects a wish to shatter bottle glass, the nemesis behind the bar in line with its brethren. Sure of itself, he would swear it is mocking him. A yawning answers his threats. "I just do what I do.

It's just my nature, s'all."

"Damn you," he steams, projecting the spirit's mocking of his empty attempt to create of it a *dead soldier*, the emptied portion of that bottle having signed, sealed, delivered a sidewalk awakening just that morning. A soupy haze floats his seething.

"Damn you!"

"Marv, what in the hell ya gettin' so hot about?" Howard, barkeep / proprietor, having watched the mild madness from afar.

"Nothing, not talking to you, H; just wishing ill will on that bottle 'a bourbon did me in last night. Swear on a stack it's tauntin' me."

"Talking bottles? Eustace rubbin' off on ya? I told ya to take it eeeeaasy last night, Marv," Howard punctuating the replay of his petition with outstretched hands, the authoritative gesture of *trust me on this one*. "But then ya ain't ever been one to listen to my reason."

"I know it. I know it. You know how I get when the parasites invade, H. Don't care if the dude is from the alt-weekly or 20-fucking-20, gets me hot, gets me to redoubling my efforts, fightin' em because they're down here, in here."

"A true warrior. Ya even make it home last night?"

"Make my home where I lie, H." Goodspeed stretches out his arms, an all-encompassing span. "It's all home to me."

"How convenient. Another'n?"

"You bet."

Howard slides out a second screwdriver, Marvin Goodspeed's late-morning power drink of choice. A desert thirst best describes his sucking it down. The tall cool refreshment of orange juice hides vodka's tooth. He sets the empty glass on the bar top, exhales contentment; the drink's mojo a timeless folk remedy. *Freedom from pain guaranteed.* A grin lights his vacant gaze, recollections wandering the haze soup....

The sun's cellular split from the horizon had reared up red just that morning, Goodspeed having awoken to the steaming blur on the sidewalk where he'd passed out. One could have expected disorientation / discombobulation. ("What the....shit, really?") But it was not the first time, and it will not be the last. The routine of it all had made of it just another morning, the bloodshot orb having pried open slits—Goodspeed's first glimpse of this new day.

"Well, up 'n at 'em," having sold himself on motivation / conviction despite the pile-on of defeats; having worked his way to his feet, having moved beyond the stonewall running the length of city avenue and puking. Only the strict regimen of devotion, dedication, and fidelity could fuel such an instinct to persist, a long foggy walk having found him here in time for opening. 11 a.m. He doesn't even own a watch, just the timeless hallowed instinct of routine.

"Boy howdy, that there's the stuff." Goodspeed savors the tingle of restorative juices penetrating deep. "That there'll restore you some faith in a hapless world."

"Take it where ya can get it, Marv."

"A slice of heaven on earth, tell you what." Goodspeed and his screwdriver: perfect harmony, *freedom in a glass.* "How 'bout some joyful noise there, H?"

"Now you're talking, son. FM radio or the compact-disc jukebox?" Howard, very proud of his most recent (if not so technologically recent) entertainment upgrade.

"Don't take to music shoved down my neck with a side of the bastards' ads."

"Right. Of course. Well, let's see. Got Loretta queue'd up in the jukebox."

"That'll do, H. That will do."

Loretta Lynn lifts his dour day. Goodspeed's grin draws a drawl. He is content here in this place. It is his place.... Welcome all, to the *Asa Inman Blue Ribbon Buffet*. Stale and stoned, it is a living apparition, its walls sealed in a film faded the color of old newspaper. One could accept Sputnik or TET as the day's headlines, the bytes of world events mired in bar side inertia. For time (we will find) is rendered irrelevant in here, relegated to just another amongst the calcified patrons drowning a thirst or a doldrum. It is a *Victory!* of sorts, regulars giving time the slip, if only for an afternoon or an evening. In here, the ubiquity of the daily grind is reduced to reviled curiosity. In here, the good regulars are free from the chattel-like shadow of corporate slavery, of manipulative marketing, of the whining mosquitoes of moral judgment and the bald-faced lies of political hacks. In here, *freedom* reigns. This is a place where regulars can gather within environs that require no explanation, no interpretation. It is what it *is* and has been that way since its start as a clandestine stop for the bootlegging-trippers back in the '20s. Hence the name; best not to advertise your sinful wares back when the *Drys* held sway.

Our man's mood lightens, his rumpled brow smoothing. Loretta and vodka, works every time. He has reconciled with his near-empty tormentor, it just doing what it does. The truce will hold, for now. But so personal a slight is long remembered. Slow to anger, once burned our man's pride tends to smolder. *A wrong lives long.*

Goodspeed looks beyond the nemesis and its brethren (for now), looking himself over in a wall-length mirror behind the bar....

"You is one sexy devil," he mutters with the half-cluck of a laugh, self-amusement / self-absorption favored tactics in this daily battle with time. Goodspeed raises a fingered V (as in *Victory!*), gains Howard's attention. Howard nods, fixes a sequel to the empty glass and serves up the potion. It is a popular tactic. The few others at the bar—Ez, Jude, Boo, Victor, Chuck—employ similar strategies. It is their time to waste. *It is freedom.* It is noon.


HAVING BID HIS BRETHREN good day, Goodspeed strides up Austin Avenue. An artery dating to the neighborhood's original design, its unkempt wilds have it coming up short of the parkway it once was. Hints of said grandeur remain: overgrown ornamentals, once precise sidewalks and flagstone medians now smothered beneath an urban jungle of vines and weeds. It is the valley of Summer. The listless air hangs as a slow smothering, full humid heat. No worries. Our man savors it, a therapeutic sauna minus the added bonus of fat naked comrades. Distant ground planes gyrate in the liquid heat. Our man walks into it unfazed, questioning the rhythms of nature as heinous a waste of time as a "yellow bottom feeder" invading his business with softball queries such as....

"If not quite lighting the fuse of revolution, your works want to at least shake down the establishment. That's a crowded field; just curious if an influential figure stands out? An inspiration, that sort of thing?"

"Jim Beam, asshole"....The encounter from the previous night having made it clear to our man, Goodspeed, that *Victory!* on that night would require steadfast dedication—a radical devoted inebriation—our man having continued....

"George Dickel, Jack Daniels, Evan Williams (on which he'd finally settled). How's that? A quartet of spiritual inspirations. What, do you expect me to sit here and cough up bullet points? Disconnected contextless quotes for the masses numbed by the yellow bullshit masquerading as culture these days?"

"Just question-and-answer, man."

"How do you know I don't lie? For all I know, it might be ol' Evan doing the talking for me. Could just be my subconscious talking itself into a lie so I can look myself in the mirror each day. The laudable, the appalling, in tandem, in conflict. There's the character we are and the character we want to think we are. And you think I'm able to tell which is which? If you ever cared to notice, you'd recognize that we aren't exactly the best arbiters of our own truth."

"You have a following. I'm on the city beat. Just curious what makes a local of some renown tick; question-and-answer, that is all."

"You want to know what makes me tick? It's all around ya. Do the legwork, chump. Do your own damned digging and stop murderin' my time, hear?"

"Crystal clear."

"Good. Now I'm suggestin'—strongly—that ya move along and let me be. Another'n, H. In fact, best just give me the whole damn'd bottle!"

\*       So, right out of the gate a signal fact has been uncovered: Compromising his free time for the "whores of yellow journalism" is right up there with this Regular's need for a hole-in-the-head. Duly noted. (Okay, can sense what you're thinking: I have to read a few hundred pages devoted to a caustic drunk? Well, we warn you now that we cannot assuage that worry. For we will not unearth heroes in the pages to follow; at most, some shallow graves revealing what they will. We're afraid that this will demand of you too, dear reader, and we do apologize for that.... That said, we set to work observing our specimen in his natural environs awhile. If game, let us let it all come out in the wash of, say, a few hundred pages? Trowels in hand, a sly grin—a squint-eye?—we set to the painstaking fieldwork ahead. What say? Game?)

Goodspeed dons sunglasses. It is an anonymity he's had to work hard for of late. As we'll find he didn't set out to achieve fame, or status, or the endless invasions of his private drinking. It was *freedom* he was after.

And he is well on his way this afternoon. Having hid the haze of morning behind the ruse of firewater, he figures a good sweat couldn't hurt either. Goodspeed sets a sturdy pace. He pounds the pavement, tacking N x NE up Bass Avenue. Beads crowd his brow. A car idles by, carving a hole through the afternoon haze....

\*       And so, discouraged of pursuing chump-like softball strategies, we set to the dig and a studied look at our man. It's hard to know where to start. Waking up on a sidewalk half-drunk offers much to go on. But we can't be let off the hook so easily, as our man would seem to imply. Simplicity masks complexity here. However, one early observation does help establish a simple / central point: Goodspeed's every day is lived within a particular brand of irreverence, a life choice that runs against the *get-up-and-go* grain of this city. As mentioned, the notion of time and society's incessant demands on it (a sprawling list featuring: "corporate slavery," "traffic-copters," and those "whores of yellow journalism") are levied like a colonial tariff on the man. *The tyranny!* A defiant backwoodsman in the regional tradition, he is following in the steps of Scots-Irish ancestors who skedaddled for the hills, sinking roots deep on the Appalachian frontier and far from the reach of uptight lowland puritans. The hills were a place where they could pursue their time and the *business of freedom* as they saw fit. In Goodspeed's case, we need only substitute Appalachian with urban and lowland with suburban, and our analogy is up to date. Out here on the urban frontier, Goodspeed can pursue his deviance from the expected norm as he sees fit. It is the pulse of heritage that drums inside his ribcage. *Live free or die!* A one-man *Whiskey Rebellion* he takes to the "pious bring down" and federal revenuer with verve.

(Be we so bold to state that after only a couple of trowels full we are already making progress? Let us err on the side of bold, folks. *Onward!*)

The street wanderer, Eustace, passes Goodspeed across the avenue. Shackled to some as of yet undiagnosed schism, yet to date harmless and self-reliant, he's as much a neighborhood fixture as our man. This here is his home too. Another car passes, presents evidence for its desperate need of a new muffler. Eustace does what he does:

"This is, this is, this is da problem with da demands 'a physics! They don't add up 'n get broken to bits, to bits. Bite the bullet! See?! Shut up! Just shut up! I hate you! I hate you! No! No! Man, I'm sorry. I love you, man! Hey Marvin, Marvin, will you tell 'em to shut all them damned cars off please? They's just too loud f'me. This is all I'm askin' of ya, man."

"I'll see what I can do, Eustace."

"That's kind 'a ya, man. See, now why can't you be more like Marvin?! Because I'm for war! Prick! Jerk! Asshole! I'm for peace! War! Peace! War! Peace!"

Goodspeed shakes his head. He understands all too well that the membrane separating us human folk from our own peculiar strains of madness is but a thin permeable veil. This legion of wanderers, harbored within the dementia of a place having evolved equal parts by-chance and by-choice. *This here is home....* And it is home to deep heat on this afternoon. No worries. It rejuvenates our man, a good sweat helping flush the cirrhotic pallor of the binge.

Goodspeed bends up onto Washita, is heading for Highland Avenue. It's a familiar course, just one of the dozens within this rare (anymore) collection of late-nineteenth-to-early-twentieth-century villages that we'll come to know, and love. It is all predictable, comfortable; like the windless heat of August....

\*     And so, we begin a look at the environment of our man, the symbiotic interplay between character and place.

Again, hard to know where to start. A locale having exalted the preacher, and moonshine-runner? An incubator for the rights of African Americans, and the Klan? A land of extremes sealed beneath a thick veneer of contradiction, at best. But for the sake of our study, let's give it the ol' college try.... This here is a land that harbors bitter memories of commercial exploitation, political tyranny and want, a history offset by a rugged (if often misplaced) pride in the ability to fight through the hardest of hardships and all that would otherwise be haunting and devastating to experience. This land, this city, they are offspring of the fabled *New South*. But their roots dig snug into the *Old*. A glance reveals the depth to which this dichotomy still drives all things. It is its kerosene, its fuel, *the old* and *the new* in tandem, in conflict. Its rending coercion often sputters in Goodspeed's ears as little more than a background hum. But be not fooled, dear reader. For it is his fuel too; and it burns white hot. *Springvale Park*, home base, the grand old ward of this *New South* city. Once the crown jewel, it is now an amorphous in-town 'hood hunkered within the DMZ inherent to metro areas, that zone separating the immaculate staged snapshot city leaders wish to portray from the cordoned-off beat down blocks no one outside them needs know exist. Out here lay the frontier. We need only substitute backwoods shacks amongst piney woods for moldering white-flight vacancies (the Queen Annes, the bungalow fixer-uppers) and our analogy is up to date. This city blows through busy days, a commercial circus worked like a mule but for those exerting an anonymity tooled by design. Irreverent, reticent, their defiance has been honed to perfection, out here. It is Goodspeed's true art.

Hunger roars in with the afternoon. The truce has halted an insurrection within his queasy guts. He knows well enough to take advantage of it. Like the Arabs and Jews, it promises future conflict. But for right then the peace stands, Goodspeed unable to hate and grateful to vodka's numbing skill (praising it as easily as he might curse it). It is the spirit's niche talent, the ability to minimize the iron-fisted regime of Summer. The despot is being held at bay, its red flags hanging limp beneath a broiler. *Just a few drinks to help deaden the aches, that's all it takes.* A little *Victory!* A little lunch couldn't hurt either, the earth's mirage melting before his steps.

He turns onto Highland Avenue and strides up to *Lou's New York Pizza* at Colquitt. A calzone with vidalias will set him right. It is his time to waste. He enters, the jangling door.

"Hey y'all."

"Hey, Marv. Sit where ya want," greets the waitress.

"Can I bother you for a domestic-in-a-bottle?"

"Be rhat out with it, sweetheart."

THE SUN REARS UP, an ocular orb riven from the horizon. Ascending with effort, it pries eyes to slits. Goodspeed breathes hard, exhales with an audible groan. He works massaging fingers down from temples, an exploration searching for new crevices and creases hanging from cheekbone and jaw. He pushes up facial skin into a joke pig face, releasing it, exhaling.

"Man, oh' man. What a night."

Goodspeed rubs his eyes with forefinger knuckles,

props himself onto elbows. He takes a look at this new day. It runs through a Vaselined lens. Hard, prolonged blinks of eyelids work to clear the blur. A humid tone advocates carelessness, its haze holding weight—an ogre's hand on the chest. He dares not fight it, lays back down, closing eyes. *Damn that ogre!* This morning rued as if closing time.

A red light turns green. Traffic rolls up the avenue like the sleeves of the hardworking. The pack motors by, funneled waves of wind trailing pickups, diesels, fleet vehicles, a bus. The whine and decline of acceleration trails their passing. A discarded styrofoam cup jumps up and over his legs, coming to rest amongst wrapper / newspaper flotsam. Just another morning, a routine no less than reading the paper on the toilet.

Goodspeed looks up as cruiser wheels bank onto the curb. A lumbering idle introduces headlights and grill before his view. Its grumbling clamor throats dissatisfaction. The door opens. The officer's form fills the frame. Door closed, riot club slid into hip-side eyelet, gun on the belt as the very law itself. A two-way radio clipped to shoulder-strap....chatter, static, chatter....cackling like a murder of annoyed crows.

The officer stands over him with arms crossed, shakes his head. The silhouette hovers as shape-only to the sight-stymied Goodspeed. But our man knows the shape well. It looms gloom and doom, the personification of badass cumulonimbus threatening lightning and downpours. But then, it's still morning. Must be the city's finest. Goodspeed leans his head back down. He grins, the half-cluck of a laugh.

"Now that I know I don't have to call the morgue, how

'bout gettin' up?" the officer hard-kicking Goodspeed's sneaker. "C'mon, Marv, get y'ass up."

He'll receive no special favors (despite having made a name for himself). He is too real a character, too many having been forced to pick his half-dead carcass up off the sidewalk. Most all Zone 2 cops know Goodspeed by name, out here. For many a step has this Regular tread / stumbled through the remote urban wilderness. He is predictable, like the snap-clap of thunderstorms in the afternoon....

\* So, it seems a good point early in our slicing up the site here to mention what may come as a surprise, this potsherd emanating from the dig.... There was a time, not all that long ago, when our man's day revolved around routine work-a-day ways; long hours served up in hope of the paltry raise, barrel-bottom insurance benefits, a lifetime bled on the whims of CEOs and COOs and VPs he'd never met and never would.... *But all that had changed.*

"Okay, alright, Pete. I'm just messing with ya there, Mr. Civic Duty. I'm gettin' up, I'm rising." Goodspeed knows all the cops by name, out here. "What's with the club? Tryin' to scare me straight?"

"What? No, no, just habit, s'pose; all y'all good-fer-nothings."

Pete extends a hand, still shaking his head. Goodspeed declines the offer with gratitude. He rolls over on his side, props up to a knee. His body creaks as an old staircase under fat feet. He rises slowly. Several years of hard drink have wrung him out, muscling out the fading traits of youth. A pallor consumes him. Standing, he seems beaten, the humid broth set to stew that day's kettle of smog. Breathing itself is enough to crowd Goodspeed's brow with sweat. He doesn't look so good.

"Not lookin' so hot this morning, Marv."

"Well, just gotta get motivated s'all. Up 'n at 'em, right?"

Goodspeed continues to ramble in a low tone, Pete hearing something about freedom, hard work, before advising the Regular: "Why not take it on home for a while."

Goodspeed places his hand on the officer's shoulder, tries to focus, nods. "Ya, think I might just do that."

"And speaking for all of us, take a shower. Ya smell like Old Parn."

"Really? Huh. Fairly certain I didn't piss myself last night."

The officer grants the situation its leave, climbs back into the idling cruiser and jumps it off the curb. His right of way is smartly unquestioned.

Goodspeed, meanwhile, is about to pass out—the closing arguments of a collapsing equilibrium. Guts churning, head pounding, he moves to a terrace of the stonewall running alongside city avenue and slumps to a seat. Hands on knees, head slung heavy and slack between shoulders like a wet shirt on a laundry line. He grapples with consciousness, cursing it. Another pack of commuters motor by....*It is 82˚ @ 7 a.m. and you are listening to The City!*

IT IS EIGHTY-FOUR DEGREES *@ 8 a.m. and you are listening to The City!* The DJ's byte tumbles in a Doppler curve from a truck cab radio blowing past. In obedience to the routine—to tradition—Goodspeed had figured a long walk might help shed the previous night's residue of excess. It hasn't. Having plotted a circular route out past *Candler Hills*, he nears its end where he began. He ambles up onto a footpath bordering the city's parkway connector. The air gloats rush-hour exhaust, preaching of *progress! (Here we see the responsible masses, the morally fit turning out to make our city great!)* The air is acidic to the taste, stewing of commuter dread. *(Here we see the miserable chattel dragging ass to another day wasted on douchebag executives they'll never know!)* The gloating, the dread, breaching the embankment alongside him and bankrolling his miserable mood. *(This miserable mood brought to you by Prozac. Pop one and misery is done!)* Goodspeed tramps the winding wend of the footpath undeterred, resolute. He has his duty. He is in the moment. *Buck up!* Every step lands as on the very ends of the earth: anxious, but with a touch of bravado. The morning fails to follow suit: windless, a touch of dank. Our man marches on, this soldier emerging from the smoking husks of dawn.

Goodspeed veers onto the worn groove of a short-cut. He walks beneath a line of juniper, a DOT attempt to pretty-up the inherently sterile. The six-lane parkway connector is seething. Connecting the north + eastern metro suburbs with the roaring twelve-lane confluence of two interstates downtown, its stalled exasperation subsidizes the daily grind. He breathes deep and hard, traversing a peninsula of DOT land carpeted of kudzu and trash. He closes the circle, emerging from a bamboo thicket back onto the length of sidewalk bordering city avenue. Once grand dwellings hunker on sullen plots across the street. Some are in the process of *renovation and restoration.* Most are not (yet). The once elite status of the old ward is everywhere evident, though it may require a piece of imagination these days. One such example: Imagine if you can, north and west of Highland Avenue, fifty-five emerald acres of parkland having opened in the year-of-our-Lord, 1898. Once known as *Auburn Hill,* it is now run through by the parkway connector, construction having obliterated the actual hill. The only realized piece of a grand pet project pushed by multiple governors during the '70s to drill an access-highway from the vote rich 'burbs straight through to downtown, the so called *Downtown Connection* left angry scars throughout *Springvale* and its sister in-town 'hoods. The path Goodspeed takes traces the worst, he'll claim, what is left of the *Springvale* side of the park, and hill, now a mile-long overgrown slope leading to a levee of embankments. The long stonewall, built by legions of WPA laborers in the '30s, traces Highland's run through *Candler Hills* into *Springvale* and is the only reminder of the park's southern boundary. Once adjacent to the prominent hill, a knoll erodes thick red sandbars of delta'd earth; the once neatly knit sidewalks of hexagonal stone broken, jumbled. But then these latter facts can be explained by the simple proceedings of nature just doing its thing. "The New South bastards and bigots are to blame for all the rest," he'll proclaim.

Goodspeed burps. The chalked vapor of alcoholic bile seeps into his mouth. He exhales, his tongue out:

"Could use some Alka-Seltzer, or maybe just a round in-the-head."

\*      Or how about a bit of fucking restraint?! Okay, alright, keeping to objective observation here.... To understand our man is to acknowledge the insignificance of codified society. Restraint, guilt, the moralistic value placed on delayed gratification and the economy of appetite, these are all concepts as foreign to Goodspeed as the Ukraine or Micronesia. The daily reckoning he faces with the bottle as bayonet. It is war out here, as he'll often tell you. And though the cost seems a reckless waste to the casual observer, this Regular presses on. To him it's a matter of *freedom*. This fight is about *rights*, a "sacrifice" his heritage points at being instinctual. To pussify oneself with moral qualms before the voracious jaws of the invaders (they being legion), is to accept Appomattox at face value—as *the end*. No, no. This here is about overcoming defeat, fighting on if only to deny the totality of defeat. This here is about duty, an underdog role he embraces with fearless devotion, however fatalistic. For the odds of defeat are of no mind when a life choice comes down to a simple matter of squint-eye conviction. *Once wronged, hate simmers long.*

And on that, let's call up a classic source of *Old / New South* mythology to help amplify our point. In his 1941 epic, *The Mind of the South*, Wilbur J. Cash attempted to define the unique (if odd) faith that drove Lee's gaunt lines of non-slaveholding citizen soldiers to make the charge at the core of southern legend. Before a skeptical, yet curious world (think southern gothic) Cash wrote:

> *The poor farmer (amongst what was an army of poor farmers)....the thing that sent him swinging*

*up the slope at Gettysburg was before all else nothing more or less than his conviction, the conviction that nothing living could cross him and get away with it ~*

Now, if this here isn't Goodspeed's guiding decree, we'll find ourselves hard pressed to define what is. For our man lives it with gusto. Obsessed with ignoring the expectations of a societal order that piques his nature, crosses him at every turn, this Regular marches on: defiant, irreverent, a one-man *Pickett's Charge* giving sure oblivion the finger.

Goodspeed seeks the running length of the avenue's stonewall terrace as a bench. Sweat forms at his forehead. It is cold and trickling. He curses silently, downlooking. He exhales.

"Phh'uh—man, oh' man," his tongue out.

He wipes forehead with the back of his hand, is pale as bleached bone. A bead of sweat tumbles down his spine....and it begins, physiology's instinct in retrograde. Vomiting twists his guts like a pretzel. He has to stand up. It's a violent jerking motion. Acidic, the burn a writ of habanero. He coughs, gags, spits, vaguely recalls performing this pleasant exercise the previous night as well. A pedestrian passes across the way. Sickened, she steps through; a final repulsed over-the-shoulder look. No, nothing to see, nothing new here. It's all part of the routine; just another day in the life.

Goodspeed hawks up saliva in an attempt to clear the burning bitters from his mouth. He sits back down, savors as if tortured release the delusion of feeling better. He peers across the avenue.

"Well, okay then."

Views cascade into the swirling mist, boil up from the vine fields and storm drains. The glib asphalt and cracked hexagonal block cloak the ground strewn steaming beneath his feet. He casts an appreciative look at his favorite sneakers, worn soldiers held together by duct-tape and shoe-goo. The old soldiers, doing their duty to the last. Goodspeed sees the day through a new light. Amazingly, he's not beat. Not yet. (Is it a sense of duty inspiring resolve? Is it trowel time?) Optimism and strength dive deep to prod conviction. He calls it up and lurches off into its open arms.

*On with the day!*


IT'S TEN MINUTES LATER. Goodspeed is at his apartment and in a bad way with this day. He has no key, no need for locked doors, entering a soul bearing hovel that would prove disheartening to any thief anyways. It's a basement dwelling, a rarity in these parts, the unintentional studio layout pure happenstance. There's the functional kitchen space, a small footprint living space, bed in the corner farthest from the door. The outside wall load bears the weight of hand-made bookshelves packed to overflowing, book piles crowding the living space itself. It is a place designed to maximize the pursuit of his *business*, whatever phase of said *business* happens to be ascendant at the moment. The space is a statement itself, tells us much about our subject: the "commercial power" urging hyper-consumption, the "moral power" paternal acquiescence, Goodspeed living it stripped-down to the beat of his own R&D.

A camel cricket scatters as he scuffles to the kitchen sink. He plugs and fills the sink full of cold-ish water, plunging his face for a soak. He grabs a towel from a sink-side rack, dries crevices and creases alike. A light-hearted sneer draws up the corner of his mouth.

"Naw, no way."

Goodspeed grabs the crotch of his shorts, reluctantly smelling his hand....*Negative, over. Roger, over*.... Not pissing himself while blacked-out, always a positive. He mulls a shower. It has been days.

"May just get around to that, will be my contribution to society."

The good philanthropist slumps into one of the two chairs in the place, elbows on knees. Sweat clings to his back as condensation on an iced glass. There's no escape from the valley of Summer, even at an early hour. It's of no mind. It does not invite longing for alternate climes. It is just doing its thing, the deep South as much a piece of Goodspeed as the notch at the bridge of his nose.

He clicks on a Westinghouse three-speed oscillating fan resting atop one of two TV trays. All were found in a roadside garbage heap. (Add scavenger to his resume.) Fat metal blades bring the *whir-whir-whirrrrrrrr* relief of moving air. The motor housing skips in a familiar hitch; a good cleaning and a few dabs of 3-in-One oil have it running like a champ. Goodspeed looks at the fan, pulls up close and hums, amused by the vocal oscillation in a way not unlike a ten-year-old and his fart jokes. He thinks: amazing what a little oil can do, can bring the dead back to life. He wonders if the same could be true of his own state, right then. Possible. Probable, in fact. He opts for sleep instead. Be this a sign of restraint? Hardly. A quick scan of his liquor cache atop countertop reveals it dry, five dead soldiers to be exact. It's all about going with the moment. For this brief moment, he is forced to sobriety.

He moves through rays tumbling in through the apartment's single window. It is the only sign of day. Light banks against the legs of a TV tray. He collapses to the bed. The frame creaks as he adjusts. His head aches, stomach in revolt. But sleep comes easy; his snoring coarse, nasally.

It is hours later, Goodspeed jarred awake by a pop-country hit blaring from the backlot. He opens one eye, is royally pissed. He sits upright, simmers, both eyes now open. His left eye ticks, the music and its source clear. He drags a hand across his face, groans.

"That freaking ass."

Goodspeed swings his legs to the side of the bed, upwardly motivating with balled fists and straight arms his 175 pounds onto legs. He stands, releases a surl-of-an-exhale. He shuffles over to the door, opens it, folds through the bear of thick air and out onto the back-landing. He stares at a school bus painted matte green (it's left rear axle up on blocks and naked) that lately took up residence in the gravel backlot behind his hovel. He casts a squint-eye at the tapestry-curtained interior, sees no one. He picks up a fist-size chunk of broken cinder block and hurls a tailing fastball. It strikes the broadside of the bus with a hollow rattling K-LUNK!

"Daing! What the—what the fuck!?" jumps in a spasm from behind a curtained veil. A hand pulls it back to reveal a freaked-out look pasted to an angular head. The deadbeat son of the brain-dead cabinetmaker in residence just down Austin, he'd driven that bus into the backlot about a month prior, its dualie-left-rears flat and riding rims. He'd tapped into a line on a nearby utility pole without electrocuting himself (a feat that still astounds Goodspeed), and has lived in it since: a green metal oven called home. A multi-generational redneck who fancies himself a next-generation hippie, the freak gathers up the situation, music still blaring,

"God damn'd, Goodspeed! What the fuck!?"

"Turn that shit off, busboy!"

"C'mon! Thought ya liked country, Marv."

"Hank, Lefty, and Buck are country. That crap is top—fucking—40. Now turn it off before I come out there and bust y'up!"

"Fine! A'right! Bet ya dented my damn'd bus."

"Gonna dent more'n that in a second!"

"Fine, a'right," he says, disappearing into the living quarters at the backend of the bus and cutting the music.

Our man rubs eyes, massages thrumming temples. The pallid tone of his skin is tangible, pasted to cheekbones like cheap wallpaper. He is not looking so well. He releases a deep exhale, scratches the sandpaper at his jaw. Annoyed, awake, what to do? He looks up. The sun's hazy blur.

"Is it eleven yet?"

As mentioned, he owns no watch, instead setting great store by the sundial of genuine importance: *opening and closing times*....

\*    And yet, as we have mentioned, there was a time not all that long ago when his days were spent "slaving" to secure his daily bread, the "life sucking parasite" of a corporate hotelier flushing his minutes, hours, days down the toilet. That job was the final straw, had set him on his course. He really should be glad for it, but years later can only recall the whole experience inside a roiling hate—the gnashing of teeth, steam slow-leaking from ears, the tedium of others' agendas....*all of which he'd shit-canned for freedom.*

Since then it's all been so clear (or so it would appear), the significance—if not the very existence—of time having settled into bivouac. Though not obvious at a glance, survey and excavation (a trowel full here, a trowel full there) is beginning to uncover what looks an awful lot like a method to the madness. We may in fact find ourselves tempted to consider: Goodspeed, the engineer? Focused, honed-in on the vibrating chaos of his nature, it is a blueprint for success. The reward for his hard work? The freedom to do what he wants, when he wants to do it. *Live free or die!* And he exercises his right to waste said *freedom* sleeping off a hangover. Sleep comes easy, busboy smartly silent.

A BALL OF LIGHT POPS. An instantaneous crash rattles front windowpanes. A mean sky boils over. Another flash and crash, rolling planes of thunder, one after another after another, like opening salvos or the fighter-wave of an air raid (pre M.A.D. era, that is). No rain as of yet, just furious anticipation. And yet, what one might call malefic intent, or malevolent design, or *(insert your own flourish here, dear reader, because why should we have all the fun gilding the lily?)* _____ _____ , our man shrugs off as nature in action. Hot humid updrafts force-feed the cumulus stack, an explosive brew blowing its top. It is all just doing its thing, doing what it must.

Goodspeed, several doubles in, stands on the sidewalk out front of *Asa's*. He revels in the foment of the moment. The storm dyes daylight a jaundiced tone, cigarette smoke swept up into the prevailing gusts. A splintered bolt rips the sky. BOOM! He can barely stand it, is feeling the need to rededicate himself, is in need of inspiration for his next chapter. A flash, an instant violent crash. "Whoa! Man, oh' man!" Just doing its thing. Just doing his thing.

A fat bead of rain pops roadside sand. Drops smack the hot asphalt. A sheet of rain drag races a microbus up Austin. The T2 VW sputters to a halt (as if knowing to do so), driver-side door opening, closing, the driver sprinting across the avenue through a rain sheet falling sideways from the west. The driver lunges for *Asa's* eave reprieve.

"Great," mumbles Goodspeed.

"What's up?" the (so labeled) yellow journalist greeting the Regular, slicking back soaked hair.

"Doin' your own legwork, or here to weasel it out of me? I tend to lean on violence a bit more the second go-round, just sayin."

"Actually, just stopped by for a beer. Still a public drinking establishment, right?"

"Right as rain. Headin' out for a stroll, anyway."

"In this?"

"A little rain and thunder? Nature's wonder, chump."

"Enjoy."

It is twenty minutes later. Goodspeed is thoroughly soaked, oblivious to the deluge then slowing to a downpour. He bends his way around *Waverly Park*, sweeping his view up a turreted tower. Angled rooflines spill over a modillioned cornice down to bay windows. Ah, the glory of *Springvale's Go Go '90s* (the 1890s, that is). *Gilded Age* castles command attention at every turn: a Greek revival, an Italian renaissance, a Tudor. A few are well-kept. Many are not (yet), one-time symbols of status having suffered the natural leveling of time. Decorative lightning rods descend on a rare pair of eyebrow dormers. Heavy and sullen, tired eyes peering, Goodspeed stepping through with purpose. He is heading for inspiration. He is heading for the *Gordon Patrick Woodruff House*.

It is ten minutes later. The storm has blown itself out. Goodspeed stands before *the house*. A Queen Anne dating to 1894 and lacking much of the inherent detail, it is his inspirational Mecca. Whenever our man feels tired or worn or lacking in duty / devotion, he sets out on a hajj to *the house*. Staring at the shrine's worn skin, Goodspeed recites Gordon Patrick Woodruff beneath tapering rain:

> *Let us attend to a creed composed of very simple demands: liberty, equity, justice for the common man. Let us not forget ah'own battle cry, my fellow men: through collective action we will achieve individual freedom  ~*

"Riding latter-day Populism and its hysteria to its grave, his only mistake. Might could have done without the bigotry too," our man thinking on *his man*: Gordon Patrick Woodruff.... *His man* would come to regret not splitting with the Populists as they lost their way in the run-up to the *Silver Sell Out* and doomed 1896 fusion with Bryan Democrats, the movement devolving from a sophisticated (if on a shoestring) socioeconomic crusade against the rapacious inequity of industrialist wealth concentration into a dark comic gaggle driven off the cliff by anti-semitic conspiratorial cranks.... Goodspeed has applied this bitter lesson. He will not long endure the crazed mouth-foaming of others claiming to speak for *his cause*. He is all the time leery of words, promises. What with his own well-spring of virulence set to a rolling boil, he wades into the "modern slave-ocracy" on his own. He will go the revolution alone, a dedication that could easily be confused with ambition; but for our man's strategic reliance on careless inaction, his finger-in-the-eye of the "Big Mules" manipulating the responsible, "running them to ruin for their own obese fortunes." He'll not long endure the rambling half-cocked conspiracies of others. For he has time but to foment his own playlist of contradictions, his own gilded conspiracies. This is his revolution—and his alone—to bury.

Goodspeed is buoyant, having been recharged for the skirmishes and challenges ahead. He moves along, waterlogged sneakers squeaking an optimistic resolution with each step.

And a neighborhood away, our journalist / interloper jots a few final notes in a small spiral-bound hand-held. He drops a final gulp of pint-based domestic (his second, if we are keeping score) and gets up to leave the, strangely, empty room.

He drops a fiver (it being $2 draft day) and gets up to head out, his warmest regards as he does: "Thanks for the hospitality. It was Howard?"

"That is right. Get what you came for?" H not one to miss a thing.

"Um, we'll see," acknowledging the barkeep's keen observation. "Might just drop in again, if that's cool?"

"Clayburn was it?"

"Clee-burne, long e."

"Alright Cleburne with a long e. You're welcome back any time, and bring some friends. Just watch yourself, hear?"

"Appreciate that, I think."


DARK GULPS THE DUSK. Here comes the nightly reprieve, the post-storm air a hazy soup unbound to gravity's bowl. Lights light up in windows and on porches all along the avenue. The dark—empower-er of the fiendish—also beckons friends (who may also be fiends) to come together, to gather amongst like kind, to vent that day's transgressions. *Come fellow regulars, be as one! A little Victory is within grasp!* A final arc of non-dark slips beyond the city's skyline to the west, night now known.

Having filled his inspirational void and fulfilled his philanthropic contribution (his rain-soaked trek shower enough), he stands again out under *Asa's* eave. Having shed soaked clothes and sneakers for a dry set, sobriety has now become a looming unwelcome presence. It will soon enough be a fleeting thought, as he sights Dorothy—D—materializing from the freshly-minted murk. She strides up the sidewalk, cycling through concentric streetlamp haloes: an obscure outline, fully illuminated, repeat. He welcomes her arrival....

Dorothy wears 40 (+/-) years well, exuding a rugged independence that is all hers despite the countless attempts of petty male egos to deny it. (She was a corporate defense lawyer.) But like Goodspeed, she'd had a falling out with the suits, defending "rapacious assholes" she'd come to loath having grown most tiresome. Even worse, its relentless schedule invaded her time in the saddle. A short stint for the other side (as an anti-trust prosecutor) proved equally unrewarding, given the incestuous backscratching and constant interference of "well-oiled" politicians. She'd left all that behind, taking on this Goodspeed cat instead. Client / lover, he is full-time enough....

"Damn, lookin' good tonight, babe!" Goodspeed gaining a smile as he sights his flame.

Dorothy, hands outstretched, shoots an *as if* look. "It's what I do," the few strands of grey running through a tightly-wound cinnamon ponytail falling somewhere between distinguished and hot stuff. "Wish I could say the same; you get some recovery time in today?"

"Enough, s'pose. How goes the thing?"

"Not bad, making headway. Should be wrapping it up soon."

"Don't know how you put up with that crap," Goodspeed, simply allergic to the average administrative chores of life and work, grateful beyond words to his *Cinnamon Girl*.

"You just need to be glad that I do, moneybags. Just keep doing your thing and rest up, let me worry about keeping 'em all in line."

Having successfully won an appeal on behalf of Howard and Martha that overturned a controversial and very unpopular city zoning-board ruling (what a few trowels full confirmed as the first step in an annexation aimed at razing blocks of private properties, including those at Austin / Elizabeth, in favor of upscale gentrification infill), her smarts are something of legend around here. But a sharp mind is buttressed by street-smarts equally sharp (a concealed handgun permit, for instance). And the fact that she took the case pro bono means she has won not just minds, but hearts around these parts....

Dorothy Harmin had shed the pantsuit for leather chaps about the same time Goodspeed had shed his "shackles of economic exploitation." She has been a regular at the Dakota *Sturgis Rally* and here at *Asa's* since. She knows loud pipes and the finer points of a deal. It seems a good piece of synchrony, the two having met the week the ruling came down, that having been the very same week that Goodspeed finished *The Book*.... To get a good deal, one could use a good contract. And for that, one could use a good lawyer. Dorothy is willing to put up with "that crap" (dedication, devotion, finds her skipping the rally this year), and more importantly: his crap. Marvin Goodspeed has drawn quite a hand....

"How 'bout a humble beau buys a beauty a drink?"

"Still make enough sense to trick an old girl."

"Old nothing, babe. Beauty, it transssscends!" punctuating his affection with a pentecostal-like hand-thrown witnessing.

Curved neon rods in *Asa's* front window advertise, entice: *Cold Beer! Hot Stew! Y'all Come!* They shove, elbowing their way through the radioactive pink of Austin Avenue streetlamps. It all glows. They glow.

"Look at 'em in there, that scene. It's a Rembrandt," Goodspeed beaming.

"You mean *Dogs Playing Poker*, right?"

The view through the front window is one of the *Asa Inman's* most familiar. Hues are lifted as from velvet paintings, a gallery of gaud for sale along the chain-link of a closed gas station: The stoop-shouldered frames of regulars = rusting pumps; hands / arms = nozzles, decaying hose. Drinks sprout atop the bar like weeds in asphalt cracks. It is fine art.

The two enter to greetings. It echoes down the line.... Welcome back, all, to the place where evenings are whittled away in an ancient way: *to drink wine, to be with like kind....* But instead of the ease of camaraderie and protocol, we are assaulted by another unwelcome presence, an aggressive cancer devouring the simple aim of timeless *Victory!*

"But see Dylan wasn't so great, he only done what Woody already done!" slurs George, a not-so-welcome newcomer.

"Woody, Bob Dylan, cain't ya just listen to the music and shut the hell up? Always trying to make a point 'n sound smart. Would you just shut the hell up for once?!" snaps Henry, a squeamish veteran regular who George has made his reluctant cohort.

A moron with half a brain originally from somewhere else, George was released from the city's Federal pen earlier that year. He drifted in and set up camp at *Asa's* in the Spring, it being the kind of place that attracts all makes / models from society's fringe. Most try to tolerate him. Goodspeed thinks he's an undeserving asshole, which he is (subjective indiscretion noted).

"But if I'd get ya to listen every s'often, I wouldn't have to always give ya facts plain as the nose on yer face. Woody was okay, see, but was nothing before Dylan. Dylan, now he was the real talent. Woody Guthrie? Please, woulda just been forgot kind likes that guy, what the fuck-hell was his name? Ya know who I's talking 'bout?"

"No, I don't. Now shut the hell up. Anything for a little peace 'n quiet," Henry placing an order: "H, how 'bout another'n down here?"

"Henry, how 'bout lopping off some of this here tab you been piling up of late. What say, friend?" Howard, stern, paternal, arms locked at the elbows as he leans on the bar. There is no question who's sheriff in here.

"I knows it, I knows it, H. Old lady took the check, again. Jeez, why don't I stand up to that evil witch. What kinda man am I? I need to stand up for myself. I ain't seen no part of that check, H," Henry's hand gesturing erratic, inebriated.

"Same excuse as last time, Henry," Howard sliding a fresh domestic-in-a-bottle before the veteran, knowing, sadly, that it is all truth. Henry: one of their own, a burdened soul. He persists....

"It's the sad truth, I swear it, H. That woman'll be my end some day."

"The plain truth is that ya ain't knowin' what I's tryin' to splain here. Guthrie 'n Dylan was like this," stammers George, swaying drunk and stupid, attempting to cross his fingers and enamored by the complexity of his pointless point.

"Just shut it up, George. Hoo! My head hurts. Just shut up yer damned hole, would ya please?!"

A-fucking-men, thinks Goodspeed, he and D walking past, making their way to the end of the bar. But the pointlessness continues, the slurred rambling words microscopic pinpricks slowly, methodically, bleeding time. Goodspeed slow-simmers:

"Some day."

Goodspeed and D file into their regular slots at the far end of the bar. A king and queen, benevolent keepers of the kingdom. Not that they would accept such nobility. For the point—if not the rule—is to blend, in here.... Annoying pinpricks fall to the background (as much as the loudmouth allows that to be possible). Goodspeed, still off from the previous night's excesses, zeroes in on the television. The set broadcasts the game, the local boys of Summer plying their trade. Baseball proves a perfect companion on this night: Goodspeed's attention span non-committal, blurry. Dorothy allows him his visual mistress without jealousy; really, she could care less about his moods (another reason they work). Sensing the shift in temper, she strikes up a conversation with Martha, known to all as "Muth." They gab, ruminate and declare, while Goodspeed wiles away. Conversations, annoyances, minutes fall to the background. It is his safehouse, *Asa's* panacea underwritten by elixirs served tall and cool. Innings are dropped and recaptured with nonchalance. Strike three called, nicking the outside corner, side retired. Six-and-a-half in the books. Goodspeed stands and stretches with the crowd.

Again, we cast an eye about the place, a lodestar

central to our study. It is a world unto itself, a self-absorbed universe where rules / laws are redrawn as what the regular wills. What *is* is what they wish, everything "out there" strangled—if only for a moment—by the physics of "in here." The place is a landmark, an out-of-the-way wonder along the lines of the *Largest Ball of Twine. (Come one, come all to Dinosaurland!)* Old tourist kitsch, the irrelevance of time itself, *Asa's* has it all. College pennants hang over trinkets from *South of the Border, Graceland,* and The Keys. Two calendars faded and fixed behind *Asa's* cash register say it all. *Classic Muscle Cars:* a '66 GTO. *Winston Cup Showcase:* David Pearson limping to victory at Daytona in '76.... It is the middle of August 1997, the stretch run of the millennium; though one might not even notice, in here. Time is swallowed in a lack of immediacy, a languor that rounds out the dank often punctuated by Dylan or Guthrie, Curtis Mayfield, K. D. Lang or The Allmans....

"Anyone with half-a-brain knows what the fuck-hell I's talking 'bout, Henry."

"Anyone with half-a-brain's got a full half more than you do, George."

"Problem's that ya just don't want to listen."

"You got that right!"

Brewery signs linger from promotions long past: coasters from Saint Louis, Cincinnati, Milwaukee. Pabst lamp cones, Hamms and Jax serving trays, a bottle of Schlitz thermometer. Promotional gadgets, hats, posters, all manner of cheap crapola lay strewn about haphazard and shellacked by an oozing ochre floated of decades of rib grease, dust, must, and humidity. Howard didn't even install window-unit AC until the Summer after Saigon fell. The effects are still apparent: stalactites of grime cling to the tin-ceiling, dust-covered cobwebs strung like an unkempt regeneration of Pollock.

But one should not be fooled. A lack of care is not the result of a lack of love. The mild madness that abides in here feeds no ire. It finds only absolution. It is a modest place. It's a place for drinking, long-guaranteed protection via its friendliness towards police gambling. Hush-hush and backroom the pots can roll big, back there—all the cops known by name, in here. *The Asa Inman:* where time sinks into the stares of its regulars, where it lay capsized in its cure....

"And another thing, ain't never met no one who's got a first name for their last name that I ever did like, like uh, like uh, a name like uh, Bob Frank. In the pen, this guy's name, it was Bob Frank or Daniel, some'n 'er other; ya couldn't turn your back on him; never can. Cain't trust 'em is the problem with 'em," George yammering on relentlessly.

"George, what's your last name?" Goodspeed, eyes still glued to the game, inquiring loud enough for the loudmouth to hear.

"What? What's that, Goodspeed?"

"Your last name, George. What's your last name?"

"My last name? Thomas, dammit! Ya knew that, Goodspeed. Fuck-hell, ya did. Ah whatever, never know what you talking 'bout anyway, always talking stuff I cain't make heads-nor-heels; pro'ly just tryin' to impress yer girlfriend over there, spoutin' off about this-and-that-

and—*blah*—*blah*—*blah*....Goodspeed having become so skilled at tuning out sonic bullshit he often feels he should patent the process and make his millions. Of course, his entrepreneurial spirit has gone a bit soft ever since he made it.

"Can't deal with that horse's ass anymore," D draining a last swallow of domestic light, getting up to leave.

"Sorry, was someone talking, babe? Was all caught up watching our five-million-dollar boys here squander another lead in the eighth."

"Got to get up and get to it early tomorrow, anyhow. Hope they pull it out. Be sure to get some rest tonight. See ya, love."

They part. Goodspeed heads for the head. Big enough for a toilet, sink, and Pabst Blue Ribbon mirror, it serves the patron equally as restroom and repository of graffitied observation. Fixed as blown dye paintings, one can read up on modern day chronicles of the hunt. Insights range from the wrath of God's fury to a rebutting guesstimate on the size of the zealot's pecker. It's no favorable guess. There is the two-parter in different colored inks: 1. *James Dean lives!* 2. *But no one can tell him from recycled aluminum*, this over top of the bumpersticker: *Who died and made you Elvis?* But Goodspeed's favorite was penned anonymously years ago. It proclaimed: *I come from nowhere,* to which he felt compelled to append: *Welcome home.*

D gone, the game now lost, it is time to get down to business. Goodspeed engineers a fine buzz. A drink is downed. A fresh pint appears. He is feeling "right," stands up facing himself in the wall-length mirror behind the bar. He hoists the pint. Channeling the irascible, indefatigable,

James Agee, he toasts: *To those wiser who do not despise man in his doom, nor in the nature of his nature!* Curious glances, they accept the man in his nature, in here, the hoisting from about the room tepid, reactive.... Time wanders, disappears. Grammar is garbled, glued to the loosening of natural inhibition. It is then, then it is now. A full glass. An empty one.... We make our way down the bar. First laughter, then a deal, a lambasting, and stoic drinking....

Victor is telling a classic:

"Preacher and his wife are rolling along in their big ol' Caddy one day. Sure enough, they come up on the town drunk and his beat-up jalopy puttin' along in the road ahead. Well, preacher says: 'I'll show that good-for-nothing,' stomps that ol' Caddy's big block and roars on by the drunk. Preacher's smiling, is feelin' all righteous and is cruising down the road. Well, he forgets all about the blind curve ahead, slams on brakes too late and goes skiddin' off the road down into a ditch. Well, that town drunk, he sputters up on the wreck. He stops, gets out all flustered and hollers down: 'Jeez, y'all okay down there?' Caddy's beat up, but preacher and wife are just fine. And the preacher yells up to the drunk, all high-minded: 'Sir, we are just fine and don't need your help. We have the Lord with us'....The drunk thinks on this a second, before responding: 'Well okay, but y'all should let him ride with me. You gonna kill him!' "

Chuck is lobbying:

"All night, H, been nothin' but that damn'd white-bred hillbilly music. All night long, H. Nothin' but."

"You callin' me a hillbilly?" asks H.

"No offense, H, but you are, ain't ya?" Sax shrugging shoulders, telling it true.

"Well gentlemen, say you got me dead-to-rights. Alright then, have been in a Doc Watson mood all day; but here and now it is regulars' choice. Here's four quarters. Your spin on the new compact-disc jukebox."

"Knew we could appeal to that reasonable side, H." Chuck, master negotiator.

"That's right, H. You a bit cracker, but still got cred," Sax concurring.

"Aw'll right. I'm in a mood."

"Some Curtis, Chuck. Some Curtis Mayfield; and some Sam Cooke too."

"Yes, sir, and the Godfather!"

Boo is cursing out progressive taxation:

"Tax-and-spend, is all. These silver-tongued hoodlums get into power, take our money, fairly earned, and give it the do-nothins who sit on their ass and only get up off their ass to go vote for them politician crooks who take our money, fairly earned, and give it away to the do-nothins. Always trottin' out the tired Robin Hood thing. Who in hell they think they are? Sayin' fair share this and that. Cain't pull the wool over my eyes. I see what's afoot here. I paid taxes all my life just to watch 'em give it away. Crooks, all; swindlers taking the hard-earned dollars of hard-working Americans and giving it away to the lazy welfare types just so they can line 'em up at the polls like so much cattle. Stick them tax-and-spenders on an island, drop the hell-bomb! That's what I say we should do!" Boo says this to no one in particular.

Meanwhile, Ez and Jude sit perched at either side of the front-corner of the bar, could care less about politics, opinions. They tip bottles methodically. Hardly a word passes....

It is growing late. Midnight hours scatter as a game of pickup. George and his mouth have thankfully left. Henry is right then being dragged off by his old lady. As advertised, she is livid, dramatic, and demonstrative on this night. She hurls an ashtray as if a frisbee, knocks over a stool and breaks a glass. Howard's booming voice nearly blows her scrawny white-trash frame out the door, advising her to:

"Get the HELL out of my establishment, now!" which she does, kicking and screaming and dragging poor old Henry off to a night of restless hate. Henry's eyes beg the late-night crowd of regulars for intervention, as he is removed against his will. But reality beyond these walls is of harsh design, as they know, all of them, all too well. There are some holes from which one must dig one's self out, out there.

Scenes cling to Goodspeed's swimming mind via the intensity of their action. He treads atop a passage written by Allen Tate: poet / writer, co-founder of *Vanderbilt* literary group, *The Agrarians*, who would claim that the #1 thing missing from the *New South* was the *Old South* (the mythic one, that is). Goodspeed clutches to a line as if a life preserver, from Tate's *The Fathers*:

*...you remember what you cannot understand* ~

Once late-night emotion has run aground on the dank shoals of drink, there is often little reason inside the act. No mind on this night, the scene quickly submerging into the lethargy roaming this plane. It is the beguiling spirit's other talent: returning the human animal to a more primitive state of senseless instinct, one having existed before we began to bother it with time....

"Hmmmmmmm, that's better," the drunken scene stroking by as a blur.

Goodspeed, sitting on the sidewalk out front of *Asa's* smoking a cigarette. The whirl of red, blue, and bright white lights frame a pair of the city's finest dragging off a pair of drunken pugilists. The two continue to spit venom despite forced suppression and handcuffs. No one had ever seen them before, obnoxious antagonists having wandered in a half-hour earlier, fucked up and yelling at each other. Howard was forced to break them up twice before muscling both out onto the sidewalk (H still an imposing specimen at 65). There they'd really started going at it. Never a dull moment....

"Have fun in the tank tonight, gentlemen."

Goodspeed stands, swerves, stumbles down the alley. Lights swirl law and order behind him. Overhead, the haze looms florescent. Painted advertisements on building walls date to the block's construction: the pandemic year, 1918. They flake from bricks. It all whirls, grey tones now: a whirling monochromatic swirl. He looks down to steady himself, downlooking. His shoe tops, the gravel beyond shoe tops.... In his basement dwelling. In his bed. The frame groans as he shifts. *Put to sleep this night. Rest thy weary soul.* The night's smoke placid, *Victorious!*

A STICK OF TNT in the exhaust pipe would do the trick: "blow hell out of that thing." Goodspeed stares at the bus with a simmering ire. He schemes as he eats breakfast out on the back landing. A half-dozen equally explosive solutions fill up his brain, heaping pleasant thoughts atop his scrambled heap of eggs.

"A doughnut-shaped plastic explosive, glazed for effect, get the peckerhead to bite into one of those—ker-blammo!" The thought brings audible demented laughter.

Finished with breakfast and, for the moment, his scheming, he ducks back into his abode. He puts on and buttons up a collarless shirt, rounds out his fashionable statement with cut-off jeans and his favorite shoes. He steps out into the day: chest forward, hands on hips, a confident grin. (A shaft of dramatic light?) He is a man on a mission; or is it an anti-mission? Well, no matter. The day wears a glaze, rescinding clarity for heavy haze. It is early (for him) and hot. Rush hour is past, but its legacy lingers as a metallic waft. He breathes it in. *Game on!*

Goodspeed strides up the inclined alley to the row of mailboxes at its end. He pops the lid to his and pulls out a thick stack. All but one envelope is pitched into a nearby trash can without a glance. One and only one mailed item concerns him. He tears into the envelope, hoists the check like a newborn king child. It is his king of consequence. *It is freedom....*

With impressive sales on an already impressive—and soon to be expanding—catalog, Goodspeed's restructured contract (he has Dorothy to thank) now features bonus benchmarks based on a percentage of copies moved, this atop set royalties. Given his recent popularity spike (thanks in no small part to the boosterism of a certain local alt-weekly, and more on this later), the spike has proven quite the windfall. It is more than the projected R.O.I. required of the whole "enterprise," really. And though many view it as no surprise, critics having hailed his first full-length as a stroke of genius (those who didn't trash it, that is), the stroking of ego stalls before the idle reality of Goodspeed not giving a shit. He'll strain no limbs patting himself on the back. The precious metal he mines from his efforts are invested in a single goal: *to defend and sustain the routine.* It is a duty, a cause that he takes to with devotion and dedication. He is writing to triumph over the "living death" of the daily grind. He writes to beat that shit senseless....

"It is the New South lie that continues to pulverize folk beneath the ruse of tradition and patriotism." (And yet the Regular quotes an *Old South* apologist like Tate? Something we'll revisit, dear reader.... )

It isn't about the money. It's about *freedom.* Well, okay, it is about the money; but only in so far as it underwrites the thin survival that defines him (i.e. *the freedom*). For in the end Goodspeed does not write for market-share, or to grace the bestseller list. He writes to be free of the lies that imprison. (He'll live by his own lies, thank you.) This Goodspeed cat is writing for *Victory!* In fact, it may be the only reason he gets up in the morning.... And the Regular steps out into his world.

He lays tracks up Austin Avenue, past the darkened interior of *Asa's,* heading east out of *Springvale.* It's an offbeat corridor: part historic district / part colony-of-the-strange. It is equally proud of both. Austin leads into the above-ground *underground* of this fair city, a place known as: *The Points.* It is here where the fringe, and those craving the charade of the fringe, rally and gather, that annexed plot within every urbanscape where the castoffs plant their stakes and stage the carnival. *(Step right up, folks! Win your purple-haired sweetheart a kewpie doll!)* A glance would suggest a diverse subversion without order. And yet, therein lie the irony of its order. It is predictable that way. Rarely will one encounter the expected out here; and that you can take to the bank. *To deviate as a rule, attitude but a tool....* And our man bolts through.

Signs emblazon vibrant hues. They roll the sparkling / whirling logos of shops alive with fads hip to the day (to be hip as retro-chic tomorrow). Commerce boasts of sex toys, odd kitsch, tattoos, used books and LPs and CDs. There are Jamaican and Cuban and mainland Mexican eats. There are shops selling leather, bongs, crystals, skateboards, and positive karma (less the dogma). There are consignment and second-hand stores, small dive music venues, alleyway theatres and numerous establishments of drink. Shops deal in the thriving trade of pleasure and contraband, places that rent independent films and pornography. It is all in the open, out here. Shocking and flaunting to some, it simply taunts others.... It taunts Goodspeed. He'd have it no other way.

Our man ambles up on *The Points'* streetside preacher-in-residence, slouched on the stoop of a closed eatery. A neighborhood institution, this here is Old Parn.... The old man with a look somewhere between elderly Jesus and Depression-era hobo catches sight of the approaching

Regular. Parn applies a tooth-challenged grin, sits bolt upright, attends to his mission:

"Ah' yes, Marrrrvin Goodspeed. Ye—soiled—sinner. Do ye feel the flames licking yer heels, Marvin Goodspeed? Is it gettin' a bit warm fer ye, son?"

"It's the middle of August, Parn, can fairly say it's warming up."

"Yes, yes, always with the snappy comeback is this Marvin Goodspeed; but alas, is the metaphorical I speak of. Is yer peace guaranteed, son? It best be, for today is the day of atonement! The time nigh! Repent ye!"

"Parn, last Monday was supposed to be 'the day,' remember?" Goodspeed not even breaking stride in deflating the apocalyptic forecast.

"Ah' yes, yes, twas but a shot across the bow Monday was, but a clarion warning to all sinners; yer last I might add as today is the day! Judgment is nigh, soiled one!"

"Could be right, Parn. No reason to think that you couldn't be right," Goodspeed striding by without pause, mining wisdom from the notion of living every day as if it were your last. *Eat, drink, be merry*, words to live by; or in Goodspeed's case, to kill yourself slowly by.... Another day, another slice of the madness however once chooses to slice it.

Steps land hard. Our man plows through the gaussian film of middle August. He lumbers with purpose, royalty check in-hand. The stench of *festivity, the morning after,* rolls up and over *The Points*: stale beer, organic rot in restaurant dumpsters, a nauseant concoction equal parts dairy sour and urine. A nebulous waft drifts over his hard-stepping progress. A garbage truck passes, its engine bitching at and arguing with itself. A vile grey liquid streams from its hold and spatters the street as the truck turns down a sidestreet. "Nice," Goodspeed pulling up short before the turning truck's discharge. The pungent presence fades. Sweat crowds his brow, stepping through "the real"....He'd have it no other way.

Austin leads into the heart of *The Points*, this commercial / residential village crouching on a roadway hub having grown up around the one-time terminus of the city's *Eastside Trolley Line*. Having run down Edgewood onto Memorial and then up DeKalb Avenue from its downtown power station, here the rails came to an end. The convergence of farm-to-market roads had long made it a natural gathering point for roadside stands and auctions. But as late as the '20s, commercial competition consisted of little more than a sleepy rivalry between filling stations—the competition for souls split between a Presbyterian and Baptist Church (both still doing God's work). The arrival of the trolley line and the resulting mingle of city and country established *The Points* as a bona fide commercial district. Over a half-century later, the place is only a long generation removed from unpaved lanes and the yeoman markets. Yet the present presides over a ratcheting up of said *progress!* Roads seethe, groping the red-dirt earth. Vehicular captives plod thoroughfares in numb devotion to the "madness of *progress!*" that drives Goodspeed to question the whole thing....

\*      Our man (as we are finding) is a self-taught student of the region. He is an observer, a defender, a critic. He will often forge a combination of all three in order to drive home a point, as comfortable within the contradictions as he is within his own skin. For instance, you may have noticed Goodspeed has a little thing against the organization of the modern corporate enterprise? And regardless of the accuracy of his exaggerated deductions, it is a well-informed critique upheld by historical fact. You see, he views *"progress!"* not as defined by Webster's — [progress: *n.* Steady improvement, as of a society or civilization] — but for its colloquial use. He knows the term to be a promotional plug once hailed as the savior of Dixie, the *Rebel Yell* of the captains of a *New South* rising from the ashes of Civil War, *Reconstruction* and the violent restoration of home-rule whites of the day christened: *Redemption.* But Goodspeed, the critic, will recount a reality sharply conflicting the rosy all-good of his native region's white-bred narrative....

"The New South? A smokescreen. The real goal of the so-called New South was to reconstitute the dominant greed of the Old South under cover of the public ruse of *progress!* Make all the saps feel important while they break their backs in the Big Mules' mills."

Goodspeed will run through an angry list of "real" results: cultural retrenchment, working class disenfranchisement, endemic race hate, penury, "a bankrupt supremacist creed that stained the honor and selfless sacrifice of rank-and-file Confederate veterans in the vitriol of thick-skulls, hooded or otherwise," that being a direct quote (romanticizing the appalling perhaps the most Southern thing he does), and the most damning offense of all, the one that Goodspeed feels underwrites them all: the exploitation of the southern people for autocratic economic gain.

"Lifting up regular folk was of no concern to all the

New South boosters," he'll claim. "Its sole purpose? Maintenance of an exclusive clique, insular fortunes, and the status quo tariffs that subsidized 'em all. If general prosperity was the goal they woulda made peace with our antiquity 'stead of reconstituting it and exploiting it for personal gain."

Goodspeed dredges up validation from revered southern chronicler, C. Vann Woodward. Our man will recite line-for-line from such tomes as Woodward's classic study: *Origins of the New South*. An animated Goodspeed will grasp the air before him as he spouts:

> *Antiquated social institutions protruded like primeval rock from smooth pavement to obstruct the traffic of progress* ~

To our man, the one-sided opportunism behind a cheer like *progress!* accomplished little more than perpetuating a crude cronyism that long condemned the proles of Dixie to a cultural backwater, and more recently, the butt-end of *Deliverance* jokes.

"Progress for the few at the expense of liberty and justice for all. Just ask the grandparent of any black friend of yers about southern hospitality. Guarantee you get an answer that's just a bit south of the pale nostalgia that is the common trope."

Goodspeed will cite as many examples as one has patience to sit through (really, trust us on this), railing on the exploitative tendency of speculators that have and continue to "prey on bloodkin." He will detail the "cotton mill gulags" and its legions of failed farmers and desperate mountaineers having been done to death in the New South slums by *Gilded Age* profiteers. He'll illustrate the economic dislocation of agricultural futures blanched by the merchant-to-market system. To anyone willing to listen, he'll detail his take on how raw unapologetic greed blurred Jeremiah Mason & Charles Dixon's line and destroyed the possibility that successive generations of Southrons could better their condition: chiefly, the tenants and croppers that the careless economic chaos of the 1870s-80s-90s entrenched into poverty. Goodspeed will quote "big city" editor Ralph McGill, who detailed the point well enough a generation later in *The South and the Southerner*, pleading:

> *Their wretched cabins and the pitiful meagerness of their possessions and existence were eloquent evidence* ~

"The vehicular hordes, look at those poor bastards," Goodspeed shaking his head in honest pity, riled traffic blowing by him as he strides through the heart of *The Points*.

"Be it the plantation, crop-lien, or multinational corporation, ya can define slavery anyway you want, even call this madness *progress!* if ya feel the need."

And so, heap one more atop the litany of examples our study will consider: the fuel firing Goodspeed's unapologetic criticism, this shade tree philosophy. He will keep a squint-eye trained on the real—and perceived— demons of his *Dear Old Southland*. (Oh, and did we mention the serene ease with which he will dispense philosophical evidence of a contradictory / specious nature?) Our man has not a shred of inhibition when it comes to such opinions, will gear up his hustings in the face of a dispute. In fact, he's likely to ask the challenger to step outside.

At the bank, Goodspeed deposits his check. He walks down the line of tellers and past a line of customers peppered-to-tastes not at all out of the ordinary: a mohawk dyed primary colors, piercings where they don't seem to belong, spider webs tattooed across the backs of hands. *Celebrate the life of the freak!* In this neck of the woods one walks hand-in-hand with the strange, the misshapen pieces to society's grand plan a puzzle of their own design. Goodspeed soaks it in. It's a unique drawl that is spoken, out here. Authenticity? The *myth* made real? Southern? Whatever it is, the accent suits our man, allowing his reclusive aims to proceed unmolested, mostly....for as Goodspeed is about to exit, the front door swings open, violently. In rushes The General. Brandishing a pistol (?), he slams the glass-door shut behind him, backing into it as if to barricade it. Sporting a government-issue winter-jacket—Summer or Winter—one gold star on both shoulder-patches, The General sets to aligning his troops....

"They're on our front! They're on our flanks! They're everywhere! You, you, and you," pointing at specific line-waiters, some stunned (those in the know curiously so), "due-south two klicks as fast as yer shit-kickers'll carry ya, secure a fallback position! Now! GO! GO! GO! You and you and you (Goodspeed pointed out as the second "you") get on their heels, but take it twenty paces at at time, covering them the whole damn-damn-damn—god-dammit! We're surrounded! We're surrounded! Fuck it! I'm goin' in!"

The General turns, throws open the door, and bursts out wildly, firing the starter's pistol, it turns out (a fact that is widely known)—*click-click, click-click, click-click*—which he keeps hip-holstered, Patton-like, at all times; that is, when not leading a courageous break out. "Suck on that, motherfuckers!" a blaze of glory as The General sprints down DeKalb away from *The Points*.

Yet another of the relatively harmless (though you never know) and ultimately tragic ill-folk that flooded *The Points* with the draconian cuts to funding for mental facilities that began in earnest during the '80s, the best guess is that he mixes in post-traumatic stress with whatever else of his in-skull milieu that has come un-calibrated. (Muckraking the hush-hush elimination of the state's safety net for the chronic and homeless mentally-ill led to a 3-part 1995 lead in the local alt-rag, *The Weekly*, and the then newly reconstituted paper's first award for investigative journalism, by the way.) Of Vietnam Veteran age, so very elusive, brandishing something that looks like a pistol causing the police to take notice, and living entirely off the land without aid of the several local shelters and kitchens, the working theory is that The General must have had military training at some point. But it is impossible to identify, diagnose, and treat what you cannot catch, as no one can get near him. (As a part of the mentioned 1995 investigation, an anonymous source at the city and region's main VA hospital claimed that if The General was a vet, he would not qualify for post-traumatic stress treatment even if he had it, as the military did not officially recognize it until the 1980s, having less than honorably discharged those exhibiting its psyche-melting symptoms during the Vietnam-era, and claiming, now, that they cannot treat something that did not exist; this, though it was in the service that the condition—which officially did not exist, even though it did—was caused? Yes, we had the same f-ing reaction, dear reader.)

So, The General makes his rare hit-and-run appearances. They are always of a defensive nature, safeguarding the public within this greater district from a phantom enemy army set at any moment to invade from just beyond the gates—a delusion Goodspeed will argue is at least metaphorically true (if not actually the case). Given his many "stands for the people," the cops settle on just keeping an eye on him, The General otherwise spending his time eluding their patrols as he himself patrols the perimeter of a place where "odd"—by-choice or physio-logical chemistry—feels right at home.

The surreality is shed quickly (though it is never far), the crowd rapidly resuming its banking and waiting. Goodspeed resumes his exiting....

"Should look into one of those direct deposit wire deals. One of these days that gun is bound to be real."

And the morning lopes along beneath the coming heat, Goodspeed's strides hitting their rhythmic stroke. The lurid hungry rays devour the last of an early mist. Our man soaks it in. *This here, it is home....* A repetitious rambler, he traverses his approach route: west out of *The Points* on the far side of Austin. Old Parn is standing and shaking both fists across the avenue, his usual fistfuls of leaflets scattering as end-times ticker-tape. He is at the top of his game, shaking violently from head to toe:

"God damn ye, Marvin Goodspeed! Ye God damn'd sinner! Atone, ye wretched refuse! Atone!"

Goodspeed smiles, waves to the boiling missionary.

Old Parn, The General, doing their part to keep the neighborhood "real." Goodspeed slips down side streets, quiet lanes, and a smug eliteness devoid of the fragrance of urine and garbage trucks streaming foul goo. He can already feel the need, the gnawing urge to keep it "real."

*Here Comes A Regular.* The few drawn up to the bar greet Marvin Goodspeed's spot-on noontime arrival. It is uncanny, executed with a balance-wheel precision that can only be explained by our man's dedication to *the routine: practice, practice, practice....Confound the stifling piety. Cross the coercive values and invasive judgment at every turn. A guerrilla insurgency slowly—imperceptibly— leeching the righteous indignation from the finger waving holier-than-thous legislating and exalting moderation, conformity, capitulation. The morning's battle is won, time in bivouac. But the war is not over, not by a long shot....* Goodspeed throws out return greetings, back pats of a camaraderie earned. He makes his way down the length of bar: his kingdom, his cockpit. He takes his usual seat. It is an earned throne.

Howard, keen to this noontime routine, uncaps and serves Goodspeed a domestic-in-a-bottle.

"How goes it, Marv?"

"At the moment, spectacular."

"So, that young reporter type, not sure what he is, Cleburne his name. Anyway, he came back by 'bout opening time looking for ya," Howard relays. Faithful H.

"My timing's impeccable, ain't it?" Goodspeed feeling the flush of "spectacular" quickly fade.

"Sayin' something about thinking through what you told him, has an angle you might be interested in, somethin' like that; said he might swing back by this afternoon. Determined, will give him that."

"Another'n when convenient, H," Goodspeed throwing a V on behalf of his empty (!) bottle, his tone assuring afternoon absence.

Having previously made things clear to the interloper, in dangerous proximity of treading on the bar side tradition of *laissez-faire* (to be explained, dear reader), Goodspeed figures the worst. There may be nothing he dislikes more than the interview, having been "forced" to physical violence in defending his *freedom* more than once. He has gained a reputation, one that continues to invite the intrepid as if a dare. And given the mentioned popularity spike of late, the horde of intruders has increased many-fold. He grits his teeth just thinking about 'em.

"Today's mass media equals fast food entertainment for the brain dead, exploiting a fad till it's a rotting corpse. Parasites just trying to sell their rags. I refuse to be their corpse-in-waiting," would be your run-of-the-mill Goodspeed rant....

\* And so, given an instinctual lean on curt threats and actual violence, it seems fair to ask: Why the interest in this dude? The intrepid dare? Or does it lie with simple curiosity (something said interloper snorts as if he had a problem)? It does seem a safe bet that when one plumbs the depths of complexity, one may just unearth a mythic reality beyond what simplistic impressions allow. No guarantee, but in this case odds favor a story far richer than: abrasive alcoholic asshole. For it bears repeating that there was a time not all that long ago when the daily grind

Goodspeed pursued as means-to-an-end, the forced necessity of a menial salary and unpaid overtime carved from the plodding vehicular hordes.... *But then, he wrote the book.*


ENTER ONE CYRUS CLEBURNE. A chump—er, excuse me—interloper—okay, wait—a young journalist for the city's alternative newspaper, *The Weekly* (there it is)— Cleburne is a familiar face to many, out here. A self-proclaimed stalker of the scene, he turns off of Highland onto Colquitt, passing by the seen-better-days building that housed his first apartment. His recent past rears up all around him. He filters it all through a misty-eyed nostalgia. Having moved to this *Beacon of the New South* in the Summer of 1990, Cleburne counts himself amongst several tight-knit staff-members who were in on the ground-floor-up remaking of the reconstituted *Weekly.*

Cyrus lopes along beneath the afternoon steam. Close-cropped hair helps to reduce the Summer sweat factor, the spine of his linen shirt soaked nonetheless. Immaterial. One must do what they must to get the scoop. For it's all in pursuit of the story: legwork, sacrifice, dedication to *the cause.* A lanky yet efficient gait powers his observational exploration of any and all things *scene.* And he is in luck, for it is on full display....

The extremes of the modern societal condition come with larger than life exclamation points, out here, the tragic and triumphant punctuating a middling *normal* that is anything but. As just documented, this place taps into that sense of security unique to colonies of immigrants and outcasts, the marginalized—the persecuted, even—a palpable sense of reveling in the shared experience of *finally* having a place where they may impose their peculiar will. Out here, the marginalized and the outcast may sculpt their reality. They can promote an unspoken hope: that though this carnival be not normal, perhaps it should be; a fantasy that has its participants (full-timers and passers-by alike) buying in all the more. See, you have what is, and what folks think is—*is*. The two perform an entertaining tango on the streets of *Springvale*, *The Points*, and the above-ground *underground* district that these urban villages anchor. Delineating fact from fiction is certainly the journalistic ideal. But what of unpacking an *ideal* conjured of an alternate reality, one that cares little for your garden variety suite of ideals? The more scoop Cleburne pursues, the more braided—indistinguishable, even—fact and fiction seem to become. They come to rely on one another: load-bearing pillars of the whole enterprise. It is an old analogy updated for our use here, fact using fiction as the drunk uses the lamp post: for support, not illumination. Shading the truth, exaggeration, the little white lies, these are but tools—the re-bar of perception. But, in fact, their use is also illuminating, hinting at non-reckoned motivations buried by-chance or by-choice.... So, shall we unearth peculiar traits unique to this odd place, or universal tics known the world over? What to make of this skein of contradiction, its furious maze of redefinition / reinvention? Is this *real v. myth* tug of war conditional to the *New South* realized? Is it unconditional East-West-North-South? It is one thing for sure: trowel time....

Cleburne is a keen observer of this little corner of *The Beacon*, its facts and fictions in tandem and in conflict. It flaunts and it taunts, running the spectrum from rib-poking jest: "hey now, just playing with ya there, chief," to squint-eye ideological stand: "mind repeating yourself there—chief?" It's a stormy lover's quarrel that often underwrites the journalist's content; well, any good journalist, that is. (Suck it, media whores!) And these days, its promising yield seems everywhere apparent. Cleburne detects truth as fiction rearing up with such natural ease that he's leaning towards it being an evolutionary instinct: involuntary breathing, the barter economy, *myth when reality won't do.* It's an interesting theory and Cleburne is wading in. To treat it as a profound truth, or skewer it as an absurdity of the human condition? (We silly conscious beings.) This is the quandary for our good journalist. He does fear that a concrete answer might just spoil his fun; but presses on sans trepidation, with dedication.... What is, and what we think is—*is*. It's a promising combustible fuel. And in one Marvin Goodspeed, Cyrus Cleburne may well have tapped a gusher.

Admittedly, our good journalist sometimes can't help but fall back on an instinct to go all-sarcastic when faced with the particularly absurd. For example, a recent lead in *The Weekly* examined the widening beltline of evidence underwriting a link between suburban car-culture and the national obesity epidemic. A sidebar column collected Cleburne's interviews with fast-food drive-thru workers at random suburban franchises (performed skillfully from a car window while proceeding through fast-food drive-thrus). According to the helpful teens and underpaid adults he'd interviewed, Cleburne ascertained that, indeed, a goodly proportion of those utilizing suburban drive-thrus probably should have chosen lower caloric options. The facts had spoken, our good journalist going deep for the story himself: having gained 5 lbs in a week. (One too many double cheeseburgers there, chump?) Determined. Dedicated.

Nothing is sacred, out here, automatic respect unknown in these parts. It is all fair game within *The Weekly's* covers. A Clemens / Mencken-style skewering in pursuit of general social commentary alongside the gravitas of going after neglected on-the-street stories often upsetting to the booster narrative of local "news leaders" (owned and operated as they all are these days by distant mega-corps), all of this guides *The Weekly's* drawl. And considering its metro-wide circulation, those of the staff who remain from the revamp days look back through the lens of magnolia-scented nostalgia at a job well done. They did more than resuscitate a wheezing source for community events / arts and the occasional op-ed slamming *the man*; they'd helped transform *The Weekly* into an institution that sports both journalistic—and—artistic cred. Strange to recall here within the halcyon gleam of these *Go Go '90s*, that the rag barely made it out of the *New Wave (No Wave?) '80s*....

\*        Having come on the scene in 1967 as *The Points'* community paper during the district's swift transformation from traditional "upstanding" commercial district to post-white-flight *groovy scene*, the vacated storefront deals up for a song and favorable zoning all ready to subsidize *the new*, the paper's antiestablish-mentarianism (real word, look it up) remained consistent throughout its first two decades of print. Unfortunately, so did its scope. That the '60s actually did end on January 1,

1970, seemed a fact unknown to an editorial bend that grew increasingly stale the further that pivotal decade receded in the rear-view. Of course, mass sociocultural-political upheavals do not heed the nice neat breakpoints of Pope Gregory's calendar; but the tectonic shifts that did remake the landscape during the mid-to-late '60s rapidly (as in blindingly) evolved beyond flower power's ability to influence this continuity of change alone. Oblivious to the fatigue of utopian ideals and the gathering storm of punk, the paper stumbled unawares deep into the '70s as a fight-the-power yawner. A lack of younger hires and its limited circulation saw it utilized much more for the local arts calendar (for which it deserves all the praise one can muster) than for any seeing-eye wit that might make one scratch their chin and say: hmmmm.... Add to it that *The Weekly's* increasingly infrequent, always predictable op-eds created of it an easy stereotype for cheap political hits equally lacking inquisitive scope....

"That rag generates unpatriotic trash like so much hippie graffiti in an underpass. It's just editorial aid and comfort to our enemies. They can take their Red America to San Francisco, or the USSR, or wherever. I'll take my America red, white, and blue," was typical of campaign season gasconade.

Small-time and amateur, *The Weekly's* mainly volunteer staff (it was a non-profit, in that it never, ever, made a profit) was long over serving as a punching bag for uptight state senate hopefuls. The '80s saw a leak of staff / volunteering leach the paper's lifeblood. Yet, watching the only local source for the arts not spewing the company anthem B.S. of arts-as-commodity go down the drain, was a fate worse than rescuing a weak local rag. *The Weekly* was on life support in 1989 when acquired by a group of metro business owners led by restaurant guru, Gibbs Frederickson.

Already a fixture in *the Points*, Gibbs was on his way to becoming scene patron numero uno—*El Presidente!*—in implementing a vision for what *The Weekly* could be: a commercial enterprise, a core full-time staff pulling competitive paychecks and going where big stiff media outlets wouldn't dare, an operation devoid of values-based (i.e. political) censorship that was wide open in its First Amendment interpretation (ads for church-run youth groups and escort services still reside side-by-side within its covers), etc. The part of the plan that would set it apart (and net ad dollars) was Gibbs' personal desire that it expand on the paper's redeeming quality—a highly regarded local music column—in pursuit of being a tireless promoter of all of the local arts scene: from live music to guerrilla theatre, local writers to sidewalk graffiti.

Again, enter one Cyrus Cleburne.... Having first arrived in the city the following Summer, his first job was at Gibb's pizza joint in *The Points*. Fortuitous? Two years' worth of a journalism degree at Washington & Lee in his native Virginia got him a shot with the new-and-improved alternative *The Weekly*. He was a staff-writer inside a year. Not bad.

Cleburne's lope makes quick work of the sidewalk. He rolls into the outskirts of *Candler Hills*, the neighborhood north and east of *The Points*. He is gearing up for the challenge, learning "the order" in order to use it to advantage. He will go where few have gone before. It may take a few curt uncomfortable suggestions to "watch yourself" and "leave, now!" But then, that's all just part of the beat, a sacrifice to be made in pursuit of *the cause*. He is no green kid. Our good journalist understands that to tread on *myth-when-reality-won't-do* is an offense punishable by fist-to-face, stabbing as it does at a raw nerve so baked into cultural instinct it might as well start with *Thou Shalt Not*.... But this here pursuit has reached an important milestone, in that he is now willing to demote better judgment beneath a fuck-it-all tenacity. Cleburne shall test his own *devotion to cause*. It is time to dig deep into the source itself. He scratches his chin....

"The character he is and the character he thinks he is....hmmmm."

MEANWHILE, BACK AT THE RANCH, Boo is doing his best to wile away the day: Zell *Boo* Hadley, having made a minor fortune in concrete before removing himself from the work-a-day world—and society. A wrinkled stub of a recluse, Boo is the elder of *Asa's* regulars, a bar side fixture since the Bicentennial. Boo shares a posthumous hope with Chuck:

"See, I've put some thought into it. It's the thing I wanna do. What better way to live on after yer dead than be stuffed? I already talked to a taxidermist who said he'd consider it," Boo's strategy to beat back time more creative than most. (Of course, he has had the most *practice, practice, practice*....)

"What'd be the clincher is if someone'd sneak my dead stuffed varnished corpse into my ex-wife's kitchen some night 'n have her wake up to that. Shoot-hell, I'd do it just to see the look on her face!"

Chuck cocks an eyebrow. A soft mountain of a man, a veteran of Vietnam and the nearby Bremen Steel yards who has spent most lunch breaks at *Asa's* going on a decade now, Chuck dials up his well-used "you crazy cracker" look.

"Wormbait, Boo. I wanna be wormbait in a hole in 'da ground. I still gotta outside chance a gettin' to heaven yet, figure that's the best place to wait around for it."

"I want a funeral pyre, big ass Indian noble type funeral pyre; burn me to a crisp and stir my ashes up into a batch of Muth's Brunswick stew," is Goodspeed's wish.

Martha, Muth—Howard's wife of 40 years and co-proprietor—pokes her head up from behind the kitchen counter. She beams, proudly. Rivulets of delta'd wrinkles and a head full of florescent white-grey speak nothing of her age, but only confirm a matriarchal status. She informs in a low-country tone: "That there's my boy. Your stew is comin' right up, Mah'vin," all shreds of patrician having been scoured from Martha's long life amongst *the people*.

Meanwhile, Howard: "Yes, yes, this is all well and good, but I'm probably gonna cash in some day standing here listening to you crackpots. No one'll even notice till it comes time for a refill, tell ya what," an assumption almost guaranteed to see its day.

Goodspeed adding: "You're gonna outlive us all, H. I say ya take Boo one step further: stuff our heads one-by-one as we kick off, hang 'em behind the bar like huntin' trophies."

Howard stands up straight and tall, hands at his side as he shakes his head: "You kiddin' me? Having had to put up with this crew while breathing is bad enough. Trust me, I'll make sure that all y'all is wormbait," a jumble of closed-lip laughs, Chuck leaning over to Boo: "sayin' it true, he said it true."

Having deposited his check into the "freedom fund" and run a strong ring around *The Points*, Goodspeed feels his domestic-in-a-bottle honestly earned. He adjusts in his captain's chair. It is his command-and-control centre. From here our man can plot time's undoing, swamping worry and general disgust in apathy....

\* Now given our most recent observations, those versed in regional history might sight an irony developing from the study of our man: Goodspeed's behavior measuring up to a key *New South* "yardstick." Trowels in hand, let's dig into this sherd field for all its worth.... *Laissez-faire*, the applied label for a hands-off policy towards the socioeconomic ramifications of free market machinations (the inclusion of big words ending in *-tion* always helping a theory to sound more plausible), was once a jingoistic maxim of the *New South* captains that Goodspeed so often spackles with shit. And as the *Populists* claimed long ago, our man in turn will finger it as THE yardstick in evaluating a wealthy white man's entry into "the club"—i.e. just how zealous one was in advocating against socioeconomic change, and how vehement they were in broadcasting broadsides sounding out support for *the status quo*. The irony? How ably this yardstick of hands-off applies to "in here." In so far as *Asa's* and the clean maintenance of *liberty* are concerned, Goodspeed is as *laissez-faire* as they come. He is an ardent defender of the peculiar *status quo* that trickles down from *Asa's* rafters. He is, perhaps, its most dedicated soldier.

Our man trumpets *Neo-Populist* credentials, and it goes to make sense. The *Populist* movement in the South—a virile socioeconomic uprising of the late 1800s—was an odd mash of small farmers with Old South (read: conservative) instincts, that nonetheless sought systemic intervention to secure a fair share of the *New South* windfall they felt their due as producers of commodities. Even more radical? They embraced progressive socioeconomic reforms (read: the guv'ment) to achieve said ends. Odd.... What was not odd was that the big money boosters of *New South* industry above and below the Mason / Dixon, and their *Southern Democratic* political patrons, saw to it that debate left economic equity in the dust, cashing in instead on the cultural currency to be mined from the threat that "un-American radical Populists" posed to *the status quo* of—you guessed it—white supremacy.

Victors sure are swell about writing and distributing history. So, it's no wonder that the "populist" label comes down to us in these modern days as a hapless crank intent on inflaming partisan wedge issues, instead of a debt-indentured farmer looking to forces larger than he / she to disperse the gross concentration of wealth and its natural result: a monopolization of political power via the cunning manipulation of that old chestnut, democracy. It should be noted that some of the labeling was fairly earned. Many *Populists* were, or were to become, hapless cranks, with many eventually retreating into vile Old South racism and Old American anti-semitism. But in the main, *Populism* and that particular late nineteenth-century *Populist* moment still present an ideological moving target. Politically, they attempted to fuse the old and new in tandem; another amongst the litany of ironies: in that it was the old and new in conflict that did them in.... The neutral historian-approved history of that moment reads with predictability: The *Gilded* leviathan of *the status quo* was in no mood for populist experimentation, only a grim racialist ass-whooping for those seeking change.

And so, having shed daylight on the historical fine print, we now realize that our man may be onto something here. Having embraced the thundering contradictions of *old v. new* (as in a full-on creepy bear hug), he defends it as he rails against it. Goodspeed will claim *laissez-faire* as one and one thing only: "the economic nail in the coffin that screwed the South for good." And yet, his dedicated bodily defense of *the status quo*, in here....Interesting.... So as to retain street-cred, his antiestablishmentarianism (no, of course we could not help ourselves, dear reader) might have Goodspeed making a public stand against our theory, letting loose a boilerplate harangue along the lines of:

"The New South was a late nineteenth-century marketing jingle; a PR dodge, nothing more. It only masked the rapacious and greedy who were fine-tuning their game for a new era, screwing their own with usury and credit 'stead of the old ways of bondage and the whip."

But people, people, please....now is not the time for ideological inquiry. At the moment, one's *laissez-faire*—er—one's *peaceful drinking* is all that matters. In here, one must abide by a set of unwritten rules. They are time-honored traditions. A newcomer's welcome is hard-earned, camaraderie a pensive act. The outsider must step lightly, pick their moments, and identify the wearing out of a welcome (lest they raise a fistful of ire). For there is an order, in here. And it is lived with an earnestness one might mistake for vigor. *Tread light and drink well.*

Howard serves up his ever popular domestic-in-a-bottle reprise.

"Much obliged, H."

Martha, still beaming, serves up Goodspeed's stew.

"My boy, my boy," scuffling her way back into the kitchen.

Goodspeed peels off a grin. It is resolute, taut, all he needs from this world sitting right there on the bar before him....*an earnestness, an intensity one might mistake for zeal....* And so does his day proceed, *the status quo* doing its thing.

After the quick hit, our man picks up where his a.m. rambling left off.... The quiet lanes emit styles unknown to an era designed for—and by—mass-consumption: a Tudor, a Neoclassic of the french sort, spandrel and finial details leftover from *Beaux Art* trends. Nuance, born of a *Gilded* past, soaks the view alongside Goodspeed's steps. Having withstood the bulldozer's wrath, *Springvale* pins its hopes to a (small 'g') gilded re-dux that's been a long time coming. Urban pioneers of the 1960s-70s-80s blazed a trail for the more general and generic (some would argue questionable) gentrification of settlers now seeping in along the lanes and avenues of this *grand olde belle*. And though this eclectic mix has reclaimed the 'hood from its original soulless white privilege, the bricks of gross profit extracted from gross inequity + aristocratic excess in the face of mass want are still there, embedded in the foundations of these one-time edge-of-urban retreats, its sidewalks of cracked hexagonal stone. With each footfall, *Springvale's* robber baron origins—*New South* style, y'all!—serve notice to a more egalitarian second-act: *There Will Be Guilt!*

Yet that does not interfere with the fantasy of *Springvale* as a *Gilded Age* theme park. Its modern holistic temper wallpapers good will over the crude lathe that still brackets its many original, if cracked, plaster walls: an artifice trading up from staid Victorian puritanism to funky and art-hip. And though Goodspeed levels a squint-eye at this settler trend—unconvinced of its implied equity, sniffing the air for hints of two-faced boosterism—he is free to wander *Springvale 2.0* as he will.

He splits his time evenly amongst the fiction and non-fiction. It is so natural a tendency that it seems (to the casual observer) subconscious, playing one off another if only for shits-and-giggles. Or is it to make a point? Hmmmm.... He will roam, mentally and physically, where he wants, when he wants. For the stultifying menace of others' deadlines, a "subservience to the modern plantation" (his loaded phrase, not ours), traffic jams, all of this is just the regressive taxation of a disposable workplace that he has neatly disposed of. These days will find him hoarding the currency of an alternate reality, time his folding-money now.

His steps translate a whim to real, rambling as he will. Splayed columns line the porch front of the squat bungalow, signature style of the more modest second-wave of construction throughout these urban 'hoods, c. 1920s-30s, and before mass production meant "mass-producing vast mountains of cheap crap"....

"Profit-driven obsolescence for a disposable world.

Suck out the marrow, replace it with cheap filler. Quantity over quality consumed by the diabetic ton."

No, this paragon of healthy living will not play along. He will not play nice. He ambles down past a block of bungalows, blockhouses along the perimeter of this urban frontier; solid and sure, yet leery of the transient. *Beware ye ne'er-do-wells, we's watchin' you....* And Goodspeed steps through.

To remain remote within a modern metropolis. A hope contradicting reality, certainly. Its achievement impossible, perhaps. Yet it is the one goal worth his energy, his dedication. In fact, if there is one thing our study has already settled it is that Goodspeed didn't write the book for fame. Money, certainly. To make a point, perhaps. But he didn't write for renown or celebrity status. His was an inspiration we all hold dear: *freedom.*

We'll get back to Goodspeed's expert testimony in a moment. But first let us let the trowel's painstaking exploration grout in a few gaps in the backstory....

\*       This drive for privacy had all started with Goodspeed's sudden fame. *Freedom achieved*, he'd not counted on the "homicidal price tag" of hitting it big. In a flash, instant recognition had found him, more like jumped him in a dark alley. Reluctant, he felt nonetheless *duty bound* to the chord he'd struck with his off-kilter epic.... Word is that his mother had achieved modest acclaim for a handful of published poems and short stories back in the '50s before he was born; and though the search for verifiable evidence is ongoing, genetics would help explain a creative drive so physiologically true that it ranks right up there with dopamine's enabling of the mesolimbic pathway. For he'd always had it in him, writing fiction / verse an obsessive automatic response. (His scribbling knows no bounds.) It was that one niche talent that if properly mined could deliver financial freedom and *liberty!* in this life. And though the charade that we all have a shot at falling into fortune is enough for most, Goodspeed's unremitting nature hoisted it up the flagpole as imperative. It was *Victory!* or bust. *Live free or die!*

But creativity as a character trait don't pay no bills. Pre-*freedom*, Goodspeed was forced into the work-a-day world just like anyone else. And therein lay a problem; for our man is an enigma cut of an alternate weave, a coarse irregular bolt not tuned in to watercooler humor. He strode the advocated path, society-approved for our protection ("they claim to know what's best for us") not a second longer than required. For when an alternate plan gelled, he was out of there—a decision made all the more easy by the "lecherous back-stabbing of office politics" and the "trite wells of displayed knowledge." Quarterly projections, the job justifying make-believe of middle management, all of the myriad greater-the-profit / greater-the-good theorems he found to be nothing more than a *Jonestown-sian* concoction that poisoned all players with the fakery of worth. To our man it was all bullshit: a premeditated murder of time. He would not drink the *New South* Kool-Aid. He was no one's "slave."

The watershed chapter was written in 1992. Goodspeed was night manager of a midtown hotel when he learned of the chain's merger with a once-reviled competitor turned cozy chum. That absurdity was followed the following week by his being shuffled into a 9-5 desk-job at the corporate HQ downtown, a questionable promotion that promoted the very bullshit he'd always escaped by working the night-shift. Late at night he dealt with the fringe of society, where the innate madness of humankind is not only an accepted fact but a notion one goes with. (Really, why fight it?) Goodspeed could deal with the late-night freaks, those with questionable tales and intent, the hookers. It was the straight-and-narrow that bent him. So, no surprise that the merger "promotion" would accelerate the eventual. For individual nature is what it is; and for better or worse, it eventually asserts command-and-control.

Goodspeed knew all along that he had it in him: an explosive creative well on which to draw. He also knew he'd go-postal (as was the in-term) sitting at a desk all day. Goodspeed's tolerance of the dead eye corporate super-culture flickered as a failing porchlamp. And so, when *that day* arrived, he knew it. The writing (graffiti?) was on the wall. Following the droning "murder" of the weekly review meeting, he'd stopped not even to clean out his desk; at meeting's end had walked from conference room to elevator, rode it silently to the ground floor, walked through front lobby revolving door, and was gone for good. Our man walked straight home that day and began putting to paper the novel he had been writing in his head for a year. He'd always had the knack. It took only two relentless months to complete; and, as impressive, a mere eight months (and *only* 43 rejections) to hook a publisher. Goodspeed had a deal inside a year. Not bad.

*That day* had been that rare day. It had all been as clear as a December morning. Some are okay with having *freedom / liberty!* defined for them. Some would rather a hole-in-the-head. Goodspeed was no one's "slave." Sink or swim, it would be of his own hand.... Since then, many who claim to know him say he's done a bit of both. Interesting in that either result seems geared for his brand of *Victory!* Goodspeed probably wouldn't even offer an opinion on the matter, his near forty-years having molded a reclusive wisdom, having peppered his sideburns grey.

Meanwhile....Cyrus Cleburne turns south out of the *Hills*, a light step as he heads for *The Weekly's* offices. His legwork seems to have found its sea legs; and that is a good thing. For careful archeology will only get him so far. He will need to turn into the heavy swells, lest he drop an incomplete picture of this man, this myth. He is working hard on behalf of a rapt audience, soldiering on, taking his cue, our good journalist learning a thing or two. "He's a walking masterpiece, this guy."
*Bravo! Bra—vo!*

TIME SKIPS A BEAT. It is Friday night, darkness weighing in. A late-afternoon storm has come and gone, humidity hovering over the steaming loam. It all seems so efficient, graphed with care, the rhythm of nature's prerogative easy, content: *mist cures the morning air marinade, heat spirals over noon summoning the storms of late afternoon, dusk acquires sky, muscles out day....* It is an irresistible tempo. It's an offer one really can't refuse.

Lights emerge from timid hovels, streetlamps spilling florescence upon Austin Avenue. Automobiles bound up towards *The Points*, headlights probing the obscure as steam-stirring shepherds....*Follow us! This way to Friday night!* they entice. *Come, join the parade of freaks!* they proclaim.

Its disciples are piling out from the inchoate grey. They are on their way. Festive chords strike in bell towers, calling to the faithful, calling them forth:

*Come forth, ye children. Heed the scripture of your desires!*

Goodspeed rights his sinking stance with the help of streetlamp post. Henry and George amble into view. They are already mid-stream of a dumb, if spirited, dispute.

"Ya cain't be serious," spouts Henry, "cain't be straight faced 'n say something so damn'd stupid."

"Pay attention to what I'saying, is all. Dickey Betts is nothin' without Duane Allman, just a back-up guitar player," George's arms flailing, stirring the dusk.

"Without Dickey there's no Duane as we all knew 'n loved 'em. They all made each other better. Ya just ain't that bright are ya? I smoked my joints up there on Rose Hill, I know what it all meant. Till you can say the same you best just shut it! Dickey wrote *Eliza Reed* for chrisesakes! It's like ya cain't help but just say stupid shit!"

"Now don't get all with the drama now. Once again you gettin' all bent, blabbin' 'stead of listenin' cuz what I just did say was that Duane and Dickey was a team, that they —

"Just shut yer hole, George. Just shut yer goddamned hole! Hey, Marv," Henry greeting Goodspeed as the two enter *Asa's*, George mumbling a half-hearted something.

"Asshole," Goodspeed thinks, a brief head shake, an involuntarily squint in his left eye. He follows them inside....

Inside, the restless regulars stir. Backlit neon paints

Goodspeed in silhouette: radioactive, stepping into his realm. It is Friday night. And on Friday night it all hangs out, in here. Normal serenities are sequestered, squirreled away under the billowing blather of those drunk and those soon to be. Jabs and barbs are thrown, followed by backslaps and the howling of inebriates. Sometimes there are words, sometimes fists. Ritual and standard are amplified in excess on this night. It's infectious, its lingo seething with a condemnation of time itself. Time's transgressions and all "freedom murdering" devices employed in their name (a sprawling list at this point of the week simply featuring: "work, work, work") are fingered as the tyrannical despots they are. The judge and jury colors damning speech, the drawling vernacular of those we know (and love?) as regulars. Feel not the need to speak light on this night. On Friday night truths are made well-known and then drowned in spirits.... *Welcome, all! (Watch yourself, hear?)*

Goodspeed does his best Moses, splitting a sea of revelry in making his way to his seat. He settles in, backslaps a fellow seated to his right: Omar, a behemoth Harley-perched Vietnam Vet who works hired-gun private security. So long as he is there, he *is* security. To befriend such a man is in one's interest, a piece of wisdom Goodspeed made his own working the graveyard shift.... A handful of parking lots around the midtown hotels were part of Omar's beat. The two found themselves kindred spirits, outsiders to a sociocultural paradigm partly by-chance, mainly by-choice. Head nods, implying all of the above, eventually led to meet-ups for a 3 a.m. flask or joint out behind the hotel's kitchen. Goodspeed invited Omar to come visit *Asa's* someday. Omar finally did. A drifter, forgotten by his country and virtually everyone else, he had finally found a home.... And he will defend it as such. Omar only cares to know a few things. But those things— loyalty, ass kicking for pay—he knows well.

And the ladies have arrived; well, the other ladies—Ez and Jude having dutifully stood to their posts (on either side of the bar's front corner L-bend) since quittin' time. Dorothy and Marjory burst through the crowd. Starting with Ez and Jude, they pay respects to a full gathering before taking either seat aside Goodspeed. Omar gives up his seat to Marge, a civility usually annulled by night's end: a face slap, an ugly sidewalk outburst. D and Goodspeed show little interest in such displays, sudden unquestioned partings more their speed. But at the moment, the love pours, elixirs served up tall and cool. It is a family affair behind the bar, nuclear, extended: Howard, Martha, niece Olivia, and grand-daughter Terry, wheeling out orders with casual indifference. A *service-plus* may be lacking, but no one feels the need to raise the point.

"Muth, how about setting up our lovelies here?" Goodspeed calling on the intrepid matriarch.

"Yes, yes, of course, my dears. What'll y'all have? Will bourbon across rocks satisfy?" Martha stepping up service for *her people*, her family.

"Bourbon?" Dorothy looking to Marge. Marge shakes her head affirmative, already looking over Omar in trying to decide what nerve to work.

"Bourbon'll do, Muth. So, Marv says you were out at your sister's?" D inquiring, knowingly.

"Mmm, yes," Martha nodding, a rumpled grin, "pretentious freeloader; had it not been for her marrying up rich she'd be cryin' herself to sleep in a shithole trailer somewhere. Should see how these wealthy folk live. How many closets and bathrooms does one really need? Livin' in one of them gilded suburbs northside of town, gated with its own security force to keep out the undesirables, even. Don't think they even wipe their own ass, probably have that illegal house servant do it for 'em. I don't know why I bother, anymore. Loyalty, s'pose. Ya just can't shed what's a part of you."

"Truth, Muth. You own your people, their past, their present, like it was your own, like it or not," Goodspeed in accord, expounding some, downing a double.

"Yes, sadly true. All she's got is her allowance and her gin. Doesn't even have her only child anymore," Martha nodding at Olivia, their niece having split and come over to the aunt / uncle's "side of the tracks" many moons ago.

"Is sad, really, the poor girl. I do still love her; older sister instinct, s'pose. But that damned politician husband of hers, SOB would screw ye six-ways-to-Sunday."

"Politicians," Goodspeed shaking his head, "hucksters pushing promises instead of Plymouths. They proclaim to the duped crowds: 'I got your back,' while winkin' to the corporate raiders just off-stage, assuring them that it is they who have nothing to worry about. Bait-and-switch, that's their gig. They can go to hell in my book."

"They all do go to hell in your books, hon," Martha grinning, so proud of their artist-in-residence, a light motherly pat of his cheek.

"No need to talk work, Muth. It is time to set to the business at hand. There are more important matters to attend to. It's Friday night. And I have a good mind to drink on Friday nights. High time we get to it! Cheers, all!"

Glasses are raised in a toast, even from a crowd of

"unfamiliars" about them. Cleburne steps in and goes so far as to clink Goodspeed's bottle with his own before draining it, giving the Regular cheers. Goodspeed awards a wry grin to boldness, casts a squint-eye as Cleburne tips his cap and moves on. Potential interlopers all, potentially treading on this here "business of *freedom*." This one, this one will be given leniency; a trial period, Goodspeed considering the potential to work a hack to advantage.... But an instant of clemency should not bring ease to the unfamilar's eggshell steps. For it only takes one misstep for it all to go to hell, just like ( * insert finger snap here). Best to watch yourself, respect hard-earned, its upkeep a constant vigil....

And Martha's grin, lighting up this dank fiesta. She is in her element, beaming: "My people, my people."

A band begins to play in the back room, reason for the crowd of unfamiliars. The music devolves quickly. Distorted and disruptive, it is more a catfight fought to a beat. A bass-player herself, it was grand-daughter Terry's idea to bring in local start-up bands on Friday nights, help Gam & Gamps siphon off the scene just up the way in *The Points*. One has to believe *Asa's* co-proprietors were envisioning something more *Buddy Holly* tribute band or classic *Johnny Paycheck*—less a bad *Dinosaur Jr.* knock-off.

"Terry kept pushin,' soon got me to thinkin' it a good idea to start the next generation off on the right foot; 'sides, could be we see the next big thing comes right in through our back room here," Howard had said in making the case to the regular crowd (presented in the format of what was to occur, whether they liked it or not). This is the second Friday, the second band; the experiment not living up to high hopes.

"Sounds like they're kicking their damned instruments down a flight of stairs; and all the caterwaulin," Goodspeed himself having wished for something more *Merle* or *Exile On Main Street*.

Rimshots and cymbals mix tenaciously with the shouts of those just trying to be heard, a frantic percussion louder than it needs to be.... The night proceeds. Empty glasses are refilled. D smokes Goodspeed's cigarettes, crossed legs, sipping bourbon: a slice of class in this hole-in-the-wall. George and Henry continue to argue. It is relentless, idiotic. Regulars Paul, Chuck, Sax, and Boo add their 2¢. Interest accrues on the argument (the idiocy?) the looser they all get. It all devolves towards tantrums. Not one to suffer the unsubstantial, Tench fades off without a word. Ez and Jude are stoic, content, drinking methodically.... And the night surges, its energy spiking. The drunk and the high and those soon to be sweep past the front window. They are heeding Friday night's call to worship, mad mannequins machined from the darkness.... A top of the ninth-inning rally, the home team letting victory slip from its grasp. A plastic ashtray is hurled at the set in disgust. Howard collars the perp, driving home a vehement reminder of the cost of a television set. George is unconvincingly repentant.... Cleburne steps to the entry end of the bar beyond the L for a refill. Terry thumbs over her shoulder to Goodspeed at the far end. Cleburne thanks her, accepting the tall cold elixir. Not here, not now. It is Friday night. One must respect the order. For on Friday nights it can all go to hell, just like ( * )...

And the music halts, erratic and sudden. A yelling roar

blows up from the back room. A loud crash and scuffling. A folding chair catapults into the front room through a back room entry. The din of chaos explodes. Cymbals and stands crash, a glass smashes, dull thuds and smacks: signature sounds of a drunken brawl.

Howard leaps the bar with the athleticism of a younger, more youthful H, exploding into the back room. He is followed by Omar and a shoving horde of regulars. Glass smashing and yelling, the sounds of backs being forcefully pinned to walls. Howard booms with authority, the back room going tightly silent. A metal serving tray, having loosened from its decorative tenure along the back wall, is heard spinning on the ground. Slowly, it sizzles to a rest.

"Alright, here's how it's gonna be! The next asshole that throws a punch gets their teeth knocked down their throat! Do y'all understand?! Good!"

Howard is reputed to have been quite a boxer in his youth.... His first bout representing a divisional squad was cancelled, the date coinciding with his battalion shipping out from Fort Sill, Oklahoma, bound for Okinawa and the "red fight" in Korea. September 15, 1950: the same day the Marines went ashore at Inchon. A hip wound he'd receive thanks to a Chinese barrage ended the possibility of boxing as a career (September 15 having since become a regular ritual: *the annual champagne curse of Harry Truman*). Howard convalesced for six months before an honorable discharge, then returned home to the city. His aunt and uncle had owned the bar—er, buffet—since opening it before the Depression, and had taken him in. *Asa Inman's* at Austin and Euclid, the one-time red-light district of *Old*

*Springvale.* The corner was known for its working girls and as a likely spot to rustle up a hit o' tea, if that was your bit. The somewhat comical negotiations at the corner were nothing to fear. Howard had seen combat. He tended *Asa's* bar for a decade before buying out his relatives in the '60s (even he is unsure of the exact year). What else was a disabled artillery corporal gonna do? Besides, it was steady work. *Asa's* had catered to a regular crowd since Prohibition and a good deal of the city's police force, to boot: cards and dice in the back room, *70 years an Asa's tradition.* One could say the same of "Friday night fights"....

And with a wrangling of collars, Howard and Omar escort the brawl's perps out through the front door. They are deposited on the sidewalk, bleeding noses / lips and all, with a demeanor non-sympathetic, purposefully hard. Neither contestants are regulars. One is with the band, the other of the brand that floats about looking for "the next asshole lookin' at me wrong."

"Ya both ain't gone in thirty seconds, I call the cops—'n voice of experience here boys: they ain't kind with arrests on Friday nights. I suggest neither a y'all show your faces around here no more," verbal flak already being fired between the two, both fully lit, finger-pointing, set to effuse more blood.

"Should we?" inquires Omar, the glint in his eye pleading for "yes."

"No, no more. If they want to fight I'll let 'em, just not in my space," Howard, the final authority, the door closing behind them.

The night sets its course on a more festive tack. The band has wrapped up, with zen in sensing their time having come and gone. The compact-disc jukebox serves up *Sweetheart of the Rodeo*, *Otis Redding*. Goodspeed drops a quarter to hear *That Smell*. The regulars seem thankful for a return to normalcy. Unfamiliars wander from back room to bar. Strange new faces meld awkwardly with strange old ones. Something new is rarely something welcome, light hearts more often meeting cold hard stares, in here.... *Tread light, drink well.*

And yet, drinks are doled out without segregation. Honing a new generation of regulars, Howard and Martha wish to start potential off on the right foot. The festivities continue. Fleeting moments buzz by: hard, blurred, thundering. Dorothy and Goodspeed share cigarettes and light company. She warms up to him. Drinking warms them both.... A timeless aimlessness wanders the hour, the fiendish blend of night / early-morning.... Last call is heard, a round drawn down the length of bar. Deep-throated huzzahs run like pirates and their plundered mead. Glasses emptied to be refilled. One last hurrah. *Rebel Yells*. Lights blur.... She kisses him. He whispers in her ear. They stand. They are outside. Neon floods the secretive night. Omar and Marge in mid-spat: he yells, she slaps. Dorothy and Goodspeed move light through the darkness. They bound across the intersection: a lunarscape carved by shadows minced, incomplete. The light grants passage to no one: green—yellow—red—green.

*Good night, all.*

IT IS SATURDAY AFTERNOON. The sky gears up for

its daily reckoning. Dark clouds soaring, the air a steam wall. Having made a stop off at *Los Alamos*, home of the *atombombrito* (1-star name / 5-star burrito!), Goodspeed plows through *The Points*. A chorizo quesadilla mixes a digestive medley stewed, toiled, and troubled by one too many tequilas, the spirit's fiendish ability to paper lighthearted facade over a violent drunk.

Goodspeed's steps land as on moving targets. He stumbles into passers-by, who push him aside. He shoves back without looking. There is a scuffle, yelling. He wriggles free from a hand grabbing and ripping his shirt. He squares up, hackles up, fists set to plant flesh and bone to concrete. It is hatred dumbly aimed.

"Alright—okay—everyone just break it up! Move it along. C'mere, Marv, before ya start something ya can't finish," beckons Bid, his bear-like hand wrestling Goodspeed from harm's way; grip like talons, his badge sparkling.

"Why would ya start a fight in your state? Guy woulda cleaned your clock, is over twice your size, dumbass," Bid illustrating the scene that would have been.... Bid, another of the high-rollers down at *Asa's* back room; uniform sharp-pressed, strewn of gear. They all watch out for Goodspeed, out here.

"Whadya mean, woulda kicked ass!" stammers Goodspeed, Bid shaking his head, leading Goodspeed across Austin, down DeKalb and away from tequila's sure fate.

"Just walk it off, Marv. I don't want to see you back here today, got it?" releasing his grip with a shove that guides the stumbling Regular on a course bound for somewhere other than there.

"Lousy no-name fucker. S'good thing 'cause I woulda dropped him like a sack 'a....a sack 'a something, sack-like, fucker!" Goodspeed mumbling a rant as he weaves diagonals resembling some naval diversionary tactic. He fosters enough motor skill to light a cigarette in stride, does not fall on his face doing it. Impressive.... It is rare to see him this drunk this early. But tequila has a way of subverting pace, moderation, restraint, undermining the focus required of duty, devotion to *cause*. He knows better. But even an iron discipline can founder on occasion, tequila in the afternoon akin to blasting the charts with a bullet: in that you come down as quick as you went up. The commercial hit machine, tequila, both will deposit you in a heap as soon as they have had their way with you.

Goodspeed turns down Euclid. He smokes as he walks, looking up at the dark sky closing in. Belabored cylinders push a dump truck down the avenue past him. Exhaust pesters the air: an irate smear rising against an irate sky. Thunderheads roll in: a reckoning in the offing....

*One day y'all shall atone for the deeds of this plane! Perhaps today?!*

The storm looks to gut Summer's stillness. *Take heed, take cover!* Goodspeed smokes as he stumbles on, so aware of nature's ability to judge harshly as to be oblivious to it.

*And through the grinding resolve of deadlined quotas the legions did toil, paper peaks stacked like a ridgeline down the length of desktops; a plodding, faceless, multi-armed vassal elbowed by inertia. Duties were made clear, an efficiency scientifically managed so as to be cleared of that most irritating interrupter of productivity....thought.*

Marvin Goodspeed  ~  *The Satellite Man*

Cyrus marks the page and closes the book. He looks out on a festive square. Spinning skirts lead up dancing curves to bikini-tops: the whirling seduction flaunting, taunting. A spectator in restaurant window, he had observed the exchange between Goodspeed and the biker, was glad to see it broken up.

"Dude would have beat his drunk ass," Cyrus coincidentally rereading Goodspeed's first novel while working on a plate of jerk chicken (the coincidence in the rereading part, less the jerk chicken).

He finishes off his plate, watching the carnival on the square do its thing. It stirs half-naked, carnal, slurring reality as a matter of course: *real v. myth*—and / or—*what we are v. what we think we are*.... Skateboarders ride rails and fall hard, pain a reward, skin loss a badge. There are the graphically-pierced, skin a canvas. There are those hip and those trying to be. A juggler juggling with skill, a dude on guitar feigning skill. Angry youth and watchful cops whirl round the midday drunks, the homeless and slumming suburban kids. Incense peddlers and motorcycles vend divergent recipes for peace: a calming scent v. loud pipes, a choice that should not be made lightly. Flaunting and taunting, it is doing its thing, a mute fervor floating about this choreography of the strange.

Despite the angry sky, young women continue their swirling dance about a drum circle then rolling in the parking lot of the burger stand across the street. *Carpe*

*Diem* and *Kama Sutra* linger as sweet scents. The spinning coven of spirits have our good journalist's attention.... But then so does the belligerent wordsmith of *Springvale*. A very different type of urge, Cyrus has realized that getting the good Regular to open up—even a few trowels full—is well nigh a *lost cause*; for now, at least. But it's of no mind. For our good journalist is plotting an end-around. It may very well be what the Regular himself would prefer. (Or had in mind all along?)

Cyrus watches raindrops smack window and sidewalk. Fat intermittent beads lead to a torrent, the sky opening up. Carnival participants run for shelter.

"The self-made myth, is it no less real?" Cyrus curling his lip in deep-thought mode, watching thick runnels swell into veins on windowpanes, beyond it now a rain wall.

The storm's attempt to wash this place pure seems futile, seems not really the root of the effort. But don't go to Old Parn with a crazy notion like "the disinterested random violence of nature." Triumphant in prophecy, he is right then the only soul still braving the downpour. He stands mid-square, yelling, sweeping an "I told you so" finger of judgment across the line of revelers packed into entryways, under eaves and awnings.

"Ah' yes, ye soiled children! Perhaps today *is* that day of atonement!"

He throws back his head, points both hands at the draining heavens. He lowers accusing fingers, aiming them at the freaks and misfits, and the normal posing as freaks and misfits. He smiles, mad with vindication—a higher order of point having been made.

A lightning bolt pops up viciously off an electrical transformer down DeKalb Avenue. It bursts in a ball, careens violently, Old Parn running for cover in and amongst the prostitutes of his ideals. The message of a higher order? Perhaps.

Power instantly leaves *The Points*, the transformer atop street-side pole left smoking like a chimney. Rain continues to pour in sheets: streaming down, possessed. All that was color is now shades of grey inside the restaurant. Cyrus stares through the rain, thinking: "pick the moment and let's just see if the Regular salutes. Until then, keep to the trowel."

> *We have a bad habit of burying the unsettled bits of our past. A useless trait, really. As all it takes is a roaring Summer downpour to wash away the red clay and lay it bare again. And perhaps you'd noticed? The deeper we dig, the harder it seems to pour.*

Marvin Goodspeed  ~  *South x Southeast*

And the Regular is marching into the heart of *Springvale* through a monsoon. Thunder explodes. Lightning pops. Hallucinations pour over him like roaring falls. Gale-wind gusts bend treetops. They turn out leaves: an umbrella caught in an updraft. The view is through Coke bottle bottoms. A delivery van churns past, shears a wave from a road-wide river of runoff that engulfs Goodspeed. Our man doesn't even break stride, grins at lightning dancing off distant antennae-tops. His mad laboratory.... He passes *the field parks*, *The Ashlands*, Alta. He is beyond soaked, standing ankle deep in a flood rushing on sewer drains. Clouds boil. Fat rain.... He makes his way through *Waverly Park*, collapsing in a heap on an empty bench in the middle of the empty park. Lilies atop laketop. The downpour tapers. He closes his eyes. Nature having its way.


GOODSPEED OPENS HIS EYES. The day is drowning in dusk. The sky is clear, some speeding clouds. He sits upright on park bench. Streetlamps are warming, the tops of buildings downtown ringed of lights: the functional designed to inspire. He is inspired. *It is the day, the night!*....And down at *Asa's*, Howard and Martha are setting out champagne flutes.... Goodspeed drags his hands across face, its hard-notched features something too common to feel so foreign. "No mind. No mind." *Buck up, soldier!* Collect yourself. See to your duty, good Regular. *For the day, the night has arrived!*....And Howard and Martha are setting out chilled bottles.... It is the regular ritual. *It is September 15!*

The earth cools, dry air. Summer has relented over the past several weeks, the perestroika of its red reign inferring reform, the coming of change, the days of long light near. A headache rings Goodspeed's incomplete buzz, an ill-timed afternoon bender is right then creeping towards a sobriety as unwelcome as the un-respecting unfamiliar, or media whore, or all of the above. But with the midday binge behind him, at peace with it having had its way, inspiration takes hold. He rises confident, sure. (A shaft of dramatic light?) He sways, a bit light-headed. It is hard to focus. "Focus, focus." *The day, the night!*....Howard and Martha are popping corks.... And he is off to curse Harry S. Truman with champagne!

Goodspeed glides through *Springvale's* guts. It is done with conviction....*an earnestness, an intensity one might mistake for zeal*.... Hexagonal sidewalk blocks are cracked and upturned by the century-old roots of water, red, white oak; these lanes, seething with the static of heritage. He vaults through. He is on a mission. Side streets pass. Alta, *The Ashlands, the field parks* all pass. He is swinging his arms, whistling. Austin at Euclid appears.... Howard rehearsing his lines, Martha pouring flutes full.... Goodspeed bombs through the intersection, giddy. He passes his mailbox: lid open, sardine-canned, whole days lost and mocking of the mail's prompt delivery. There could be a week's worth in there. He has lost a whole month: vague bits of night's dim succor, the barroom scenes and grey awakenings strewn across non-linear hours. It is a piece of strategy, the man feeding the myth. It is his true art. *Come one! Come all! See the Great Illusionist render time irrelevant! Viola!*

He beats down time, submerging the strangler of *liberty!* in spirits. Oh, the conspirators behind closed doors, the smoke-filled anterooms, cooking up ways to steal time—the time of others, his own. It is the "New South conspiracy." It is despotism. It is slavery....

FUCK TIME.

And Goodspeed is bathed in neon hues spilling from window-front brewery signs. He opens the front door with a jangle. They all turn. *Here Comes A Regular*....

"Damn, sorry y'all, nodded off in the park again. Did I miss it?"

"Couldn't start without ya, Marv. Grab one of them glasses," flutes grabbed and raised round the room. Champagne anticipates. Howard leads them all:

"Okay, all. Ready? 1, 2, 3....

*It was a government-issue September when that fresh-faced dupe got the call*

*Said, boy, we got more than boxing in store for the likes of y'all*

*Get familiar with kimchi and Panmunjom, 'cause we ain't gonna use no nukes*

*Harry's got his own ideas, says its time you kill Red gooks!*

They howl and curse and laugh. And they drink, as they are wont to do  ~

GO OUT WITH A BANG!

IN MORNING'S STILLNESS SEETHES *the potential of restless desire. In the yawning groggy dawn its instinct reigns. Is it then just dumb luck that both desire and instinct drive the cause, whatever that cause might be? To the carpenter it is a construction that withstands time, to the rocketeer a flawless lift-off. Yet to those who view society's master plan as little more than a profound set of burdens, the cause is something more immediate, more personal. It is freedom at any cost, independence from the yoke of lies murdering time and liberty. Lock step salutes of corporate overlords are replaced by middle fingers, out here, a response designed to intimidate and distance one's self. That which is lauded as mainstream or upstanding or responsible will encounter an instinctual skepticism on these streets, the delusional ideals behind "that slavery" heaped atop the shitpile of its duplicitous order. Bargain your time with the Big Mules and yer just digging your own grave, a certain Regular might say. For the greater cause of freedom, said Regular will claim, is not the aim of the modern socioeconomic landscape, these Go Go '90s. No, no. Freedom is reserved for those with the balls enough to fight for it every bloody day.... And so does the potential of restless desire propel the works of one Marvin Goodspeed. He is writing as if the cause hung in the balance. He is writing as if freedom depended on it. He is writing for Victory!*

*It's game time, y'all.*

STIRRING, STIRRING UP COFFEE. Thinking, thinking through thoughts. The space between his ears roars like a hurricane, ideas and characters swirling, emerging, converging. A nascent plot is beginning to gel. "This dog'll hunt," this writer's instinct—powerhouse of *the cause*—up on the high-wire, traversing the snarling dog pit of his nature.

Grease pops in a pan, the diner's kitchen sizzling up bacon, eggs, toast burnt to black as he takes it (his coffee taken regular, of course). Gold print star-fields sparkle atop the '60s style countertop, a future filled with hopes and dreams, then and now. Ideas are taking shape.

He shifts on the counter-side stool. It creaks. He arches his shoulders. They creak. A hard lean figure. His eyes are deep tunnels, a focus untouched by glasses clinking, plates clanking, *"Order Up!"* Restless desire bursts through the griddle-fried aroma then meandering up nostrils; an idea horde forcing itself on revolving doors. Goodspeed channels the internal roar.

"Got to find the groove. Some unscheduled wandering

will deliver. Need to fuel up first; sculpting the next mah—sta—piece be hard work," our man laughing to / at himself.

Stirring, stirring up coffee. Speaking, droning, diner chatter like monks chanting. It is all filtered to inconsequential, no more than a dull background hum secondary to the work at hand: the sacred work of *freedom creation.* This immaculate creator, *The Big Bang* alight in his eyes, Marvin Goodspeed sitting at the counter awaiting breakfast.

*"Order up!"* and breakfast is delivered. Five minutes later, Goodspeed leaves an empty plate. He throws down a ten and makes a hurried, yet anonymous departure. He steps through the front door out into the fray. Commuters skip by, the "servile herd" powering the whole charade. Roads seethe, asphalt tentacles groping the red earth. A bus hustles by, the somber expressions of those interred within passing with it. Goodspeed shakes his head, dons sunglasses despite the grey.

Our man lights a cigarette. He strays onto DeKalb Avenue heading south. He sets his steps to meander, a pace designed to maximize thoughts, potential. Smoke rings the emerging creation thrashing about inside his head. It is a crazed beast, a peaking addict locked in a room and forced to sobriety. He channels the chaos into the maintenance of *the status quo*: his duty, his art. To engage the man while in this state is to come face-to-face with a creative flurry so intense it should be visible thrashing about outside of his head. This brusque laureate, stringing his style of beat poet / local color / social commentary like barbed wire, rusted. It is infectious (that of the lockjaw variety). Predictability and formula are shown the door, roughly. When he's on his game, words careen from the page. They grab you at the throat and clench, certain suffocation giving way to a mad grin. "Ah, just having a little fun with ya there, chief. I'm just messin"....He is messing with his readers. He has smacked-up a vein: an alternative to the stacks of formulaic crap that his niche audience has been jones-ing for. Writer and reader, they're in this mess together.... He walks on through the mist, insistent ideas in-carom between his temples.

But for an otherworldly discipline leading to occasional bouts of sobriety—and dumb luck—he'd be just another streetwalker, he'll claim (a bona fide freak-of-nature in lieu of the physiological / chemistry-altering mind-fuckery of alcoholism). The line is that fine, he'll claim, having well-observed this societal microcosm, these in-town neighborhoods, out here on the outskirts of real and gentrified *myth*....

Goodspeed walks up on a homeless woman, another *Points* presence since the late '80s: Sheba, *the Scientist*. She sits on a bus stop bench, all her possessions always in a series of curated plastic bags.

"Keepin' it real?" he asks.

"Marh-vin, oh Marh-vin, I slept on my arm wrong last night, feels funny."

"Keep moving it around, pro'ly just a nerve thing."

"Marh-vin, oh Mar-vin, why did science do this to me?"

Goodspeed shrugs. No one quite knows. It is entirely possible that science DID do this to her: shock therapy, pre-lithium pharmacology, eugenics inspired indigent lobotomization; shall we continue? A gentle soul, if fiercely independent, it is hard not to feel for the woman; many attempts to wrangle her into shelters unsuccessful. "Dumb luck," Goodspeed mutters.

Our man banks onto Euclid. He is the critically-acclaimed author of an underground sensation, a style that has a growing audience buzzing. Some have gone so far as to call his first full-length: *The Satellite Man*, a contemporary masterpiece. Strangers in line at the bank, at the convenience store, at the diner, will occasionally point him out, gee-whiz looks on faces. Yet as we have seen, notoriety wasn't the goal. He didn't set out for fame. On the contrary, this writing gig was simply the most direct route to *freedom*. Still, trading vocational isolation (re: Thoreau's *quiet desperation*) for one of his own choosing (re: Thoreau's *Walden*) hasn't translated to reality quite as he had envisioned. All he'd wanted was to escape *the machine*. He would not be party to his own "enslavement," would pursue his own manias as he deemed fit.... It seems predictable; inevitable, even. It's a heritage thing. The evidence of our early trowel work points towards this obsessive pursuit of *freedom* turning in familiar eddies. For we are talking now of a Goodspeed tradition, his ancestral clan having installed itself deep on the Appalachian frontier out of similar motives: to be rid of the tax-levying God-bothering buzzkills. Our man's one-man revolt is just the relentless march of history finding its legs, a virulent independence spelled: D-N-A.

"A Goodspeed having made good. Only took a coupla centuries," our man laughing to / at himself and his insular clan. "Alright, to the task at hand," there being much work to be done, a *Victory!* to be won....

\*        Goodspeed's conviction, his devotion to *the cause* (shall we call it: *progressive laissez-faire?*), resides on the order of sacred. Its self-delusion—and the resultant self-destruction—a minefield when broached by the hapless busybody. Careful steps are advised. The interloper need only be "down here" to provoke a spirited defense of "home." Addicted equally to heritage and instinct, it is a nature that cannot help but be in conflict with itself (and all that around it, for that matter). But then our study has already dusted off a maxim to help launder the contradictions: *questioning one's nature is equivalent to the murder of one's own time....* To engage in the shooting of one's own foot means you bring it on yourself, make of yourself chattel—that you are, in fact, in collusion with the executive pricks shoveling said chattel like fodder into *the machine's* boilers....

"Those who would exploit you by promising the sun and moon are hidin' beyond every oxbow in the muddy waters, descending on the dirt-poor miners of nineteen-teens-and-20s Appalachia and this here latest New South just the same, anywhere there's an opportunity to create indentured servants of those born free," a certain Regular might say. "The whole point is to brainwash ya. And if that don't work they'll just brain you outright. If the latter, why provide 'em the shillelagh?"

Our man: fighting the power; fighting it in order to maintain his thing as it is, that is. *Go ahead, fuel the contradictions*: "I'm for the radical realignment of the distribution of power in society" / "I'm for fighting to the death to keep things the way they are"....Shovel in the white-hot coal of character and environment. Compress the bellows of fact meets fiction. Nature will have its way. Make no mistake there, chump, it will have its vulgar way with you. So, knowing that, why not revel in it? Why not roll around in the filthy business, thrash about in it madly. Love! Hate! What you love and what you hate pesky sidebars to doing it all with gusto. Live the truth. Live the *myth* as if it were truth. Love with vigor! Hate with vigor! Drink with a vigor some might confuse for virtue....

The fearless mid-century reporter William B. Huie wrote a work of fiction titled: *Mud on the Stars*. In it, the incorrigible *Old Mis' Ella* counseled:

> *Get you some things to love and some things to hate....and then love 'em and hate 'em with all your soul* ~

Now if that quote doesn't map out the very roadway of his nature, then the reference is just dumb luck. For this here is the petrol that fires Goodspeed's steps....

Okay, maybe not so much with the unscheduled wandering. "Eyes on the prize there, pal; publication equals dinero equals *freedom*," our man prioritizing, an impressive (honorable?) *devotion to cause.*

Goodspeed's steps angle into *the field parks*, once the core of the stately *Ashlands* of *Old Springvale*. "What once was, what could have been still." (A tear shed for a world, *a cause*, lost?) His steps and thoughts ply a past erased, carriage step blocks and hitching posts now pointless sentries of homes long since demolished, the voids of cratered foundations swimming in kudzu. Victim of a politicized D.O.T. plan never realized, this now barren half-mile swath of land deep in *Springvale* underwrites the never-ending (never-learning?) attempts of whims to disregard the past.... The stated goal of the *Intown Byway* plan had been to hook four controlled-access lanes veering south off the (at the time new) interstate parkway connector into the stadium complex just south of downtown. Over virulent community protest, it was decided that the best route was to drill a byway straight through the down (but-not-out) 'hoods of *Springvale*. The worst part: the project was fast-tracked and had already demolished three dozen late-and-post-Victorian homes along the planned corridor before the scheme behind it was outed....

\*         In the Summer of 1979, that troublesome "hippie-rag" dropped a bomb (of the word-brand, being pacifists and all). A whistleblower had appeared at the paper's offices, unsolicited, with a memo hand-printed on state governor's office letterhead. It stated clearly (too clearly?) that the I.B. was no more than a public-funded attempt to win the votes of suburbanites (non-urban blight access to sporting events) and deep-pocketed roadbuilders (who stood to make a killing at taxpayer expense in the year before an election). The necessity of the road versus the staggering price tag, at a time of oil embargoes and stag-flation, had been disputed by officials and activists across the political spectrum. It cocked more than a few eyebrows considering the existing and adequate north / south downtown interstate access that already overfed the stadium complex. The story was soon pouring from all the city's big news outlets, the original source quickly forgotten in the chum-like feeding frenzy.

Of course, the governor's office claimed the notion absurd: "a charge political in nature" / "planted by enemies as an underhanded attack in the run-up to an election cycle," and such. And indeed, it may have been. But whether fudging the truth or not, the leak itself properly nailed the project's true intent. (Produced only once, the memo was never seen again. These days, those who broke the story claim it may have been a plant, if only to leak the real corruption. Pursuing the truth: so fickle, so slippery a slope.) It would prove just another steaming pile of government corruption in the post-Watergate era. The project and its funding were abruptly frozen, but not before the core of the c. 1890s *Ashlands* of *Old Springvale* had come down. And what's worse: it was all for naught, the controversial governor having been tossed out the following year. (The brazen cronyism soon produced an actual smoking gun: taped telephone conversations linking the governor and fundraisers to insider land deals, at the public's expense, on a proposed, and once again, unnecessary, airport runway.) The sordid mess fizzled out in a bitter coda: *Springvale* property owners, having been compensated on deflated appraisals (it was soon discovered) in lieu of the eminent domain rulings on their land, suing en masse—a miserable mess that played out in the courts for over a decade. The reality was these barren fields left running a highway-width channel through south *Springvale*.... And yet, at the end of all this lay an ironic benefit: the justified shitstorm and lingering outcry in wake of the I.B. debacle has left the remainder of the *grand old ward* largely unmolested, despite the rough edges, to the present.

Almost two decades later, man's small influence is on full display in *the field parks*, having been used by locals since as recreational, if overgrown, havens. Nature is having its way, out here. Old stone steps lead up to phantom front walks, weed-choked cobbles in turn leading as gangplanks into the crumbling foundations otherwise draped in muscadine, ornamental ivy gone feral, the all-consuming kudzu.... And Goodspeed is taking care to keep nature at bay (jerking that hire-wire taut). The whims of vice taunt his every move, his every thought, every moment of every—bloody—day. In an instant it could swallow him whole, the thin membrane of sobriety rupturing / dissolving into the bottom of a bottle. It is October 1. He could wake up tomorrow and it would be December 1. He is not without free will. But he is no fool, either. Nature is what it is; and (so goes the logic here) it will have its way despite your puny will....*whole months lost, vague bits of night's dim succor strewn across non-linear hours as if dreamed....* Goodspeed knows his manic nature can devour free will and spit out a corpse. It is not like him to question nature. But the next "mah—sta—piece" deserves airtime before nature has its way. He is taking care to keep nature at bay. (Well, more so a robust reallocation of energies: substituting intensity for intensity, but more on that later.) The maintenance of this state is, in fact, taking all he's got: channeling restless desire, devotion, dedication into the maintenance of *liberty—writing for Victory!*

"Dissent from within the belly of the beast: a one-man Trojan Horse. Yes, yes, that's the glue. Onto something here. No sequel, no sir. Yes sir, this dog'll hunt," our man prioritizing, lining up the "idea crowd" to pass through in an orderly fashion.

"Alright now. Focus, Goodspeed. Focus."

Goodspeed exits *the field parks*, passing over Alta Terrace: demarcation line of D.O.T. demolition. The stately mood, if in some disrepair, reappears: a Neo-Classic, a Gothic, the later run of Craftsmans. He motors past the landmark *Carriage House*. He slices through *Springvale's* soft underbelly. He is onto to something here. He can sense the spark of inspiration. He is heading for inspiration. He is heading for the *Gordon Patrick Woodruff House*.

BACK AT THE DINER, the usual weekly production meeting continues over (round the table clockwise): Cyrus (news and city writer) omelette, wheat toast; Kelly (art direction and photography), 4 eggs scrambled, biscuit, hash browns smothered not-covered; Anna (arts and culture editor), short-stack swimming in syrup; Grey (news and culture—stress on the culture—contributing writer), coffee black. The projects (running counter-clockwise): Grey finalizing a compilation of down-lo deep background statements delivered by members of the force for an upcoming piece (more on this later) + an idea; Anna, stressing a six-month dip in ads, ramping up a by-neighborhood eat out feature—one per 'hood per week to add a little competitive spirit, pump up ad-bucks as they pump the local cuisine scene; Kelly, her plate full of asset production for *The Weekly's* first real (not lame single page excuse for an) internet website—version 2.0 of *theWWWeekly.com* to include the curious experiment of selling ads on *the world wide web*; Cyrus....uh, Cy?

"Hey, space cowboy, think I already know what you are up to this week—but, what are you up to this week?"

Anna adding a snap-to-it snapping of fingers.

"Yes, what? Sorry. So, there's the usual, which is blessedly near to complete. Also, been working a new angle on the Goodspeed thing, been tailing him, digging into his background; stalking him, really."

"Didn't he tell you to get lost recently?"

"Not....exactly. On second-glance, actually seemed like more a test, or challenge?"

"And that means what....exactly?" Grey sipping black coffee, eyes on Cy.

"That's what I'm trying to figure out, almost like he was inviting a very specific type of coverage; tailed him from here the past three mornings: same exact routine, same exact timing, same exact course, even, but with one interesting omission—no *Asa's*, three days running."

"How could you know that for sure? You have been in-office a lot this week," Anna, the only other staff-member with Regular experience, fact-checking.

"Got an inside source."

"He was leaving the diner right as I walked up this morning; looked intense, kind of huffing to himself, y'know?" Kelly, eating as if she hadn't for days.

"Ya, got here early this morning to observe the specimen in his environment. He rolled in right on time: 8 a.m. sharp. Orders the same exact thing each morning and aside from occasional verbal jabs at the waitress and cook interacts with no one, is all the time impatiently scribbling, talking to himself, chows down and is out-the-door, all in about 25 minutes. It seems—disciplined."

"Scientific," Grey tipping the hat to a rigorous application of standards.

"Stalker," Kelly pin-pricking any cheap inflating of

self-worth, shoveling in eggs and taters.

"Gonna run with it, see what shakes out. But yes: still got some loose ends to tie up on the ol' stemwinder first; think it needs a more provocative title: *In Case You Didn't Notice*, maybe? Still thinking on it."

"It's gonna set the roof on fire," Grey, sipping.

"We don't need no water, let the motherfucker burn! Burn, motherfucker, burn!....What, nothing?" Anna incredulous at the lack of respect for a well-placed—and aging—and over used—hip-hop pop-culture reference.

"Fine, I'll just enjoy it myself."

"Please do, and to yourself."

"Done," Kelly dropping the fork to an empty (as in crumb-less) plate, a metallic ceramic rattle as the fork comes to a rest.

"Crikey, been fasting, girlfriend?" Cyrus seriously impressed by the caloric intake their thin cohort can absorb daily.

"Really, felt the need to pull my hands in for fear of losing a digit," Anna's assessment of Kel's voracity dropping between "funny, weird" and a mild case of awe, herself not halfway through a short-stack.

"Mmm, love me some breakfast," Kelly smacking lips, ready for the day.

Anna, project-managing: "Grey, a reminder not to forget that *Prez* picked you to run out a follow-up on the FCC ruling." (Said ruling essentially gutting the commission's long-standing rules against cross-ownership and majority-share of media outlets in a single market, the worry for independent purveyors of creative arts being that this is about to, and has already begun to, unleash a tsunami of acquisitions and mega-mergers of everything "arts"—from print and radio stations to live venues and ticket-sales—and that it will, as part of the intent, flood out all small players in the resulting ocean of over-priced / over-hyped pop pabulum crap designed to sell crap to audiences numbed into subservience by pop pabulum crap....and you are welcome, Grey, as we just composed the intro to your column following up on the recent FCC ruling.)

"Yup, already on it. Right up here," Grey light-tapping the ol' brain case.

"And what of that tech-culture idea you had, the playmate thing?"

"Right, so check this out: A Playboy centerfold from 1972 becomes the image of choice for testing digital image compression algorithms in the '70s, '80s; almost entirely hetero-male sub-culture; of course the image of choice is a hot naked woman, right?"

"Of course, dorks without girlfriends," Anna, shooting straight.

"Harsh, probably true. Certainly true. But anyway, Lena Sodenburg was the model; and because her image was so widely used, she became an underground star with the early computer-programmer set. But here's the kicker: She had been kind-of famous for a quarter-century and had no clue about any of this until someone, out of curiosity, tracked her down about a year ago and told her. She's a happily married mother-of-three living in Sweden!"

"Creepy, and cool? Is that possible?" Kel shrugs, looks to the others.

"Well, she seems to have owned it, came to the States for some sort of wired-like conference back in the Spring.

She was a main attraction."

"S'pose you know what you're getting into as a Playboy centerfold?"

"To be a cheap thrill for drooling masturbatory compu-geeks? Can anyone fully prepare for this?" Anna, chief tangent-straightener.

"Well, like I said, she seems to have owned it; and it's not like anyone was stalking her, or anything."

"Really? Someone tracked her down—in Sweden—25 years later!"

"Ya, but more out of a sense of respect, maybe?"

"Right, as in: Hey, back in 1978 I use to jerk off to a naked picture of you late at night in the computer lab. Can I get your autograph?"

Cleburne doing his own breakfast-shoveling, settles up, gets up to leave.

"And on that note, have some stalking of my own to get to."

"Will there be masturbation?" (Okay, so it must be noted that this was group-think snark and Grey just happened to be the first practitioner of said snark to get it past his lips....)

"Pro'ly not, but one can never tell," Cleburne drawing in shoulders, hands out, palms up: "Gotta go where the story takes you, eh?"

"Just keep the sticky details to yourself there, kid," Anna turning to the other two, "so, how about: *The Chow Down Low Down?*"

"How about: *Eat Me?*" Grey's raillery urged on by black coffee.

"Cute," smart-ass retorts being the most common of managerial potholes @ *The Weekly*, it being the kind of place that draws said practitioners, is really a by-product of the skepticism of institutional / societal norms that defines their editorial through-line. It need not be encouraged, but neither can it be discouraged, Anna moving things along: "Anything else?"

"No, I'm serious."

"I'm sure you are, Grey. Anything else?"

"C'mon, why the hell not?"

"Because we're actually trying to hook local restaurants and sell ad-space, not drive off the smarter and far better-looking half of their customer base?"

Cleburne takes leave of his fellow practitioners. He steps through the front door out into the day. It is moody and grey. And they say, each great journey must begin with a first step. He can envision many steps-stops-starts to come—just hanging in there, hanging with this story—the most challenging aspect of all. Gearing up for a marathon, he is a chump with an angle; endurance, gumption, extra-strength aspirin his tools. *Onward, to Victory!*


WE RETURN TO OUR MAN—Marvin Goodspeed—and trowel a layer deeper into his reverence for "the man." Spend any amount of time with the Regular and it will become crystal clear: Gordon Patrick Woodruff informs the man our man is, or (at the very least) *the man he thinks he is....*

\*      The life of *Gordon Patrick Woodruff* has been lost to popular / regional history, which is surprising in that he had an outsize role in his day; but not surprising given that he wound up on the losing side—twice, actually. A Confederate war veteran, Woodruff lied about his age in 1861, enlisting at sixteen. He miraculously survived the butchery of our Civil War, serving in the west from Shiloh to Franklin only to be shot by skittish comrades while on sentry duty during that army's desperate retreat from Nashville. That was Christmas Eve, 1864. Woodruff lost his arm to amputation but beat the infection that followed. He eventually found his way home: one-armed, penniless, but alive. A bloodbath had gurgled up all around him, receded, and left him still standing. It would instill in him a fearlessness that would be put to use. In a journal entry (Woodruff a diligent journal-enterer) dated August 14, 1866, he dropped this reflection: "The rest of this life is to be an unexpected surprise." The one-armed sinewy Woodruff was able to farm as a tenant, marry the neighbor's daughter (Eliza Roe), and eek out enough scratch to buy acreage by his twenty-eighth birthday. With his own farm—and more importantly, as his own boss—he defied the indentured cash-crop trends driven by lending merchants and their "colluding bankers," splitting his fields between subsistence and a diversification of marketable crops. He watched the rapid slide towards dependency of all small farmers forced to farm only cotton. In open defiance, he championed the more traditional method of crop-rotation over a reliance on increasing amounts of purchased fertilizer: guano—bat shit—the preferred soil-enricher of the era (no joke). It was a stance that won him no friends in "town / city." He was not afraid to stand in public against these "homegrown carpetbaggers." He was urged to run, did so, and was elected as an agricultural commissioner. The kind of parasitic exploitation and graft that he encountered led Woodruff to take up law on behalf of all small farmers (white ones, that is) shackled to the crude inequity typical of the system. By 1886, Gordon Woodruff was a civic leader popular with the people of the piedmont town where he'd lived his whole life. He was "their man."

But despite Woodruff and like leaders in their corner, those years were lean ones before the juggernaut of *Gilded Age* concentrations. Agrarians, plugged into a global economy whether they wished for it or not, were earning less yet working harder; all while the merchants and creditors in town / city speculated on crop yields until they could sell at inflated prices. The more farmers produced, the less they all earned; while the bankers and merchants all seemed to earn more just as they were doing less. How could this be? The public face of this *New South* vision was talking out of both sides of its mouth: selling the universal benefits of unquestioned loyalty to this "new improved construct of business," while the benefits clearly streamed uphill. "There's something aside from just bat shit that smells about the credit manure the merchants are sellin," Woodruff is said to have said. If more regional, a second civil war was brewing.

Given the long tradition of neighborly aid and the extensive network of *Grange Halls*, clubs, and secret lodges, (arrayed, of course, along a blood-red color line) it is no surprise that the mother of all socioeconomic clubs— *The Farmers Alliance*—coalesced prostrate southern agrarians into a true people's protest movement. It would be so bold (and unwelcome) as to found competing capitalist models, shoving its way into the "den of corruption and thievery" itself: politics. However brief, the "producers" of the *Gilded Age* felt they had a voice.

Fiercely independent, Woodruff was initially reluctant to take on a leadership role in the *Alliance*. But everywhere Woodruff saw exploitation and wealth contraction in the merchant-to-market system creating a new kind of servitude. His neighbors, friends, extended family, war veterans, they all seemed expendable chattel, crude capitalist fodder. To Woodruff, this was the reality of the *New South:* an exclusive trust designed to benefit fat cats, not the average citizen. It was a selling out of the southern people. Woodruff's duty to his "fellow patriots" led him into the ranks of the *Alliance's* aforementioned political movement: *Populism.* Many of this movement's figures were self-made men like Woodruff. They were skilled agrarians, but proved poor leaders. Woodruff stood apart. He proved his ability as an agitator and, once elected, as a legislative leader. He knew how to manage processes, how to take an idea and give it real breath within the constraints of the moment. It seemed, to Woodruff, not much different from growing or tending a plant. He would come to pose such a threat to *the status quo* that he was specifically targeted by the ruling *New South Democrats,* whose sole aim was order, an order achieved only by everyone—white and (especially) black—knowing their place. *The Bourbons,* as they were called (often with a hiss), in turn derisively labeled Woodruff a "hayseed." But this figure popularly unknown to the modern era was a political natural. Woodruff was fearless in the moment. Without missing a step, he turned negative character attacks to his advantage. He wore the "hayseed" rank as a badge of honor. An 1892 speech he delivered at a rail stop just outside this city propelled his rising star:

*The merchant lays about like a lazy pontiff, shrugging his shoulders, saying 'that's tough going' when the small farmer has to plead for equal return on that year's harvest. And all whilst that merchant gets him a new lounging room put on the back of his house, already the biggest house in town, mind you; and gets himself a few more smiling white-gloved negroes to serve up the afternoon tea. Then these types get and grease up friends in high-up places to bend all the laws and make this exploitation all just and legal. Well, I'm here to say that when they deride me, a man that comes off the land, has actually swung the scythe and pitched the hay--a man of and for the people--when they deride me as being a no-good traitorous one-armed backcountry hayseed, I say this: The words that pass my lips and carry on the warm breeze are those of the small farmer that those rapscallion reptiles in the courts and legislatures and banks and stores seek to oppress. And I'll go on to say this, my fellow patriots: It is true I got only the one good arm, but it's of no mind, because I got two good legs by which to kick their backsides black and blue! ~*

Goodspeed will recite the harangue word-for-word; well, excluding the racist word (let's just say "negroes" was not the word used in the original text within the *Gordon Patrick Woodruff Papers*). Yet having already identified that contradiction, as endemic to the environment as are the town square memorials to the

Confederacy facing north, it does not deter utilization of "the man," and the majority of his words not leaning on vile bigotry, as a wellspring for our man. It is inspiration for the task-at-hand. And be not fooled: Goodspeed is hard at work here. He is not one for idolatry, but reveres Woodruff for having trained sights on the bullshit of his day—the "phantom *progress!* masking a first-degree murder of freedom."

"Cubicles, gridlock, the homogenous mega-culture and its fat-belt of 'burbs is the end result of corporate America's vision: the *newest New South* slavery."

Goodspeed channels the forgotten *Populist* firebrand, serving proudly as a late twentieth-century bullhorn for the unfinished work of the late nineteenth-century sociopolitical fight that our man will argue was about nothing more and nothing less than *liberty!*....

"Real freedom comes with real money. Get the scratch and set your own orbit, a satellite to the hungry madness and ruin."

Robust sales of *The Satellite Man* and several recently published collections of shorts / verse (a good deal of which was written prior to TSM), could argue that the people are listening. But despite his justifiable claim as a modern *tribune of the people*, it seems as plausible that the wandering guru of *Springvale* simply has his audience hooked—more candyman than Robin Hood. Of course, it is just as likely that Goodspeed couldn't give a shit either way. So long as it is profitable, he'll continue to fuel the *myth* that sells; this, of course, in the great *New South* tradition.

Goodspeed stands before the house: a moment with

the master (or at least the master's house). It would seem an odd choice, Woodruff moving from the small-town piedmont to here: in-and-amongst the *New South* aristocracy. And yet in that light, it can be viewed as his greatest act of dissent: choosing the life of an urban pariah, substituting the stump and the rail stop and legislative scrum for pen, paper, and press in-and-amongst "the den of thieves."

Shingles are coming away from the turret's roofline, porchfront cornices fouled by black mold. Goodspeed has had his eye on the house for a decade. It pains him that the house shows more than chinks in its armor. This is heritage. Duty calls. The house has gone through a series of owners since the '60s. It has been for sale and vacant for two years, the elements having taken the opportunity to reinforce the natural order....*It is simple arithmetic: that which is borne of the red earth is destined to return to the red earth*, the driving Summer torrents remind us. *Tough love, that's all this is*, the virile vines jeer.

"Think I'll have the scratch pretty soon, once that second printing hits the ground."

Goodspeed is feeling optimistic. A brimming bank account is a new thing to him. It has him brimming with hopes and dreams, free (for now) in his orbit. He takes a final longing glance. Girded for the day, he steps along.

"I'll repair ya, old friend. We'll take it to that damned rapscallion [ *time* ] yet."

He turns a corner, this flesh-and-blood dynamo rolling through the *Druid Heights:* past the rows of servant shotguns down by the tracks, the soaring Greek Revivals well away from the tracks, the hints of *Beaux Arts*. This is where the truly loaded once lived. He breathes it in. The grandeur of *New South* achievement, the sprawling appalling fortunes extracted on the working man's spine. Nostalgia. Disgust. A two-sided tendency as regional as the soft rolling hills of dialect. He breathes it in.

Goodspeed aims steps for his hovel, charged for the work-at-hand. Each and every step seems calculated, engineered—the twenty-car pile-up of nature and freewill behaving itself, for now; the truce holding. With purpose, and a bit of ego, he walks on. Walking, marching through the fog of creation. Thinking, apprehensive: unconvinced that all this success hasn't just been dumb luck.

> *Human beings are engagingly absurd, we oscillate between being insignificant and imagining ourselves God.*

W. A. Percy ~ *Lanterns on the Levee*

RUSTING LEAVES HANG LIMP. Listless air recalls the torrid Summer having recently passed. It is October 10 and it is 92°, one final melting reminder. In his hovel—his lair— the fan motor skips in its familiar hitch. Goodspeed's expectation would find him commanding cadence with the precision of a sharpshooter. But there are those days when the mojo just ain't working. This day's investment has so far been wasted; and by now we all know this to be a capital offense (stifling *liberty!*, a suffocation by one's own hands, no less)....Focus, Goodspeed! *Buck up, soldier!*

Soaring operatic song, at first distant, comes closer, louder. A light *da-dat-dat* knock at Goodspeed's screen-door. Gid, the mailman (and part-time regular), shields his eyes, ducks, and peers in through the screen after no response. He understands, tones down his song to a rhythmic hum. Courtesies are extended instinctually amongst the brethren. He enters just long enough to exchange the mail with $60 laid out on a door-side end-table, a quarter-ounce (pre-seeded just like Goodspeed likes it) nestled tightly within the folded / rubber-banded parcel. Postman, conveyor of staples: royalty checks, pot.

"Can see you's busy, friend. I'll leave you to it," Gideon Burns exiting, filling his lungs and resuming his song.

Goodspeed doesn't even notice the drop-off. An obsessive, near-manic passion propels his pen. Channeling intensity—intensely—frenetic strokes drop line-after-line.... But our man is unimpressed, irritated by the day's results, or rather the lack thereof. Sweat meanders down his neck, a v-shape stain soaks the spine of his shirt. It is hard work under such conditions. Focus! *Buck up!*

Humidity terrorizes the coming cool-down, smearing the lengthening light of Autumn. The thermometer shrugs it off. It performs its duty dutifully, indifferent to mortal grumblings. For this newest *New South* is the deep South first-and-foremost, sultry days accepted vis-à-vis the mad uncle a family feels it too cruel a fate to institutionalize. Nature will have its way. Seems best to just stand down, make your peace. (But what if your nature predisposes self-destruction? What of the instinctual drive to fight-on no matter the futile cost, no matter the wrongs littering the wake of a *cause* once deemed righteous? Yes, what of all that? And so does the restless trowel continue its painstaking survey.... )

Goodspeed begs off self / regional reflection for the

moment, breaking his focus only for a quick nostalgic nod to his lucky stars, whatever cosmic grace bore him to this mystical Southland where....

*Imagination holds sway; nothing seems improbable save the puny inadequacies of fact.*

W. J. Cash ~ *The Mind of the South*

But despite said grace in his corner, Goodspeed is right then pretty well unimpressed with his inadequate puny efforts. *The cause* demands more. He must give his all here. It is 3 p.m. He fears the day lost, fears he is *losing the cause* all over again. Through the open door, downtown buildingtops glisten in the steam. The heat boils his distress. Grumbling, apprehensive—unconvinced—he presses on....

*Fight on stalwart Southron: For liberty! For rights!*

It's an hour later, the notion of a kinder-gentler world having gone and gotten itself all tangled up in a barbed-wire reality. It is all part-and-parcel, nature's instinct to tack when expected to stay the course a trait Goodspeed understands, respects. Thespian in its motivations, it is a sucker for "the drama." Only the outrageous will do, the coroner having arrived to seal the deal....

Four cruisers, an ambulance, the coroner all crowd into the half-lot / half-dump behind *Asa's* and Goodspeed's hovel. Rooftop lights whirl a red, white, and blue that is swallowed by the humid mist. It is 4 p.m., the heat still rolling. Cops stand about an area being marked off with crime-scene tape. An investigator scribbles notes.

He notices, theorizes. A camera snaps, documents. For years the lot has been a junkyard: the rusted hulls of dome-topped pickups near buried beneath the gutted waste of renovation projects, drum barrels, broken-wheel shopping carts overflowing with all manner of trash-ola. It would seem the perfect lot in which to bury a homicide: the strangled victim having been found in the trunk of an old totaled Corvair.

"All's I know is I leaned 'gainst the car 'n that trunk opened 'n I see a hand 'n that is it, had nothin' to do wid it!" pleads, Eustace, who discovered the body.

"I get it, okay? Tell me one more time, I'm gonna think ya did have somethin' to do with it, alright?"

Trey was first cop on the scene, Eustace having flagged him down and having relayed the path to his discovery over and over and over. Trey is near to out of patience....

"We got your statement, Eustace. Now for Christ's sake, move it along."

"Okay man, alright, alright. No need to swear the super Lord's name in vain, cop man, just tellin' ya that I sat down on that there car 'n I —

"Go, Eustace—just—go! Go away from here!" Trey grabbing him by the arm, guiding him up the alley and releasing him with a shove inferring the necessary route-of-march (that being anywhere but there).

"Alright, I'm goin'....damn'd cop man."

"I heard that."

"Good! Shoulda been more careful cop man. The super Lord is good and great—ohhhh, but it's so loud out here, so damn'd loud. Hot damn!" marching to the beat of polyrhythmic delusion.

Meanwhile, having withstood Eustace's piercing

screams ("Holy blessed super Lord! Body dead! Body dead! Someone get the helio-copters! Body dead down 'ere!") and the invasion of emergency vehicles that followed, Goodspeed's robotic absorption has finally dissolved. He flicks pencil across the room, exhales. Annoyed, but nonchalant (homicide being not an unknown quantity, out here), he emerges from his hovel in time to join Trey heading back to the group standing about, kicking stones.

"Guy's a bonafide genius, Trey. Sure he didn't do it and just employ his cunning to get himself off the hook?" drifting across the patio, lighting a cigarette.

"Dude can't figure that he avoids pissing his pants by unzipping his fly. Gang-bangers again, Marv." (They all know Goodspeed by name, the cops that is....)

"How 'bout you hang it on busboy. I'd swear to that on a stack!"

"The stringy cat livin' in the bus?"

"You're right, no one'd believe that either. Pretty sure Eustace could drop 20 IQ points on that .22 shit-for-brains."

The two meld with the milling fray guesstimating time-of-death, smoking, loitering. The sour whiff of death lays languid on the air. The coroner calculates the body 36 hours dead. It would seem open-and-shut due to the victim's gallery of gangland tattoos, a piano wire the likely device of death: grotesque lacerations, a crushed larynx, severe bruises ringing neck area—a $ crudely carved into the dead man's chest. Open and shut, it would seem. And yet that he was strangled has the investigators puzzled.

"Why not just shoot the bastard?" one asks, chin-scratching, looks thrown at the sky in contemplating clues.

"It's a statement. They're putting their stamp on it.

Remember last year? The *South End* x'ing out eyes? Bet it's just a statement," Cleburne, on the scene, offering his gruesome 2¢. He nods to Goodspeed, who looks him over, smokes / exhales—a passive stare in return.

The question and theory are pondered, the body bagged and loaded. The coroner leads the slow vehicle-by-vehicle procession out of the normally quiet plot / dumping ground. The absence of on-the-scene news teams is evident; only Cleburne, who wandered in (as if having just been in the vicinity). Given the terra firma beacon of flashing lights, one would figure the major outlets send out at least a news chopper fly-over. But minus the shirtless guy jumping fences, sprinting down garbage-can-lined alleys, city's finest in breathless pursuit, nothing newsworthy here it would appear. Just your run-of-the-mill inner-city homicide.

"No buzzards, must be a car chase somewhere," notes the *Springvale* bard, Goodspeed bidding those who are left good day, heading dutifully back into his hovel.... No, gang murder just doesn't capture the imagination anymore. It is so '80s. And besides, "advertisers don't want to go disturbin' suburban sensibilities during the nightly news, er nothin'...." This is the second banger's body found in the lot this year, the second news cycle snub....

Oh, right, and Goodspeed recalls that his day so far has been for crap. With a grumbling sigh, he settles back in at his TV tray post. Despite the hazards, the discomfort of Summer in Fall, he is back at it. Devotion / duty keep him in the game, keep him fighting despite the losing trend. He simmers. His brow: a) knitted, b) furrowed (your pick, dear reader). *Buck up, soldier! Fight on! For freedom!*

The rapping of his pen accelerates. He scans the waste of words committed to paper: lethargic, shiftless, lazing about on the TV tray before him. Weak! *Liberty forsaken!* his temper alone dissolving the thin membrane. He flicks his pencil at the wall in disgust, knocks over the chair in standing up. He paces bookshelves that line his apartment's back wall. They are strewn of a working collection. Show volumes are absent amongst broken spines, torn and abused editions acquired from yard sales, antique stores, library give-aways. The stacks run the gamut: from Camus to Mark Twain, Kafka to Mickey Spillane. The crafted works of Carl Sandburg and Woodward fold into a magazine heap equal parts *Popular Science* and *Hustler*. The magnolia-scented Sidney Lanier seems taken aback, out-of-sorts alongside the impolite candor of Langston Hughes and Lillian Smith; a rare 1860s Bill Arp (his one well-cared-for volume), the local color of Joel Chandler Harris, all of it strewn about—Shelby Foote's monumental *Civil War* trilogy blending peaceably with the *Howl-ing* Ginsberg.

In a *Weekly* column the previous year, Grey had summed up Goodspeed's first short-story collection as "controlled fury," likened it to *The Subterraneans*: the short novel anthem Kerouac belted out inside the barbiturate-haze of a few days—or so goes the legend (and if entertaining, why not let fact / fiction blend peaceably, hmm?). The two do seem cut of a similar cloth: beat, manic, alcohol-fueled. Goodspeed angrily stabs at his worn copy. He flips through *The Subterraneans*, stops at an earmarked page. Goodspeed reads Kerouac:

*Now this warm thought of greatness is a big chill
in the wind, for greatness dies too  ~*

"Damn, Jack's right. Ah've killed the day!"

He stares at the ceiling. It is decided. He helicopters the book, stands down the vernacular assault. He mutters, rants, searching for his favorite shoes. The thin membrane ruptures. Instinct swallows him whole. Shoes on, he kicks open the screen-door, lurches up the alleyway.

*Let it be done.*

Some time has passed. He is drinking and has been for some time. A bottle rests atop the bar before him. He doles out his own poison, a day to live in infamy.

"A whole day lost. A lost cause!"

And the inference is not that Rome (or the next mah—sta—piece) was built in a day; but that the battle for *freedom* is fought to be won every single bloody day. This bender could, in light of our study, be viewed as proof of his deep investment. This is a personal grievance—against his own person. He has let down his brethren, his clan, himself....

And he drinks. Shot follows shot, a repetition he drives home with force. This is not maintenance drinking, this is vengeful. It is an absolution of the self-flagellation stripe, an intensity that might be confused for resolution.

And Goodspeed slides from his stool, the liquidation of a collapsing equilibrium. He meets the floor with a thud, the floor's tile cool on his face. He smiles, purified. A gaggle of head-bobbing laughs gurgle down the length of bar.

*There Goes A Regular.*

IN CASE ANYONE CARES is *The Weekly's* latest investigative feature. A three-parter, it will lead the coming publication. It is two years in the making. It is provocative, and not for light causes, but because it's a story that needs to be told. The backlash could (strike that), will be ugly. It is a big risk. Big establishments with clout—government, media—will be implicated. It should be an interesting three plus weeks....

"Could never have anticipated the sleight-of-hand to be so cynical, and that's saying something. It wasn't even on our radar."

Cleburne stands with a group of off-duty officers milling about out back of the Zone 2 precinct located just beyond *Springvale* and off the main drag in the *Old 5th Ward*, yet another once elegant in-town 'hood having been white-flighted and red-lined to shambles (if trying to crawl back).

"All the project-dwellers with no access to credit? No chance that they're movin' on up to a mixed-income development. Move 'em on out was the plan all along."

"Is it ever done any other way?" jabs Laverne, a warrior build, a second-degree black belt making her a walking weapon as well. She has all the respect you'd expect from those on the force, and at *The Weekly*.

"No, s'pose not. But that it was integral to the plan? And a plan publicly shilled as social uplift? That civic leaders sat down and actually plotted it all out; that is severely fucked up. And I can't believe that I fell for it as long as I did," Cleburne incredulous and forever grateful that this group of hardened vets let him hang around long enough to deduce it.

"Hits the stands Wednesday, then I'm movin' on."

It is the end of a long shift having begun in the backlot behind *Asa's* that afternoon and having ended with a mop-up of the remains of a running gun battle around the Oakland projects south of downtown. Cleburne had known what Trey was thinking while standing around the dead body in *Asa's* backlot that afternoon: "payback is certain, it will be ugly." Word of the ritualized hit would have spread to the street—if someone hadn't already boasted about it—and it would be all-out war. At that point, as Cleburne had recorded in multiple interviews he'd held with former gang members, the number one goal would be: "to create as many funerals as possible." (Side note: the second of these interviews scared him so shitless that he'd quit the story for weeks before being urged back to it by Grey Stinson.)

Sure enough, the guns opened up at 10 p.m. A drive-by wounded two gang bangers and killed a middle-age woman waiting for a late bus. This horrific mess had been creating scores of pre-meditated and un-meditated funerals for years now, a graveyard shift living up to its name. The wounded bangers were dumped out of still-moving bullet-riddled SUVs at an emergency room entrance just after midnight. Both were pronounced before sun-up. A retaliatory hit was said to have produced additional casualties (the rattled eyewitnesses unwilling to talk, but in clipped passing detail), but no more of the wounded ever showed up.

"You see it in there, you see what goes down. That's a problem without a solution; hard enough to neutralize it, let alone fix it. It's hard to argue against anyone just wanting to up and move along," Trey: Chief Rebuttal.

Cleburne offers counter / additional evidence: "Okay, but then purposefully exporting it? Unloading that problem on suburban cops with no clue how to counter that kind of artillery? That's a dick move."

"Alright there, muscles; but still, don't seem like it's put a dent in things here. Still plenty of the little fuckers to mop up; all that money rolling through these days."

"No question, no doubt," Cleburne easing off, deferent.

Having hard-earned contacts on the force, Cleburne had received a call from Grey telling him that Trey was on the scene of what seemed another hit-job: "Gang war returned to Austin, back of the Asa Inman. They're on the scene now." Just so happened Cleburne was right around the corner at the time. Both Cleburne and Grey had been regulars in the patrol ride-along circuit, one of the very few media outlets provided anything like routine access; largely because they were one of the very few outlets who'd actually asked—and—when allowed in, did so with some respect. (Add in the fact that they can both handle a piece.) They put in their time, did what they were told. And when both came under fire inside a week on separate ride-alongs with Bid and partner Darius—and did not stop submitting ride-along requests in its wake—it was clear they were willing to put themselves in danger to get the story. That gained them carte blanche on ride-alongs (just not with Bid or Darius, who considered both to be bad juju).... Cyrus had gone out with Trey and Rollins this night hoping against, but knowing there would be a body count....

The article about to hit stands was an offshoot of that original investigation, it all having started with them looking into what seemed, at the time, a massive escalation in gang violence. But the more the two dug into the dirt, the more this story sunk into a mire deeper than just the frightening sophistication of the city's gangs and the drugs they were dealing. The sociopathic element verified, the facts continued to clamor for further review, it all knocking about in a restless display that indicted other parties—other high-profile parties....

"That no one pulled the plug? That's when we knew," Cleburne shaking his head. "We weren't the only ones in-the-know. And, as embedded as we were by then?"

"Y'all like those dashboard bobble-head dolls, right there every time I look up," Laverne stating it true.

Trey refining: "naw, naw, more like one of them little dashboard hula girls, right? The way you shake that thang, Cleburne?"

"What? Fuck that; c'mon, check out these guns?" Cleburne dropping his best Macho Man Savage puff-up: "Yeeaa-hhhh! been working out."

"That is impressive. Well, if you all blow the whistle, brass gets to step aside the political shit-storm. Of course no one pulled the plug. Not sure it's out of some urge to do the right thing, more ass-covering, I'd say; but still," Laverne with a finger on the pulse.

"I still cannot believe elected officials thought, and I guess still do think, that no one was eventually going to check into all this? Once you adjust your sights, it is astounding how brazen it all is."

"But is it really a surprise? There's no cameras down there. The media certainly doesn't give a shit. No one fucking cares what goes on down there, just so long as it doesn't start appearing up here, right?" Trey, the realist.

"Apparently. But hey, trying to clean up and make the downtown livable, who can be against that? We were all for that 100%—until now. All a big fat lie to cover a big-ticket fleecing, might as well be raiding the Federal Treasury."

"Hey, everyone's gonna look the other way if they like the outcome. Don't want to know how, just so long as the poor and the gangs disappear," Laverne, a co-equal realist.

"Well, we're banking on the very mention of misappropriation of tax dollars getting some attention; but that ain't all. The lazy toe-the-line complacency of big media outlets? So focused on their mindless entertainment push that they can't be bothered? That this could go on in plain sight, investigative instincts going all soft since the FCC removed the cap on local market-share; all about shareholder distributions now, locking in eyeballs. Well, that and they're all clearly blinded by the sunny day promises of the re-dev."

"So were you," Laverne telling it straight.

"Yes, but at least we are course correcting. Those assholes in leading posts all knew, and still do know their actions caused this mess. I don't give a shit if they didn't mean it to go this way. It did. And we got the stat to prove it."

Confirmation of a theory came earlier in the year,

Cleburne and Stinson having parsed a clear pattern from the annual and, for them, morbidly anticipated metro homicide stats. (Now it can't go without mention here that picking needles from haystacks became Grey Stinson's claim-to-fame after he, amazingly, picked up on a serial arsonist's tip-offs wrapped in daily requests phoned in to a noon-hour all-request line, Grey actually teasing out the next likely target, which was thwarted, the dude caught in the attempt—*really!*) But first, some backstory....So, targeted revitalization was moving into the more stable intown neighborhoods such as *Springvale* and *Candler Hills*, while federally-funded mass-redevelopment programs—the re-dev—had begun to enter even low-income neighborhoods at the core of the inner city. Yet despite all the potential of that *progress!*, a brand of violent crime associated with the urban dystopia of the post-mass-suburbanization 1970s-80s was reemerging all around it. Just as Cyrus and Grey had predicted, the city's murder rate increased for a third straight year. But what really drove the two to go deep was the wafer-thin coverage it received. This here should have been treated as a stain on the city's conscience. And yet, the metro area's large, increasingly consolidated and suburban-centric news outlets reported it as no more than a passing stat, anchors acting out their head-shaking dumbfoundedness as if they were all reading from the same script: *How so, in our fair city?* Worse, some ignored it altogether. This was all too real, too complex, too complicated for their market, it seemed. It certainly put an asterisk on the old adage: "if it bleeds, it leads." *

( * offer not available in poor urban 'hoods )

Perhaps it was best put by a certain Regular: "Well, of course. It was no high-speed car chase down the connector."

"No surprise the gang war turned out to be a turf-battle; aren't they all? That was the easy thing to figure out. And why this was all getting increasingly worse? No surprise either; getting packed into ever-smaller chunks of turf, fighting over pathetic little scraps of undesirable land; the tensions flaring up at the same time the Benjamins are flowing in. The re-dev just put the squeeze on."

"Those that weren't being squeezed out," Laverne, having been the only one they could really consider an inside-source during their investigations (it having always checked out).

"And all the real criminals and sociopaths that got pushed out to the 'burbs in the process, bringing their arsenals with 'em."

Cleburne and Stinson, feeling compelled by this lack of coverage, looked beyond the dreary headlines to deduce the larger surround of the gang wars and swelling homicide stats. It told of an affluent '90s creating mass discretionary income for the purchase of recreational drugs, a development turbo-fueled by highly-productive Asian sources of smack and continental sources of MDMA (ecstasy, y'all), all of which worked to cumulatively swell the cash caches of inner-city gangs dealing said Schedule-1 controlled substances—and, in turn—using this wealth to arm themselves to the teeth with automatic-weapons, a resource even easier to come by than cheap narcotics. Turn all that loose in poor urban ghettoes fenced off from the rest of the metro area (on purpose, as per the campaign to spur downtown investment), and then heap on the extra pressure of those places getting smaller and smaller and more tightly-packed due to the bulldozing of huge swaths of, admittedly, shitty project housing in the downtown's core and—*presto!*—you get a "hard for suburbia to understand" spike in the city's murder rates, and even harder to understand direct-line role that the highly visible, highly touted inner-city re-dev, with all its purported benefits, was playing.

At that point in their research, both Cleburne and Stinson could only hope that all of this was coincidental in so far as the re-dev was concerned; this considering the solid cheerleading that they and the entire *Weekly* staff had given it. In fact, no media outlet in *The Beacon* had been a bigger booster of intown neighborhood revitalization. In older 'hoods that nonetheless had good bones, like *Springvale* and *Candler Hills*, it had taken on the form of sales of single-family fixer-uppers fueled by great deals, tax incentives, and the multi-hued reverse of white flight. Amongst the low-income section 8 housing downtown, revitalization was more comprehensive, taking on the form of these "mixed income re-dev zones" fueled by massive federal grants, and the never-ending efforts to crack the old problem of institutional poverty. So, starting (you guessed it) just over three years ago, the first of several dilapidated housing projects were bulldozed. This was the first step in the process of replacing them with thousands of new condo / townhouse units. Ideally, it would attract urban dwellers across the economic spectrum. And it continues to be a wholesale effort with a broad base of support. Billed as modern *progress!* this here was taking the fight for equity in housing to the slums. Or, so it has all been advertised....

What did occur, and still is occurring, is the wholesale relocation of an entire population segment displaced by the bulldozer's work. They have since packed into those remaining low-income urban areas outside the planned scope of the re-dev—causing a massive overnight uptick in gang violence—or for those accepting relocation vouchers (a program which in a piece of cold cynicism was initially titled: "Live the Dream") were set up by the thousands in cheap apartment-blocs out on the far edges of suburbia. The property values out there have since sunk despite the booming economy (subsidies having not followed the relocated poor, with a certain set of whites again in flight), which has knocked down the county's revenues to such a degree that they are without the ability to beef up certain public services now breaking under the strain....

All of which serves as a fitting segue.... As mentioned, there was THE other stat in the yearly homicide report which seemed to eradicate all hope for Cleburne and Stinson that the re-dev was anything more than a massive real-estate grab on the Fed's dime, one with fatal consequences. For the city's plan was not just exporting the poor from the inner-city, but the urban gang-bangers who lived amongst them. It was now clear, THE stat was supporting an emerging, and uncomfortable, side-theory that *The Weekly* duo could no longer ignore.

"Gonna bring a world of shit down on your head. Don't know, man. I just can't focus on how those fuckers got there when I'm out there; gotta do the job, root 'em out," Trey, trying to keep it all in front of him.

"None of this falls on the force, Trey. No question that sociopaths on the streets need to be neutralized. But this here goes beyond that. This was no organic thing. It was manufactured. And whether a direct or an indirect result, doesn't matter. Intent follows the bullet, right?"

"Hey, see, they have been paying attention," Laverne winking at Trey, who shakes his head, throws in a dig....

"There is a brain sittin' atop that spindly frame."

"You kidding? You want some more of this?" Cyrus gritting his teeth: a redux arm curl, muscle pump and grunt. Impressive, indeed....

"Trust me, we didn't want to be right about this. It may have all started as a back-door real-estate deal too good for the greedy to pass up; but it's now directly to blame for suburban cops getting gunned down by TEC9s."

The inner-city homicide stats had predictably been left in the dust of dense amazement that met THE heavier stat in the same report: the murder-rate having also spiked—radically—in a suburban county south, and far from the inner-city. This here was different. It got the attention of the Bigs. But both the inner-city spike and the suburban county spike were being treated as separate events. One local newscast actually sandwiched the latter stat (not even mentioning the former) in between the idyllic suburban worries of the understandable "gridlock blues" and the dangers of pre-teens heading soccer balls. Now, those at *The Weekly* were not unconcerned about the life-sucking effects of the metro area's intractable, legislatively languid congestion issues (the tradition of road-builders buying public policy to suit their bottom-line being so institutional that it has become hard to even muster the effort to mock it in print anymore), nor were *Weekly* folk without heart about studies inferring developmental problems in the still-gelling brains of kids heading soccer balls. But that said, *The Weekly* scene-stalkers were left shaking their heads at the mass journalistic failure to dig out a deeper context worthy of that year's appalling stats.

This was not the narrative with which news conglomerates wished to worry their core demographic, it appeared. It was simply not sensational enough and / or was just lost on those blasé about problems un-suburban and working-class poor. It didn't even seem all about latent racism (though there was certainly some racism), but more boardroom decisions on the kind of content that would sit well with advertisers and / or symbolic of a culture too engorged on comfortable consumption to muster a care. But for one—and only one—major newspaper editorialist, one—and only one—state rep, and of course the police (who had to deal with the real results every day), no other investigative sources in the South had even pulled out their trowels. Not only was the inner-city spike explainable (given that it was just explained), but so was this new troubling flare up far beyond the urban downtown where folks "just expect that kind to thing to happen." Not only were the two tallies related, they were one-in-the-same. The pattern had come clear to Cleburne, who started writing that Spring: a vicious gang-war three years running, certainly the oddest by-product of economic prosperity, was being exported to the edge of the 'burbs. And mass inner-city revitalization was to blame.

"Relocating the poor under guise of a progressive re-development housing program? Does it get more cynical? It is covert eminent domain on the Fed's dime. Push out the poor and the gangs, open up some sweet downtown real-estate. Everyone on the in makes a killing."

Rollins, having stood by silently smoking, finally throws in a few cents: "Yeah boy, you all openin' up a stinkin' can-o-worms. Best get out an umbrella, 'cause it's gonna start raining down shit as soon as that thing comes out."

An attempt to suss out a reason for an odd spike in gang-war violence had instead led to uncovering what was the worst (certainly the bloodiest) instance of political corruption, misuse of taxpayer dollars, and general social malfeasance by elected officials since the mentioned late '70s dust-up gutted a swath of *Old Springvale*. Cleburne is so put off by it, and perhaps smarting a bit in the pride department (common when confronting your own gullibility), that nothing short of lawsuits and convictions will do. He has held nothing back. *It's game time, y'all.* His three-part *Weekly* report (a co-writer's credit having been planned for Grey, which we will revisit) is about to blow a big ol' income disparity-sized hole in the public's rosy view of the re-dev.

"You hear what they're talking about doing now? Lotteries. Picking out a handful of project dwellers, givin 'em credit lines and movin 'em up into re-dev apartments instead of shipping off to the 'burbs."

Laverne adding, with a disbelieving lip-curl: "Ya, and

lines are out-the-door; what other chance do these folks have? Those not in gangs want out."

"Elected officials taking huge chunks of taxpayer dinero in the name of combatting institutional poverty; help the poor to help themselves, right? The real game: funneling massive housing grants into subsidizing a downtown real-estate boom, in which they all have a stake. Lotteries, damn. What cynical assholes. They'll probably have a ceremony and photo-op."

"Yeah boy, big time can-o-worms."

But people, people, please....it is getting too late for such hard-boiled socioeconomic discussion. It has been a long night. It is agreed upon without saying it.

"Well fellers, as usual, ya sure know how to show a girl a good time."

"Hasn't been my experience," Laverne, tired and out-of-there, leaving them all without another word.

Cyrus bids the city's finest godspeed. He walks a few blocks alongside the tracks, glides up Delta Place and into the heart of *Springvale.*

Cleburne's side research has Goodspeed on-the-wagon, which can only mean one thing: he's writing as fast as the pen can scrawl whilst sobriety stands. In fact, Goodspeed had seemed more irritated by the commotion over the dead body in the backlot behind *Asa's,* than by the fact that a dead body had been found in the backlot behind *Asa's.* But then: *It's game time, y'all.*

The night is thin, expressionless: the hum of streetlamps only. Having spent two years looking at / thinking over / reporting and writing on the pathologic solution-defying black hole of urban poverty, gang violence, and unconscionable politicians using the chaos to their advantage: yes, Cleburne's looking forward to a change of speed. He steps on through. It is 2 a.m.

SEVERAL DAYS HAVE PASSED. A drizzling mist spits, low clouds a rippling grey: heaven's under-sink corroded, leaking.... Out along the avenue-of-strangeness the vibrant hues force-feed this starkness, reality being given a dose of the *alternate real* that abides out here. It's a pervasive blend. See, you have what is, and you have what is also *is*. Or in less cryptic terms: You have your real, and you have your *myth* hoisted up the flagpole play-acting as *real*. And let's give credit where credit is due: its wind-ripped salute has the power to convince others and, most importantly, itself. This quadrant: a virile hothouse having organically evolved to breed a persistent, if peculiar, demographic. This quadrant: a refuge carefully engineered to elbow out space for society's "not so normals." Its not so subtle message aims bullhorns at the "responsible chattel" imprisoned within a soul-crushing gridlock, imploring the tired masses to drop the daily grind bleeding life, liberty, the pursuit of happiness....*Come, declare your inner-abnormal! You are one of us at heart!....The Points* exists to rub "normal" the wrong way. It does damage to the venal establishment via attitude alone: the *un*-fashion / the sneer / the jeer, all the sandwich-board it needs. An old mythic conflict once solved via inquisitions, drawings-quarterings, loyal sadists, pogroms, and pitting those who would control freedom against those who would be free, defines (via spray-paint tag?) this avenue-of-strangeness, its commitment to the fight emblazoned in its whirling vibrant hues. This here (or as it has been hoisted up said flagpole) is an existential stand against the soul-crushing ways of a "corporate slave-ocracy" out to "perpetuate its plantations via the self-absorbed lies of *noblesse oblige.*" Out here, a certain Regular takes his last stand for *freedom.*

> *The blank faces and expressionless forms: belabored human gears droning repetitive tasks that fed the leviathan of the pedestaled profiteer. Starve thoughts, maximize utility to flood the bottom line black. The rules were clear. And so were the threats. The voice that spoke in extracts all its own a threat clear as day.... And yet, despite repeated threats against just such lapses in judgment, he'd talk in his own voice, often.*

> Marvin Goodspeed  ~  *The Satellite Man*

The diner is bustling. Patrons and regulars come and go like a time-lapse sequence. He sits at the counter on his usual stool, one in from the first on the left. He stews.

"A warmer, Marv?" asks the waitress behind the counter. A half-grunt half-salute infers: "and best keep it comin."

Goodspeed bores his sight into the pad of paper on the counter before him, a manic desire to stab through words. His ambition force-feeds the day's starkness, a roaring energy dueling the overcast drear. Determination and dedication alone seem enough to carry the day....but our man sits, stewing, the scrawled results before him an insult to craft, failing high expectations. It is at this point where heritage serves him well. When he finds himself here, at his lowest, down next to out, that inner pull to push-on seems its strongest. It is instinctual. It is tradition....*Stand, fight for the cause! For your fellow patriots!*

"Don't dance around it. The key is within this character, what the dude thinks he is. Go all in, Goodspeed. Just dancin' around the edges here. Dig in, dig in," our man muttering to himself, urging himself on, knocking back cupfuls of coffee regular as fast as staff can refill. He rifles off sentences. He is pouring it on.

Upon the spine of this stamina Goodspeed is stacking up a second novel. He has planned no sequel, nor even a riff off the successful formula of his first: *The Satellite Man*. "The market" can sell a sequel. It can sell formula. But our man seeks the violent destruction of expectations and limits. (He is a *freedom-fighter*, after all.) It's been said that there is a running, often heated argument with the small publishing house who took a chance on him, has seen that chance pay off big and has him, in principle, signed through this book too. But to Goodspeed, our besieged hero, their perceived pleadings for a sequel or formulaic series are of no mind. Despite the perceived pressure to conform, he will talk in his own voice. Goodspeed alone will pick his targets. (Legwork would reveal this "argument" to be a simple humoring device that is all about strategic antagonizing, back-channel sources admitting: "Marvin thrives when fighting against something. We view it as doing our part for the best of the client. Whatever works.") And with this—his second full-length—he aims to detonate a *hell-bomb* of diction. The tyranny of market expectations and conventions will calcify beneath the mushrooming maelstrom. Sand will turn to glass, steel facades melting like butter! *Annihilate the duplicitous lie via the written word!*

> *They had tried to get inside his head, shape him in the company mold. But unlike all the others, they could not crack this one. The old stand-bys of coercion, trickery, even public humiliation; nothing worked. The man was impregnable. He was a fortress.... This, this would not stand. It would lead production astray, incite others to think freely. This was an existential threat that would leave profit-margins vulnerable.... And yet the more they worked him over, the less phased he seemed— smiling in spite of their efforts.*

Marvin Goodspeed ~ *The Satellite Man*

His verve alone seems enough to dissolve the leaden blues of this day. Words pour....but they are haphazard, lacking verbal glue. "Focus Goodspeed, focus." He is on edge.

"Grits 'n eggs, how long could that take?"

"Pipe down, Marv. Servin' it up now," the cook, a routine agitation, Goodspeed resuming his work without rebuttal. He sets thoughts within crosshairs. They are dead-to-rights. He snipes, they dodge, remain at-large. "Dammit! Focus!" Two eggs over-light, buttered hominy, a biscuit. Goodspeed shovels it in. For there is work to be done. *A cause to redeem!*

Five minutes later and Goodspeed is finished. He

throws down a ten and exits. He melds awkwardly with the morning rush-hour pushing through *The Points'* crossroads intersection. He is going against the grain of the expected. He is purposefully out-of-step. He lays tracks up Austin. It is an entirely expected move....

\*　　　So, a lot to keep track of here. We figure that most of you—our dear readers—have been taking dutiful notes. But for those in the back row having dozed off during our presentation (and you know who you are), let's take a moment to review our latest findings: *1) one's nature is a present moment manifestation of one's heritage; 2) one's heritage is equal-parts organic chance and engineered reality....* So, in applying this to our field study we see a pattern emerging from the murky hangover of poetic license: In consciously utilizing his instinctual natural born talent to free himself from the "daily madness" that shackles so many to a rote work-a-day "serfdom," Goodspeed lands a staggering flurry of blows to those forces who would consciously manipulate that instinctual need for all to provide for one's self. And though we may have just lost those in the back row, again, for those still following along it must now seem obvious: Our man's successes are not just his alone, but those long denied *his people....*

Here, at the murky intersection of real and *myth*, is pure motivation. Our man consciously channels chance talent in order to consciously redeem the chance hardscrabble life forced on so many of *his people*. He calls up inspiration—his man—channeling the *Populist* firebrand and all that he stood for as a tribune of the people (of the white people, that is). Still, Goodspeed's duty is clear, updated, and improved (kind of) for the times: He will take it to those who would strangle individual liberty for profit and power. Our learned Regular calls up the bitter cultural knowledge of exploitation and want having been heaped atop generations of Southrons. In the normal course of his abnormal efforts—when the chips are down, the odds at their longest—he needs only recall the acrid history of those used as cannon fodder by those others that stacked fortunes on bent and breaking backs, the engineered humiliation of the common agrarians kept down by the plantation aristocracy, by damned Yankee aggression, by the scalawags and their carpetbags, by the *New South* Bourbons—by the *Gilded* fucking *Age.*

Goodspeed is stewing as tacks onto DeKalb. The morning's efforts have been for crap. But he is in the thick of the fight. He is remembering why he fights, why he writes: redemption, *vengeful redemption.* He aims tracks for the Highland end of north *Springvale.* The daily grind continues all around him, its plodding vehicular hordes prodding him to redeem the day, redouble his efforts. He looks on at those mired along the avenue....

"A living death. Puny, unimportant, no less regressive than the crop-lien; look at all those poor bastards."

A strong genetic imprint, natural and environmental, runs deep in his marrow. It roils up grey and bitter. *Burn through the drear. Fight on!* He lights a smoke, is seething. *Beware those with the painted on civic smile, glad-handing, promising. They'll pull the old bait-and-switch: trade your freedom for feudalism!* Our man's hardscrabble ancestry had trusted their political leaders, held close to the rigid cultural confines imposed on them, put faith in their economic captains. And for their efforts they'd been thanked, in C. Vann Woodward's summation, with: *the annual defeat of the crop market, the weekly defeat of the town market, and the daily defeat of the crumbling barn, erosion, illiteracy.* Heralded Dixie raconteur, George Tindall, documented this profit-less toil in his tome, *The Emergence of the New South*—the flotsam of generations: *bent under the burden of perennial defeat.* Under fire, our man shares a trench alongside Lyle Lanier, another of the Vanderbilt *Agrarians* who in his *Critique of the Philosophy of Progress* took aim at the "venal establishment," denouncing: *man's virtue being measured by his social utility....* Goodspeed will detonate the inequity, the destructive omnipotence of profit over common liberty that has bled his beloved Southland white....*for freedom!*

"The madness of today attended by all the madness of yesterday. Sad. True. But they won't get to me, that I know."

Goodspeed looks on at a stalled line of cars, pickups, diesels, fleet vehicles, a bus. He is actually moving faster up the sidewalk on foot. He shakes his head. He feels contempt and pity for *the people*, the concept fueling this particular madness so foreign to his fiber it has him as alien as "a Stonewall Queen in Jeff Davis County." The rush hour smokes, seethes. He skims along the avenue's fringe beneath sky spit, seething, plotting.


IT IS AN HOUR LATER. The sky's mood is still morose, sunken, hollow. Token stabs of light punch through the dank of Goodspeed's apartment. His morning power walk complete, he has settled in at his *new* old metal desk recently found discarded amongst the ebb-and-flow of the junk pile out in the backlot. He has replaced a broken leg with a cinder block and is dealing with its missing drawer just fine. (A landmark event such as mah—sta—piece creation certainly deserves such minimal material support, eh?) Goodspeed holds a special place for the TV tray, but feels the bargain is his. He is moving on up. He is plowing through his second full-length.

"Feels like a crapster-piece at the moment. C'mon, Goodspeed, dig in; yer just dancing around the edges here. Stop fucking around!" he grumbles to himself, rapping a pencil obsessively, violently, atop desktop.

Caution: artist at work.

\*      So, we have tried, but we just can't let this one thing go.... A slow-gelling theory of our fieldwork is that we are all weird walking contradictions, the sociocultural worlds we build up around us little more than that individual truth writ large. These are such predictable traits one can bank a theory on it. So, what say we admit to the ubiquitous weirdness (why fight it, really?) and take our trowels to a few of these contradictions proper. A prime example: A regional scholar might cock an eyebrow at Goodspeed sharing ranks with *The Agrarians*. Aside from attempting to bleed the soul-crushing industrialization of society with a thousand slices of the pen, the side of their work our man conveniently quotes, they were also apologists for the very plantation ideal that Goodspeed instinctually plasters with shit. In their collection of essays, *I'll Take My Stand*, *The Agrarians* cite the Civil War's breakup of the plantation as a tragedy near equal to the late nineteenth / early twentieth-century decline of small independent farmers caused mainly by the monopolization of supply and credit, and technological advancements in the agricultural process itself. They mythologize a harmonious happy (white) Southern family that fails to synch with an inconvenient fact: The old economic aristocracy, who controlled with iron fist the distribution-of-wealth in the antebellum days, simply gave way to a new one that used cover of the idyllic *myth* of reconciliation and *New South progress!* to indenture a generation of small-time agrarians—black and white—in a debtor's prison called tenant-farming. Just ask our man. He will rail on and on and on about the "bitter inequities of absentee combinations and trusts directing the country's demise from town and city." But then, he'll quote an *Agrarian* as if gospel. And this, after having lived about as urban a life as the South can offer. Weird.... And yet within the weird jumble of artifacts strewn about the base of our excavation pit lies this common nugget: the contradiction of ideas is to conviction as the competition of ideas is to democracy. It is fuel. *It is his fuel....*

It is a big tent that can boast of such either-ors inside the genes of heritage and not simply implode. But there stands our man. And we are beginning to suspect our man knows it all well enough: not just triangulating the coordinates where the survey-line of *real v. myth* falls (with pinpoint accuracy we should add), but purposefully leaping back and forth across that boundary as if a porous wormwood fence put up only for show. Dare we say our study is paying dividends, people? *Contradiction memorialized as heritage, reconciled beneath the wind ripped standards of tradition.* Strange. Genius?

And now, back to our regularly-scheduled artist at work.

A newly acquired desk lamp, about the only new thing in a room full of old things, is the only substitute for sun. Having stalled for the moment, the day's efforts are nonetheless going well—in that he doesn't yet feel the need to fire it atop a pyre and give up this "masochistic writing gig" for all time (a thought he's certain to have at least once inside the next hour).

"Spur revolt, an active revolt from within; a touch of anarchy, even. Tacit anarchy? Is that even possible? Do not rehash Orly. Gotta bust through here, Goodspeed. It's on you. They are relyin' on you."

Sebastian Quentin Orly, the central daydreaming character in *The Satellite Man*, is at the moment casting a long shadow over the aggressive boat-rocker (as yet unnamed) emerging at the centre of this new work. Goodspeed is fretting, cold-sweating. Obsession needs its fuel. It needs results. It cannot fathom the threat of sobriety—as much as it should be fucking praying for it, for fuck's sakes! (Yes, okay. Excuse the subjective interjection, dear reader.... ) He has yet to find a voice for the still formless figment at the heart of this new work. The day grows long. *Victory!* is in doubt. *Buck up!* Our man pins some measure of hope (the hopes and dreams of a long-denied people) on the bromide of dialog....

"No sequel. What is past is past. Either he's gonna speak for himself, or it is game over."

His fear is that *The Satellite Man* is infecting this new obsession. Whereas TSM told of the dark comic tale of desk clerk Orly's accidental triumph over the hegemony of a soulless corporate culture—a *Victory!* deploying a passive resistance more clueless than planned—our man now fears his newest of notions, turning its sights on the "chattel support system" of said corporate leviathan: *suburbia*, is being swamped in TSM's wake. He fears he is still too close to that ship having sailed. For this is to be no sequel. That will not do. That is worry #1. Worry #2 involves the subject-matter proper, that the fictional indictment of suburbia is a rut run to death by a generation of uninspired takes on its most obvious theme: the facade of secure contentment masking the steep spiritual tax of arid convention, token diversity, and the expectation of puritan morality. No rehashed plot of adulterous malaise, no cheat-and-deceit within a tranquilizer haze. This newest notion cannot be a "hitting close to home" melodrama. That will not do. This work must root out the obvious angles root-and-branch, taking it to the do-good lie with blunt force....

"Shining light on the hollow predictability, the painted-on smiles of a mass numbed by material excess and pills? Posers have done that crap to death, just Cheever copy-cats. Go in obliquely. It is day two at Chancellorsville. Time to detonate the whole obese mess."

Many critics continue to dismiss Goodspeed as having gotten lucky with *The Satellite Man:* the satirical epic starring S. Q. Orly that fell somewhere between George Orwell and Terry Gilliam's classic film oddity, *Brazil.* Two years have passed since TSM was published. Yet critics continue to pile on, pinning Goodspeed as lucky. It's a claim he will not dispute; though he will often drop an outrageous response to a critical piece. And though our study would indicate this stirring-of-the-pot is performed with purpose and as provocation only (nothing personal, y'all), it is his schoolyard taunting that makes it hard to distinguish the actual target of the negative criticism. Is it Goodspeed the author, or Goodspeed the man in the sights of the potshots leveled? I mean, yes: The guy can come across as, well, a dick. And those critical don't hold back, a trend our man stokes. He is loathe to miss an opportunity to give the "feckless creative establishment" the finger. It's a kind of disinterested sport for Goodspeed, like fishing or politics.

Anna, mentioned culture maven for *The Weekly*, is one of the few who has interviewed Goodspeed, having gotten in by telling him up-front she didn't want to talk about his writing. But it was Anna's strategy put into action over several domestics-in-a-bottle (she can hold her liquor, people) that unwittingly laid out the blueprint for our study here; in that she asked him what he wanted to talk about. The first 74 seconds post-question proceeded as an uncomfortable stretch of silent-drinking, all of it leading up to a rant lasting 13 minutes and 15 seconds with hardly a break. "A harangue for the ages." The central theme? "Corrupt establishments," generally. Here's a 30 second snippet (a discreetly positioned NT-1 having recorded the whole thing):

"I need a focus-group definition of quality in art like I need a hole in the head; just a bunch of operatives, parasites without a creative bone in their body who do not create art but simply slick up their hair, sip chardonnay at gallery openings that hawk art-as-commodity and discuss who-the-fuck-cares esoteric bullshit so as to: a) look smart, b) feign creative skill, all while their whining drivel betrays both—*you see, the radical decompensation of later-*

day post-modernism has led to a state of—blah—blah—blah....the whole charade papering over the fact that they're in bed with big money speculators who corner their markets so as to keep the producers of real art down."

But then, all this vitriol can appear planned. Goodspeed goads his critics wherever and whenever possible to reload and let fly. The old maxim still rings true: bad press = press. And by inducing it, our man reaffirms his street-cred out along the world's many avenues-of-strangeness. Again, we're led to consider: *Goodspeed, the engineer?*

True or not, what is known is that our caustic son of Dixie done took fire. He's had five works published in only two years. And they are selling at a clip sufficient enough to support his thin lifestyle, and then some. A collection of short-fiction: *Tin Roof, Rusted*, and a novella: *South x Southeast*, had just been published earlier in the year. Two other collections: *Sin-r-gy* and *Welcome to Penitentiary Company, No. 3* were both written prior to, but released after TSM. All four were initially ignored, along with TSM, his fat file of rejections providing him both proof and inspiration. Goodspeed will claim bad reviews are nothing but boardroom decisions:

"It's about discrediting the competition, smearing anything and anyone that might just compromise the stranglehold of monopolies reliant on sweatshops to churn out their mass-consumable crap. It is all a public relations play."

Yet proving this conspiracy seems beside the point, if not irrelevant. For proving that he believes it—or even cares—comes to seem like a pointless exercise. Beyond recognizing and documenting his conscious pot-stirring, further study dead ends at his irreverence. Goodspeed hasn't been committing the first-degree murder of his own time thinking over ways to smite critics. He's been drinking.

As for that front, the truce holds. (Our recommend-dation of scorecards to keep all this straight must now seem clear, dear reader!) It is a tenuous truce. Nature stands impatient, arms-crossed and glaring threateningly across that thin membrane of DMZ. It is itching to blitz Goodspeed's attempt to put this novel to paper, something our man does frantically (an anxiety that one might actually confuse with ardor). Goodspeed knows well enough to take full-advantage of the cease-fire. For it promises future conflict. And that right soon.

It's an hour later. Goodspeed is stuck. Several attempts to bust through writer's block have resulted in nothing but an angry pile of paper balls and a virulent run of cusswords so loud they were heard upstairs in Asa's. (Oh, and he also broke his new desk lamp. It had a good run.) Anxious pacing has failed to help. One can see the steam venting out his ears. He is so very close. One missing ingredient, that's all. But like a name you can't recall when you need to, the right word, the right phrase, the right turn, eludes him. It inhabits his skin like an itch. Dammit, it's on the tip of his brain. FUCK! FUCK! FUCK!!! "Alright, dammit! A quick break." The world, humanity will provide grist. A quick stroll never fails. He throws open the door, kicks screen-door, exits his hovel. He rants, dons sunglasses despite the grey. A quick stroll will provide....

Goodspeed is not sure when this latest idea came to

him. Short stories come and go. But a novel is an infectious presence, inhabiting the skin like an itch. He can't place the inspiration, most of the previous six months having been spent with the binge. Grey spinning scenes flay his memory, a.m. radio signals sputtering under a bridge, low days, the non-linear trance of nights....and then, like that: *restless desire percolating through the haze, our hero awakened, inhaling the gilded vapors of inspiration! Of freedom!* When the idea came to him is of no mind. It is here now.

He walks on, scanning for the spark. Non-fiction underwrites his fiction. In his view, the two are kissing cousins—if not just doing it on a public park bench. Our man is a keen observer. He is always hard at work, really: scanning the world, scouting humanity, drinking its mad vigor. Pedestrians pass, a side-eye glance. You never know when you'll walk right past a storyline. And then, like that: BANG! Words cut loose like a stampede. Time is stunned, dazed, exposed for the lying little fuckhead that it is— inspiration transcending that abused corrupt tool of the lying official: TIME. Inspiration beats time senseless, *the cause won!* (For the moment.)

And he's got it! Of course! It was so obvious. Goodspeed does an about-face. He runs for his hovel to detonate writer's block.... Again, Will Percy:

> *Only the faintest wavering glimmer of the shouting light of creation penetrates our dark diminutive cell ~*

It's several hours later. Goodspeed has relocated to *Asa's* backroom. The truce holds. But even the most disciplined can only be without Martha's brunswick stew for so long. He goes at the stew and pad of paper with equal gusto. Disturb at your own risk, even a friendly *how do ya do?* sure to provoke an object thrown in the vicinity of the inquiree. Stew, cigarettes, writing implements: all the camaraderie that's required.

His pen is sprinting down the page, driving home that spark—this novel idea making haste in delivering something he can work with. Pen is hammer, paper is anvil, Goodspeed forging the firebrand of his musings. It is high professional skill. The title's a strange fit, but it fits. An extraordinary discipline channels manic obsession. The two traits set aside all past differences they might have had, coming together for *the larger cause.* (The strange alliance of poor farmers following aristocratic slaveowners into war seems the apt regional comparison?) As mentioned, without the friction-of-conviction our man would surely fall flat on his face. (*Here's to friction!*) Sparks scatter before his swings. He pounds out sentence and stanza and chapter-upon-chapter. It is relentless and best to give it a wide berth. For fists might fly if disturbed.

"Another'n Boo?" asks Howard, the length-of-bar empty but for the two.

"You bet, H. He doing that writin' back there?" inquires the regular.

"Sure is, gets that fire up in his eyes. Will burn a hole in ya, swear," Howard automatically wiping a clean bar top.

"Sure's intense, that boy," Boo reminded of his stint in the Marines, Goodspeed's wild look akin to that of the natural born killer. *Oo-Rah!*

"Whatever works. The boy seems to have what it takes. I can't say I can get on board with, or even understand what in hell he's talking 'bout in those books of his; but he pays the bills, ahead of time too."

The two bounce a slow banter. Respectful of the talent and the light-of-creation burning white hot in the backroom, it nonetheless passes to inconsequence. Goodspeed could be penning the next masterpiece or running up a high score on the pinball machine, either would pass for fine, neither altering *the conscious maintenance of inconsequence*, in here.

And right then it is possible that the furious Goodspeed dynamo has burned off the drear of this day, singlehandedly. The afternoon spills the first visible rays of the day through front windows and doorway. It penetrates the dank, rings the regular and proprietor. Conversation floats to the background like a wallflower.... The compact-disc jukebox is scratching out *Neil Young* beneath heart of gold sconces....*I've been in my mind, it's such a fine line*....Haloes drift across Goodspeed's work-in-progress, a high-wire act at the moment putting on a show. And it is something to behold, synching fury with the pen in hand. The bowed paneling and tile of his immediate surroundings—everything beyond stew, cigarettes, writing implements—it all drops off into oblivion. Two scenes: indifferent to the other yet bound inextricably. It's a self-contained universe holed up within these jaundiced walls. It is a masterwork. (Hmm, perhaps some enterprising young soul should write a book about this.... )

And just then, the front door opens. It creaks with a pang. Cyrus steps through. Backlit, he appears as a sheriff seeking his prey. He steps to the bar. Howard casts a glance, pulls up a smirk as Cyrus Cleburne takes a seat.

"Pick'd a sore time to drop in," Howard advising, "Marv'll be less than pleased if ya interrupt him here 'n now."

"Wouldn't think of it, just haunting the area this afternoon, put on a good thirst. Anything on tap'll do. Howard, right?" Cleburne's view glued to the all-sports channel on the cable TV.

"That's right," Howard accepting Cleburne at his word, pulling down a pint glass, filling it full, serving it up. And the inconsequential acts of day drinking and masterpiece creation proceed unmolested.

YOU GET THE IDEA that busboy isn't all that bright. Having been told in no uncertain terms to turn off a portable stereo blaring "corporate pop in cowboy boots," busboy has instead, it would appear, asserted his right to blare said music when and where he wants. Having tromped over to the portable stereo on the ground under an awning strung over the open front-doors of the bus, and staring at Goodspeed the whole way, busboy has just turned *up* the volume. Yes, the decision was a poor one, the tick in Goodspeed's squint-eye the ocular equivalent of a mega-ton detonation.... If he has any brains at all, busboy will view Goodspeed coolly striding up to and violently deconstructing the stereo into mangled exploding bits with aid of a baseball bat as the best outcome he could have hoped for. Busboy stands aside without protest, without a word, as Goodspeed lets fly a final flurry, wipes his forehead and disappears back into his hovel. Wise choice, busboy.

For Goodspeed has reached a milestone. He has the end in view. It is still a horizon line, critical miles yet to cover—but he has it in sight. To stand in his way now, by-choice or chance, will induce the near certainty of physical violence. The additional time required to beat busboy seems the only reason Goodspeed left him unscathed. For the end is in sight, and the only thing standing between him and that end is his old nemesis: TIME. Goodspeed plans on beating it senseless instead.

Our mason of diction is back at his new / old desk. Paper, pens, pencils, are strewn about. He pitches forth. He is a conductor. He pins words with the precision of a knife-throwing act, verse bursting onto the page as fast as his pen can scrawl; and at the moment, it is having trouble keeping up. He is a steamroller. He is unstoppable. It is the blood, sweat, and tears of *his people* that pours onto the page....*Hoist the standard of the cause! Fly it in the face of the Big Mules who denied his folk their earned share, all those bastards past and present! Remember, remember! Each word a bullet fired into the riddled corpse of freedom denied!....*

> *About my head the thundering storm beat like a heartless voice, and the crazy forest pulsed with the curses of the weak.*
>
> W. E. B. Du Bois ~ *The Souls of Black Folk*

*Detonate the past, all undue pain and suffering, the weak betrayed! Payback to take the form of a mushrooming firestorm: blasting, atomizing all those smug greedy grins!....Target acquired, over. 3 − 2 − 1. Bombs Away....* And his words explode onto the page.

Goodspeed can and has kept up this pace for days without rest, hunkered in his bunker, hunched over dwindling pads of paper. He is fueled for the long haul: a resolution, a commitment to a process so deep that it owns him. It is so mercurial, instinctual, a substitute addiction whose product—creative diction—he consciously brow-beats into serving the ultimate goal. For it is just a tool, no more or less important than the pencil in his hand sharpened to a nub and recording furiously, the many more scattered about in pieces, the dead soldier ink pens, cartridges drained, having given their last full measure of devotion to *the cause.* But not in vain, not if he has any say. For the end is in view, *Victory!—freedom—*within grasp!

This here is binge writing: paper, pens, pencils, momentarily sub'd out for the "bottle as bayonet." Terms of this turbulent truce stipulate fifths-of-bourbon be replaced by a cycling intake of coffee, cigarettes, OJ by the gallon and two joints a day. But whether the fuel of the moment be spirits or words, either could easily be his undoing but for one trait we find crossing the DMZ with impunity: a manic time-bending resolve. On this, the terms are unconditional:

"Compromise and ditchdiggin' are one in the same. Bargain an ounce of your time, your freedom, and you're just diggin' your own grave."

And he is buried in his words.


Since the last time our study made a point of knowing such trivial detail as what day it is (and it bears repeating, lest we forget: time = the undisputed heavyweight champion of douchebags), October has lengthened. Summer's stretch-out has finally blown itself out. It is a more lackadaisical temper these days. Autumn redefining, inverting thermal expectations. Canopies rusting.

Century-old white oaks stand fast around the edge of *Springvale's Delta Point Park*. The noble spires can only speculate on the commotion jostling hostile along the avenues, boulevards, and parkway connectors below. It is the resounding clamor of *progress!* The wise lumber shakes heads, scatters leaves methodically and without worry on the manic hustle rolling the pavement of this new *new order*. At the edge of view stands its flagships: buildings spiraling resolution and the delusion of control, this new epoch promising the world as our oyster. And yet, these century-old oaks and maples and poplar, they have seen it all before. Always the promise: "give us your faith and we'll give you the goods." They have seen generations of suckers left holding the bag. They have watched "town" (modern translation: mercenary corporations) rake in *Gilded* fortunes as "country" (modern translation: everyone else) was left to the servile scraps. They have seen it all before. The buildings preach their anthems of *progress!* but spell it: p-o-w-e-r. They preach this scripture as *liberty!* but spell it: p-r-o-f-i-t.... Yes, yes, it all seems so clear to him now.... This newest *new order* has simply plastered over the old. It was always about gaining the power-to-profit off enslaving others' time, just tweak the definitions for successive generations and you're good. A tried-and-true method: play the game or be played. *("Sound like those Marxist-types with all their equity-talk, these here Populists....")* This new / old order inherits its condescension. It looks down at "country" as sacrificial regiments to be thrown into the meat-grinder, those who failed to achieve the appropriate levels of rich. This latest take needs only substitute company-store credit with "flat wages stifled under the cost-of-living index" / mill-town shack with "tract house in the 'burbs" to update it for the modern-era. These newest *New South* captains, spying down on all those not singing the company song. They plot their hostile takeovers from behind cascading walls of glass....*Oh yes, this is what they're doing!*....A playground power struggle delivered to top-floor boardroom: "The trick to winning, to supremacy? Bend the free-will, the time of others, to your own purposes; unless, of course, you can enslave them outright." It is about power-and-profit masquerading behind a flag-waving patriotism, filling the mills full of wistful suckers wanting an honest day's labor and a house of their own. Sound earnest, honest, compassionate, all the while entrenching an interest-fueled indebtedness.... Yes, yes, this game is an old one (and seems more clear by the swig). The burnt leaves of a parkside maple spiraling down, a soldier of the ages shaking its head. It has seen it all before. Sad, really: these humans enslaving their own, defiling the *freedom* of their own.

A bus deposits two workers at the *Delta Point* stop, takes on two more. It is an equal exchange mapped out carefully at the most minute levels of this rat race; and here is the proof, stretching-out the most efficient route to profits. It's an old strategy, re-dux.... He sits on a park bench in the small triangular park, leaves raining down. He sights the bus shuttling off two more "suckers." It lurches off behind a black-and-blue screen of exhaust. The deposited suckers amble home: bruised, tired, the shock troops of this newest *new order* heading for bivouac.

He unscrews the cap from flask, draws a full pull. The sky minces swirls of orange-red to the west, texture glowing as the heart of fire. Dusk is on deck.... And he is coming to see this complex conspiracy more clearly: "the rapacious greed of freedom deniers" theory, having driven the *live free or die!* crowd into the Appalachian backwoods, having migrated through antebellum and *Reconstruction* and *Gilded Age* days to have infected the crowning achievement itself: *The New South.* Well, this will all require diligent observation to unravel, getting down on hands-and-knees with trowels and handbrooms and getting dirty, peeling back the layers, hoping, hoping that one half-buried clue leading to theoretical elucidation will poke up from the red dirt. Yes, our man was right. To understand we must put in the legwork. We must fully immerse.

The day comes to a close. He sits on a park bench in *Delta Point*, inviting the requisite lubricant *(freedom oil?)* to sooth his mind into theories and concepts not so readily apparent. He is immersing himself fully, is getting lit! ("Oh bourbon, you sly miscreant. Are you tryin' to get me advantage so you kin take drunk of me?") The oaks, maples, poplars skirt this small plot run round by the forked lanes whose angles gives it its shape and name. It stands defiant, as does much of *Springvale*.... And Cyrus Cleburne stands up. He sways, rummaging about the swell of inebriation for an elusive balance: "steady boys, steady." To fully understand, one must do the work: one must walk—er—stagger a mile in another man's duct-taped shoes.

Cyrus steps on down Edgewood Avenue. Cracked

hexagonal stones reach up to trip his slurred steps; the knots of century-old roots follow suit. He continues unfazed by the missing steps (as if they were unnecessary all along). He is heading towards Elizabeth Street. Sky swaths supersede the maple with evening redness. He is thinking it all through....*Cruel greed crushing hopes, dreams left smoldering. How then to gain back control, to win back time? Where then to turn but the bottle?*....It is the regular way: proven, dependable—like a faithful pickup. He can comprehend an aversion to working one's self to death for the perceived ill-gotten gain of others; but can only cock his head at the alternative: drinking one's self to death and calling it *freedom*. Even under the influence of its chief (liquid) patron, that there still seems "funny weird."

But ever the objective journalist, he'll leave snap judgments aside for now. He must keep to character, observe, persevere in *the cause—his cause*. Perhaps he must more fully immerse. Perhaps. Our study is taking a turn. (Intellect, meet visceral. Visceral, intellect.) There is much more ground to cover, context (pretext?) to uncover. Cleburne draws a full pull to help him understand, our charlatan of *the cause* walking on.

OUR STUDY HAS TURNED into the heart of the matter. He turns north, lays tracks up Elizabeth Street beneath warming streetlamps, dusk staggering towards night. *Renovations and restorations* are underway, *renewal* possible—probable, even: the late gutting of a late-Victorian, the revival of a Revival. Time is being hailed only in its defeat, out here. We cannot deny nature's franchise. But, perhaps, with some elbow grease its indifferent "tearing down of what we build up" can be held in check, a DMZ established. *(Beating time senseless, if only for a spell? Can we get an amen, people?!)* And what with the economic verve, the bravado—nay, the sheer braggadocio!—of these *Go Go '90s*, *Springvale* and her sister intown neighborhoods are positioned to be gentrification hot spots.

Withered facades mask one-time desirable residences having been made undesirable by economic desertification, racist housing policy, and urban blight (i.e. whites wanting to be as far from "urban" as possible). But fast-forward a generation and these pads are being made desirable again by their more tolerant kids and an instinctual Gen X skepticism of the stultifying yawning sprawl. The combustion-engine-fueled tide that has spent half-a-century flooding the 'burbs is showing signs of reversing course. "Settlers" have been showing up in *Springvale*. Deals abound. Fixer-uppers are being returned to their former stateliness for a song. We see nature being denied its best attempt to tear down the weathered Tudor, the unkempt bungalow—for now at least (a thin membrane, indeed).... But for journalistic rigor and the sake of our study let's consider the either-ors: Is time being beat senseless—or—is the gentrification of *Springvale* and the *Old Fifth* and *Candler Hills* denying nature its timeless *liberty?* Is the revitalization of intown 'hoods an evolutionary step, an expansion of a more equitable, diverse, and free future—or—just the financial shit-slag of a "rapacious new *new order?*" Is it time to oil up in order to more fully understand? Most definitely.

Cyrus Cleburne unscrews flask cap. He is putting in

the time. He has aspirin at the ready, is getting into the story. Our charlatan draws a full pull. It's not yet 5:55 p.m. (And already lit!) An uprooted slab of sidewalk stone trips him up: grinning, loaded, all in a day's work. It is *Armistice Day:* November 11. Cleburne has been hard at work at the bending and beating of time for weeks now. (Or has it been months?) He can see a vast improvement: the more inebriated he is, the clearer it all seems to be. He is grasping, more fully, at this *winning* strategy.

A sound from out of the blue, something like an unhappy cat being accordion-ed under the arm. Eustace walks opposite Cyrus, up from the intersection with Austin.

"Mwwaahh-wah, that's what you get! Mwwaahh-wah, yessir, that is what you get!" Eustace actually making an accordion-like motion with hands and arms. An air headlock? If so, to whom? Who knows, really. We are not the clinical psychologist he needs. We know all we need to know.

"Mwwaahh-wah, that is what you get, you lover No, no, you is a fighter! And I told you, I warned you, do not bring that down h'yere! Mwwaahh-wah! Don't be bringin' that shit into my house!"

Cyrus continues down the hill toward the intersection. Gravity's pull makes a mockery of his equilibrium, a wise law doing its best alt-*Weekly* style "smart-ass"....*How is your hubris going to help you now, human? Dominion over nature? Sure, believe what you must....* It is its franchise, its prerogative—the impish delight of nature to fuck with we foolish mortals.

A car passes, stirs the fair Autumn air. Another strides up in its wake and slows down alongside Cy's slurring stride. Anna Coffee cranks down car window.

"Still going tonight, kid?"

"Hey, what's up there, Anna-bo-banna?"

"Funny, and—of course. You're drunk, aren't you?"

"A bit."

"You realize it's not even six?"

"Hey, hey now. I'm workin' here."

"Right. How you convinced *Prez* of this I have no idea. He must have been drunk too. He owes all of us in the wake of this little stunt. You better make it pay off there, chump. We're all meeting at Roy's at nine. I'll see you there, if you're still standing."

"The what now? Oh, right, right! Afterburn @ The Point! Ya-ya-ya, still goin'—will see you here, uh, there."

"Ya, later dude," Anna pulling away, the smirk of disbelief pasted to her face, knowing of Cy's "R&D" and spelling it c-o-m-p-l-e-t-e-f-u-c-k-i-n-g-b-u-l-l-s-h-i-t. "Cover for daytime-drinking on the clock, no wonder he hooked Gibbs."

Cyrus walks it off, heads for his pad in the *Candler Hills*. The study is coming to him. He knows more for his efforts (despite actually remembering less of it); and perhaps therein lay an important discovery. In the blurring of recollection, via misty magnolia-scented filter, or the bottle—or both—is planted the seed of that dysfunctional regional sport: *nostalgia*. All the better to remember it as you wish to remember it, once the real has been conveniently misplaced.

*[Mrs. Blake] lived upon lies....thrived upon the
sweetness she extracted from them.*
Ellen Glasgow ~ *The Deliverance*

Our study has taken a turn. Cyrus Cleburne turns east on Austin, twilight redacting daylight. The black out a-coming.

It is 9:30 p.m.... With no Cyrus in sight, an unsurprised Anna, boyfriend Roy, Kelly, and occasional *Weekly* contributor, Lou, had started out for the club.... And they are walking up on the club, Cyrus in sight standing against the wall outside front door and hassling the large native Dominican, Abraham—Ab—at his usual post working the door. The wall vibrates, the opening band having just begun. Sidewalk crowds are gathering up-and-down DeKalb. The nightly festival kicks into gear.

"C'mon?"

"Really."

"Now, Ab, level with me here."

"Hello, all," Ab ignoring the slurring scene-stalker, welcoming the familiar posse having just strolled up.

"Roy's at nine?" Anna fixing a look on Cyrus.

"Said I'd see ya here, or there—right. So anyhows, Ab here says he has no interest in my tight virgin ass; and this, though I am havin' to resist his many advances. I think he be lyin.' This here, fresh meat!" Cyrus slapping the ass in question.

"Take heem inside, now."

And they do. The darkened room is filled with a textbook blend of youthful abandon and chemically-altered states: music louder than necessary, songs ending haphazardly.

"Ab's a good sport for not dropping a beat-down on your virgin ass," Kelly looking over Cyrus' lanky frame, ordering a drink.

"Kiddin'? He loves me, he's on my side. Pro'ly wants a tea-baggin' too, just can't admit it. Hey, beer me, Kel!"

"You (insert the laugh of disbelief, or disgust—or both—here), are on your own tonight."

"Harsh! No respect for the hard workin' man, still workin' here, people. Gettin' to the meat of the story, the nougat centre!" the blur of drink rolling him....

Many recent days / nights he has lost in a similar fashion. It is proving quite the journey: doing the legwork, walking / staggering a mile or two. He is getting to the heart of the matter, wandering the avenue-of-strangeness (madness?) in-character.... And yet, there is a tipping point once one veers this deep into *this* study. Will he recognize it from within? Will he recognize the neck-deep water as a Rubicon crossing where the act begins to square-up as reality, that salient point where reality really comes loose from its moorings? (And yes, perhaps this *is* the point; but let us conclude our research, sans rushing to conclusions.) Strangely, or perhaps not so strangely, this deep dive has proven vital—essential, even—to *this* study. It is, at the moment, making all the difference: the thunder-crack of contradiction no more than gentle heat-lightning brushing the sky, the counterintuitive blend of fact and fiction having become so clear, the daily reckoning, the bottle as broadsword. "It is all a beat down of time." A beat down of time = a beat down of your history = freedom. *The past redeemed! Inequity erased! Victory!* Of course, it is all so obvious now!

And Cyrus has lost a whole hour: this time-bender in training. He comes to as the main act takes the stage. They serve up the swelling roar of post-rock. They are going places. They have come here. They bring sound like a wall. *Brother Jim*, an imposing gentle giant of a scene-ster to be seen at most shows (most good ones, that is) has propped Cyrus up against a wall, the group having disowned him for the night. Cyrus dons a stupid grin, is mighty fucked-up. Stage-lights whirl, windmill streaks across sight. They bend, strobe—the club at the point of Austin / DeKalb packed. Crowd heads bob, a bubbling mass. The music goes right through him. Cyrus understands. It is all so clear: "as all get out." The blur rolls him a final time. He slides to the floor in a slumped mass of gelled flesh-and-bone. Ab takes it from there.

SUN UP BREAKS FAST. Sunrays seem cellophane-wrapped. They pry at his eyelids: the white-knuckled strain of fingers pulling open heavy doors. ("C'mon, man, open up! I know you're in there!") Determination meets resistance: a slit-eye view. ("Go away. No one here.") He peers through slits skyward, does not like the looks of this day. He props himself onto elbows, blurred shapes run through a Vaselined lens: a tree, a lamp post, the accursed light of day.

"Shit."

A semi lets fly a great hydraulic fart as it throttles down on parkway connector beyond the embankment. A sharp sudden pain pricks his brain behind left-eye. Squinting, it is absorbed by an omnipresent gloom. Consciousness comes to in languid steps, a print in a weak batch of developer. Focus, focus, having woken up on the stonewall terrace running the length of city avenue....*Nice*.... A headache looms, as does the onset of grey Winter.

The parkway connector writhes with the restless vehicular hordes, the day seized of *progress!* Incoming traffic creates its own wind. It washes over the embankment, over his prone position. It seeks to coerce, apparently, to bludgeon resistant ne'er-do-wells into the company mold. It has its work cut out for it. *Springvale*, this haughty *old belle:* an intown district having begun its days defining "the grain" to be most beneficial to the expansion of status and wealth, having been redefined of late by pioneers amongst these urban 'hoods going "against the grain"....And so, what of this new *new order?* Is *renovation and renewal* a clandestine attempt to redefine, or simply re-ingrain "the grain"? (Scorecards, people. Don't forget your scorecards.) Either way, the shift whistles do bray, calling the corporate slaves in from the 'burbs.

"Nothin' but modern day mill towns," our unreconstructed *New* New South man would say; "late twentieth-century sharecroppers trading their freedom for credit and a two-car garage, sellin' out to the whims of CEOs / COOs / VPs they have never met and never will."

*Do not listen to the mad drunk. Ours is the path to responsible citizenship. Nature is what we make of it. Fall in line or face societal excommunication,* this new *new order* of *progress!* informs us (apparently). All of which begs the question: Has gridlock become the "yardstick" of loyalty? Or is it just the shit-slag of all the suckers left holding-the-bag?....New orders, old orders, the villainy of gentrification....

"Phh'uh—man, oh' man."

It is all so clear through the morning fog. He drags

hands down his face, pulls facial skin into something resembling Munch's *The Scream.* The scene is a corporate-productivity dream, everyone busy getting their productive-ness on. Traffic helicopters hover, carhorns yell foul, gridlock pouring the masses into the "modern day mills." Convenience-culture litter skitters in the man-made breeze. It is all proceeding to plan (or so one would have us think).

And Cyrus Cleburne is smarting with the by-products of R&D. There's a chill in the air. (It is November.) Waking up on the stonewall terrace running the length of city avenue, still a bit of a buzz on.... He recalls nothing about the show, only Ab taking him outside, telling him to go home, making it as far as a bench in *The Points* plaza. There was puking at some point, hopefully not on display in the plaza. It would appear there was a random blacked-out trek to this spot too....*Super*.... He laughs. It so hurts to laugh. He curses silently instead.

*Calgon, take me away!*

A garbage truck squeezes down the alleyway. It comes to a wrenching halt in the low lot behind *Asa's.* It strains hydraulic arms in hoisting a backlot dumpster. It is emptied with a clang and a crash: industrial, rude, a tremor as the empty dumpster is dropped. Goodspeed comes-to long enough to curse the distraction and sharpen a pencil. A day earlier such an intrusion would have our good Regular out back hurling vitriol and chunks of broken brick at this gross violation. But here, now, such a trifle waste would be a notch in time's "victory belt" (a waste not of his own choosing, this being the grossest of gross violations). For he can see the end; and at the moment, duty compels him to beat time senseless with words and meter instead of flung objects. A smelter of diction, he pours hot fiction into the mold: sentence-stanza-page-chapter. This here is personal. *Fuck the Big Mules! A chattel system masked in the subterfuge of patriotism!*....If Goodspeed has slept two minutes in the past three days it's been done with eyes wide open, pencil scratching out sentence-stanza-page in rolling through the final chapter.

And beneath this new day beckoning wanders the salvage of a midnight reckoning: Cyrus finding his in-character study fork-to-face visceral. He has come to discover that this turn in his study is less a cerebral thing, more something to be felt. Treading in the steps of the Regular's daily routine has (surprise!) proven raw and relentless....

"Phh'uh—my fucking head. Aspirin or death!"

\*      Or how about accepting the finite bounds of in-character study there, chump?! One should not stroll casually into the ring of a freedom fight in-progress. *Live free or die!* is no place for the dabbler. It is zero sum. It is a grudge match. It is "fight dirty" time. It takes all one has and is best to know one's limits, this particular "live free" method subsidized by a fundamentalist strain beyond simple play-acting....*It's the bastards. Always has been, always will be....* You cannot fake this. You cannot come and go as you please. This isn't reading a book, or researching microfilm or observing the specimen in his natural environs awhile. Step lightly, scene-stalker. This here is dyed-in-the-wool, the sweetness extracted but a veneer walling over the dry rot of contradictions and leaving only *fidelity to cause.* This is no place to go slumming, dear Cyrus (and a word to the wise too, dear reader). You may be saved under the revival tent-top on Saturday night, but you will awake Sunday morning a sinner once again....

> *Always we had the feeling of punishment about to fall upon us....*

Lillian Smith ~ *Killers of the Dream*

This battle begins anew with the rooster's crow each and every morning. So, if you are not all in, then as the saying goes down here: *You wouldn't understand....*

Our good Cyrus is contemplating Plan B. His steps land tentatively, even walking a chore. He traverses D.O.T. land, browning kudzu unrolled as a burlap carpet across all things. He emerges from smoking vapor, a cool down having rent these days with premonitions of Winter. And yet, he has sounded one dark mysterious depth in that there is a kind of courage to this here life choice. It is, of course, not of the role model brand; but the grudging sort you award the grunt in a foe's trench. Their motivation may be beyond comprehension, but zeal applied to fighting for it is sloughed off at your own peril. Goodspeed does not just accept the weirdness, the un-square-able contradictory claim-staking. He is quaffing it down by the fifth, distilling it into a high-test fuel that fires the furnace of fatalism....*S'long as you take the bastards down with you....* Right and wrong is a philosophical milieu for another time. For *freedom*, in this instance, is a telos free to detonate any / all moral distinctions in its being realized. It is hanging judge and jury, all in one....

Cyrus thinks it through. (It hurts to think.) He is learning of this extraordinary *devotion to cause*. It is a crash course. The chill in the air meets warm rays as a handshake in truce, making his way down sidewalks bordering city avenue. His head pounds, palms sweat; guts are speaking of revolt. He drags a hand down his face, sits down on the running stonewall terrace. He wears pallor as a tangible pain, slumping over: arms locked at the elbows, hands on legs. Cold sweating, the onset of retching.... *On with the day!*

And the days reap the harvest of Autumn now unquestioned, rustling leaves winded by the lateness of the year. It is a reflective time, a season for contemplation and stock-taking. But such meditation will have to wait. For a *freedom fight* is in its late-rounds, and we're about to declare a winner.... A bite in the morning air has him rubbing his hands together, a blow of hot breath into hollow-balled fists. Focus and persistence have ruled his days. But for speed-walk sprints to a hole-in-the-wall down in the *Old Fifth* for smokes, or depositing the latest quarterly check in the "freedom fund," he has not been seen. And he careens towards the light at the end of the tunnel. *It is near!* He brings it. *It is here!* Marvin Goodspeed drops the final period of the final sentence onto the final page. It is done with finality, resolution. An absolute act. A *hell-bomb* of diction! BOOOOMMMM!

He exhales, leans back and lights a cigarette.... *On with the day!*

HIS MIND IS SWIRLING. Streets are roaring rivers, a whirlpooling sky. He has to sit down on the flagstone curb fronting Austin Avenue in the square of *The Points*. It is 8:44 a.m. A heady buzz pervades, the moment sure to be brief. This dedicated soldier, pursuing this *pursuit of freedom* from within: "Imbibing towards a greater understanding." The jury is still out on method (though it seems to have endured just about enough evidence). Undaunted, "committed" despite the legion of "misunderstanders," he takes a deep slug from a metal to-go cup. Fueling up on the *breakfast of champions* ("Jim Beam, asshole"), he is taking a deep tack. He claims to have found the trailhead, is dropping down into the fog-shrouded thickets where cultural haints lurch about the half-buried razorback-devoured corpses of the past. Down here, these hauntings dog the present with an unreconstructed glee they feel not the least bit compelled to explain or reconcile or apologize for. Down here, it seems a fine enough strategy to simply line up sere arthritic myths shoulder-to-shoulder and march them out—time and again—across fields that the present and future hold in enfilade. Yes, he can see it now: having adjusted his focus, unlocking that which sober reflection could never decipher.

Some have begun to question his tactics. They point to a worrisome "what's up?" drop off in his work, several stormy mood swings, a string of unexplained (and apparently) unapologetic no-shows. He waves it off, all a fluke of his having not committed fully enough, having not given enough of himself to *the cause*. He takes another swig, committing more fully....

"Should pro'ly be recordin' some thoughts, be productive 'n all," rooting around his inner-coat pockets without looking, a futile rifling through outer-coat pockets to follow....

"Fuck, d'I forget the recorder again?"

Yes, he can see the strategy, he'll claim. Secure inside a deep instinctual righteousness, it would seem sufficient enough to simply close up the gaps being torn asunder by the artillery of a rapidly evolving world that has found the range and is thundering away—with its own sense of self-righteous glee, it should be noted. (Mencken, *Sahara of the Bozart* anyone?) And yet, in the face of these devastating volleys, it is deemed enough to simply hunch shoulders, lean forward and press on—as if its ranks were merely walking into a stiff wind. How is this so? Its fate was sealed a bygone era (or many) ago; and yet this charge lurches on. How is it so?! Perhaps another deep swig will help clear things up. For he is on the trail, he'll claim. He has stumbled across the pipeline of inertia that, tapped into the bubbling springs of *grace* (it should be noted), has this assaulting column stepping off—again and again and again—to engage a future it does not understand, and does not care to understand. It marches out beneath the rippling bullet-riddled colors of honor and pride and nostalgia for a myth. It does so without a second thought, without an ounce of sober reflection on the devastation to body and mind that will surely result....

"Mencken was a cultural sniper. Hey, tha's good; gotta 'member that one. Course he was an anti-semitic asshole, mmmm."

Yes, it is into this hazy domain of the living dead where our scene-stalker dares tread. Sure, he has come to understand and respect *the order,* "the ways." But this little stunt here has him wending and bending down amongst the dark cackling thickets of commitment without a compass, casually strolling amongst a place where living actions and unmarked graves come along as a package deal, are just accepted as the price—the sacrifice—of one's *duty.* This place, confounding our good 'ol college try at every turn, where death be the only silencer of notions so long deceased that their continued acceptance can be held up as evidence of the existence of zombies amongst us...."But see, they're just products of their generation, s'all" / "Such drinking, well, it will just change a man; change him in body, change him in mind"....The signal danger here is that while the living dead run out the clock, they infect the living not yet dead.

The fearless journalist George Washington Cable spoke truth to this old tired power, knew it all too well: *those whose thinking still runs in the grooves of old.* He knew that as long as they drew breath, they would continue to fire their spent useless shells: *the antiquated artillery of an outgrown past.* Cable knew what should be known to all over a century later, here in these *Go Go '90s,* having ably—courageously—pointed out in the 1880s that these types make no case for a past on which to hang a future, but are only for making a big god-damned racket in the present. It is nothing but a tragic addiction that will find its end, in one wasted way or another, under a mound of red earth freshly-turned....

"Wait, what was that other thing I was thinkin'? Uh, oh, fuck it. It'll all come back to me," light tapping his skull, self-amused. "Steel trap, right here."

Yes, it is here, 'round the ledge of this shallow hole in

the ground, that he has decided to do his little tap dance towards "a more visceral understanding." That he is a crappy dancer is at the moment secondary to a larger concern: the all-eclipsing blind-spot having served up a zeal that, fed with enough alcoholic fuel, could be confused with commitment (re: "the jury is still out out," first paragraph, seventh sentence). It is driving him to turn down deeper, commit more fully, ever more deeply, ever more fully. His brief foray into reevaluation, contemplating a Plan B, has been swamped in this: field research of a more physical sort, a quarrelsome strain of zeal that has him out on the square of *The Points* at 8:48 on a Wednesday morning already fairly fucked up. It is not the first time. It is not the first time this week....

"Fuck the recorder. Got Jim-bo Beam to remind me!"

He leans forward, is pressing on. He sees the unconditional daily war for what it *is*. He can see the desperate straits spawning unconventional long-odds tactics, a high-risk strategy he himself is riding hard. To grasp *freedom* in your clutches, if only for an afternoon, an evening; living for *Victory!* each and every day. It is addictive: the *freedom-fighter* dialing up a daily commitment equal in depth to "the powers that be," engorged as they all are on their grotesque fleecing, unwilling in the deepest cells of their marrow to relinquish the present to a future not driven by entrenched constructs profiting off of the past. Oh yes, this *is* the backdrop of our times. This *is* the reason why those committed get up each and every day, sell themselves on conviction and begin the fight anew. The formidable greed of those forces aligned against you will show no quarter. He can see it, he'll claim, the scalawags swindling you of your time, your *freedom*, their overseers looking to crush your spirit. Oh, that *is* their aim! Defy those who would enslave you. Defy the aggressors because they are down here. Slay the despots, the tyrants! Conquer or Die! *Vince Aut Morire!*

Cyrus is deep-probing this story, taking the trowel—'er—metal thermal to-go cup (?) to it. It is taking both barrels to him in return (re: "whirlpooling sky," first paragraph, second sentence). No quarter will it show. Our good journalist, getting at the character at the heart of our study; the one fighting for this *freedom* every day (in his own special way). Contending with the methods of the force of nature behind *The Satellite Man*—a work of cutting originality that some have pegged as "Orwell with a drawl, y'all"—is indeed taking his all. What all it is taking in return is the verdict pending, the jury filing in as we speak....

"Oh, for chrisesakes—again?" asks Lacy, having wandered up and now standing next to Kelly at the front window of *The Weekly's* offices, both looking out over the square at the scene playing out.

"Ya, again," Kelly, having come in early with only a day left before that week's issue goes to press.

Having noticed Kelly standing there alone, hands at her side, looking out the window, a low simmer sparking about her silhouette as a visible atmosphere, Lacy had made his way over. A glance out the front window had him quickly up to speed as to the root of discontent, reminding him of his own....

"He's on a deadline. Do you even think he remembers that? Needs to pull this together, as in now."

"Ya, he does. The clock is ticking down. I am not waiting around on this bullshit."

"You alright?"

"Suppose I'm just fine. Disappointment just comes with the turf, right? Why should I be surprised to find myself an accessory, again. To be taken seriously, now that would be a surprise."

Kelly takes a deep inhale, a deeper exhale, watching a candle of hope dim in the dumb wind blowing in off this scene on the square. She turns and walks back to *Graphics*.

Lacy mulls this over a second, a light bulb connecting dots as he looks at his shit-faced staff-writer on the square. He looks up at the clock on the wall: 8:51 a.m. He gives a "what the fuck was I thinking" shake of his head, having given the go-ahead to this thing on a busy day months ago when he was not really paying attention....

"Lacy, my man, got a second?" Cyrus had said, hand gripping door-frame, half-leaning into his office; as if just ambling by.

"No—what?" Lacy's inattentive response.

"Hey, was just thinking over an idea, would have me diving in deep to develop an insider perspective on that Goodspeed profile," Cyrus's casual lean-in approach masking a concise plan-of-attack....*Defenses down, over. Attention diverted. It's go time!*....as if the idea had just dawned on him while ambling by.

"Alright, sounds moronic. Clear it with *Prez*. So long as he's willing to bankroll this stunt. I want something tangible by Thanksgiving. No expenses, either. You pay your way," Lacy, admittedly, having not processed the details, wrapped as they were in the sausage-skin of conversational obfuscation (i.e. you really don't want to know what's in it)....

Lacy casts a blank stare at the ceiling, releases his own deep exhale and heads back to his office.... For Cy does look committed, out there—*as if he has bought in*—as if the increasing volume of concerned pleading has mustered but passing recognition, a fleeting momentary notice akin to the streetside preacher's handout warning of apocalypse, urging *repentance!*, yet shoved nonetheless with nonchalance into the recesses of pant's pocket. It is as if none of the "what the fuck are you doing?!" looks have intervened in this so-called totality of duty, commitment. For all the busy people do seem lost to him, the rush hour some grim funeral cortege. He has (for this brief moment) slipped time's penal grip, has found another strain of "reality" lurking deep, deep down. Down here, where an oft-repeated fiction reads as fact, where mythic apparition will do as historical record. Down here, where a unique tradition holds sway, where in the words of the odd-man-out New Dealer, Ellis Arnall, believers: *prefer to listen to gaudy lies.*

Cyrus watches from within the dim of his incredulous stupor: all the frantic scampering, lusting as for their own ruin. *Yes, it is working!* He is under the spell of an ancient remedy, its forked-tongue promising clarity, *freedom.* (Side-effects may include: job loss, willful ignorance, divorce, renal failure, etc.) Cyrus takes one more deep swig. He can see *it* clearly now. From his flagstone perch he laughs at them all, stupidly. For this one brief giddy moment, it is all working. It is 8:53 a.m. and it is all *crystal clear....*

*Stand before the prophet of big enterprise, make it your idol and pray, watching from deep in the bowels of utility as the duped all drown in the day....*

"Hoo lawd," Cyrus standing up beneath the whirlpool, centering gravity as if to counter heavy swells. "Justa bit fuck'd up. Alright now, what was I thinkin' now? There was a thought in there, somewhere. Ah, will 'member all that later—or sooner," Cyrus laughing to himself, stupidly.

THE EARLY MORNING HOURS float a rare calm, the rhythms of darkness having lulled the mayhem of our daily grind to insignificance. Here, within this late-lateness, nature's steady unflinching nerve is on full display. It makes the case that it will ultimately prevail....*While you rest, we march. Resist if you must, but do so knowing that you shall come back to the earth that spawned your birth just as sure as the dirt is red....* And it is hard at work in this moment of late-lateness, nature with resolve in plying its irresistible logic.

But oh, we foolish humans: this calm but a reprieve inside our ongoing offensives. For come the rooster's crow, the human war on nature—both nature *proper* and (more importantly?) our own—is back on. It is a conflict of such restless resilience, and in the same beat one racking up such a predictable bloody calculus, that *some* might be inclined to peg the whole effort as delusional. There comes a time to fight. There also comes a time to concede inevitable defeat. But at the crossroads where these two instincts cross paths you'll find waiting that ol' instigator:

pride (or as one might label it for the purpose of our study: *duty to the cause*). There it is, our contradictory self, stepping up onto the stump and pitching its pledge with verve, with something you could mistake for zeal. And you force yourself to listen, as by instinct. You listen intently, transfixed to its harangues, listening as it disparages all naysayers. You listen to it go on and on and on and may do this just long enough so that even you, yourself, are eventually convinced by the worth of its immutable slow-motion death march—it's interminable, inexplicable call to "fight on, fight on no matter what"....But after what now seems like enough legwork (and a touch of comeuppance), our scene-stalker is set to call the aforementioned *some* dead on.

It is December 1, er, actually, December 2. The moon throws silver light through branch-ends, slivers scattered as a land of needles. He steps through. Streetlamps wash down across the dark hours, steps passing into and out of diffused haloes. Down the avenue, veering down a side-street, into the park. It is the earliest-early it can be, or....yes?....you have something to add, James Agee? It's, it's the what now? Ah, yes indeed! It could also be considered:

> the latest lateness of the night, and of such ultimate, such holiness of silence and peace that all on earth and within extreme remembrance seems suspended upon it in perfection as upon reflective water
>
> ~ *Let Us Now Praise Famous Men*

And so, with humanity at rest (and nature hard at work), the exploding commotion rips this holiness, detonates the calm. Cyrus is stopped in his tracks, heart skipping a beat, the calm peace consumed by that split-second anticipation of being struck by blunt object, the wielder in search of a wallet or pawnable rings....but no, only momentary confusion / surprise minus the assault / larceny....

"What—the—?!"

The culprit? The de-calmer of night? A heron. Cyrus, standing on the path alongside the lake in *Waverly Park*, the thrusting strokes rippling the late-lateness / early-earlyness. A blue heron in the urban piedmont with the solstice imminent? Odd, yes. Unheard of, no—the fowl's in-flight outline blending with shadows. *Go South, young avian! Go South!*....The night, the suspended perfection and his steps all resume. Silent again, it is 1 a.m.

Cyrus has taken to these post-witching-hour treks of late. He shuttles along the lakeside gravel trail, approaches the wide stone staircase at the park's southern end—sober, mind you. He is thinking through the conversation (intervention?) dropped on him a week earlier. His so called in-character study into its second month, Kelly had confronted him at *East Bay Ray's*, the bar club fronting DeKalb just up from *The Weekly's* offices. He would deduce, ex post facto, that this was impromptu, an unplanned drop-in; which considering the contents of the exchange made it, ironically, all the more authentic. It has him cringing thinking about it all the more, which is all the more to the good: Kelly, walking home that night and happening by EBR's front window at the moment that Cyrus, alone at the end of the bar, was knocking back a double as if a single. She did an about face and busted in....

"What—the—fuck? It's a Tuesday night and I already saw you hitting a flask after lunch out on the square. You are dead wrong on this. You are on the wrong trail, Cy. All of this (having pointed in a circular motion at the empty lowball glass atop bar)? Complete—fucking—bullshit."

Cyrus had refused to let go of the notion that this most recent "turn" in his fieldwork was anything other than deep (if painful) research. After the night at the club, and the rude wretched morning / day after, he'd actually doubled-down on the effort instead of, you know—*not*. Fast-forward two weeks and there he was: still under the impression that such R&D might deliver fault-line insight. It had not, but was instead providing a thorough understanding of what so self-destructive a routine does to body and mind. He was still committed, if not fully understanding why. For even he was wearing of the ceaseless hangover cured daily by "hitting the flask after lunch out on the square." As for getting inside the Regular's head, he had little to show. And yet this commitment had him all the while feeling the increasing urge for full-time "research." Red flag, anyone? (Now, for those readers who took our advice and have been keeping score, Cyrus' claim to moments of clarity in the preceding chapters? Ya,' that was the *pop-skull* talking.) Was he on the wrong trail, casually strolling out onto a high-up narrow ledge with naive disregard? Was he "wasting his fucking time, big-time?" Kelly, done with this stunt and for the moment with him, uncapped a firehose....

"Of all people to trot out: 'hey, I'm just living my art, man.' You make a living calling out that crap. Yet it's okay for you to dabble in it, to fool yourself into thinking you can drink your way to a better understanding of this guy? Complete bullshit."

"Wow, tha' was a dramatic entrance, is there —

"Ya, I'm not done. You really have convinced yourself that getting shit-faced will spark a light bulb moment? Well, this just in: You are full of shit. Drinking and being drunk is his thing, not yours. You were out to prove a hunch, one that seemed fairly developed back in, what, August? You told me, apparently without even realizing it yourself, that he's employing all this to some perverse effect, knows the contradictions well enough, but obscures them in an ocean of alcohol. The whole Orwell dressed up for the '90s, this redux freedom-fighter thing? It's just the autobiography of his alcohol-fueled fictional life; or at least, that's what I thought you were trying to prove with all this (again, the circular pointing motion)."

"Right, wait, wha's this about?"

"What's this about? Well, let's forget for a second that you have stood me up twice in as many weeks without so much as an explanation, let alone an apology, and let's make it about this: If I can figure out your character stone cold sober, then what the hell are you doing? Did you actually tell Lacy that the more you drink, the more clear it all gets?! Ho—ly—shit! You put him in a tough spot. You did that. He doesn't know what to do. No one does anymore. Even Gibbs is over this stunt. It's a wonder you haven't been fired. It doesn't matter how many doubles you knock back, you're not on the trail and you're about to fuck up your whole life."

"Now, jus' hold on, been doin' some serious legwork here."

"No, you've just been drinking—a lot. Everyone is over it, you have been completely blowing me off, and this after what I had thought was a really great Summer, and that we might actually have something here. And now, according to Lacy and Anna, you've missed three deadlines."

"No, well, shit; but I'm putting this thing together. It's jus' that, I'm sorry, jus' been slow-going."

"So, you admit it: You have been at this for months now and still have nothing? You said a published sketch by Thanksgiving, that was your promise to me weeks ago. That's two days from now and you don't have crap, do you?"

"Hey, dude's a moving target, okay? Alright, alright, I'll focus on the column. I may needs to backs off some."

"Backs off some? Ho—ly—fuck, you can't even see through this dumb drunken haze that you had him pegged before you embarked on this half-baked, I don't know, what do you even call this? Walking a mile in Goodspeed's drunken duct-taped shoes? You've been drinking your way right past the storyline for, like, two months now. Cy, there's the guy he thinks he is and then there's the guy he is. The shading that blends those two? That is the story. And the fact that he can, according to what you said, slide from one to the other seamlessly; or what's even more insane: that he is consciously leveraging this delusional alcoholic self as grist for his fiction? That is the story!"

"Ya, yes, you are right. That is all part of it. But I have to go where he lives to fully get it. This is jus' background, like method acting, er gettin' into character. Fuck. You know what, fuck this. You and no one is understandin' it like I do."

"I don't? Sounds like I just nailed it, and the only reason I did is because you have told me all of this before, apparently without even knowing it."

"I'm jus' sayin, the complexity, the—it's jus' takin awhile to unravel, ya know? It's jus' takin me awhile to get there."

"You were already there," Kelly's fed-up look sealed by the mock-grin that she drops on senseless things deserving little more; "but you can't see where you are because you're fucked up all the time. I'm over it, over this dumb charade. It was mildly amusing for a week or so. But getting obnoxiously shit-faced, getting up, doing it again? And now, just blowing me off like I'm some accessory to your genius? Ya, it's getting old, and quick. And I know you, Cy. You're on a ride that might be hard to get off. Remember how hard it was for you to stop smoking last year? You look like you haven't slept in a month. You look terrible all the time."

"Well, now, thanks there, girlfriend. You lookin' good too, and —

"Just—enough with the smart-ass. You are screwing with your health and a crack story. You said just last week that you're certain Goodspeed's wrapped up another book, did it in about 60 days, or so; and that he was on-the-wagon that whole time? How is that even possible? You completely fuck with brain chemistry drinking like he does. How could anyone who needs a half-dozen shots just to settle in at 'normal' stop like that, cold. Trading out an addiction for an obsession? That is something way beyond a functioning alcoholic. That he can endure the physical toll enough to drag his hungover carcass out each day without fail, or so you keep saying, to keep up this so-called fight of his? Whatever that is, *that—is—the story*. Do you even remember telling me this last week, right before you blew me off Tuesday night?"

"Okay, alright, jus' back off! I'm sorry I forgot the date thing; but we can go do dinner any time. I'm dialed in. I'm fine-tuning my research, s'all."

"Get a grip, Cy. This is his thing, not yours. Drinking and its delusional 'clarity' is just a tool to Goodspeed, no more or less important than a pen or pad of paper. It *is* what drives him. Setting aside for a second that he seems to be consciously killing himself, you are right, there's no denying it: he lives it as if he's upholding some sacred duty; and that's a direct quote—from you! Do you even remember saying it? Doubt it, 'cause it was last Wednesday morning about 10 a.m. and you were already shit-faced! You expect me to look the other way and believe you when you say you're just being authentic, going deep undercover as an alcoholic? No, no more. Slumming as an alcoholic? You have bought into a lie."

Of course, Cyrus' final retort was helped by the numbing (dumbing?) effect of a double-shot of bourbon; which, by the way, was his third in the twenty minutes he'd been there....

"Alright! Damn, girlfriend. But since we's tallying up bona-fides here, would ya even know authentic if it bit you on the ass?"

"Really? That's gonna be your dumb-ass response? Okay, fine. Fuck you," Kelly grabbing her bag and heading for the door....

"Shit. C'mon, Kel. I didn't —

"No, no, I didn't have to stop in here. I did because I believed you once, that you were onto something big; and that, I guess stupidly, we might be onto something here too, the two of us. But instead, I see you investing in a slow-motion train-wreck and killing whatever it was we had in the process. Don't treat opportunities as disposable whims. Don't you dare pass me off as a whim and try to talk your way out of it. That's what an alcoholic asshole does. That's why alcoholics who are also assholes eventually fuck up their lives and drive everyone out of their life. Just, you know what (Cyrus recalling an exasperated head shake about this point), I'm just gonna leave the genius to his 're-search,' " Kelly, the air-quotes hers, busting out the door....

FUCK! FUCK! FUCK!!! Of course, she was right. She was dead on. It all clicked that night, all of it. All he needed was to hear it told back to him in a linear string of bullet-points, a thing he'd denied himself because, well, he'd been fucked up for the past two months. He had fucked up telling this story. He had fucked up with her. *Fuck, fuck, fuck....*

Cyrus thinks it through as he ascends the stone stairs. He sets a crisp pace beneath the crisp air, the staircase aged yet holding fast. A masonic construction, it is memorialized like a citadel. It seems to mock its peers inequitable decay, shocked by the ring of blight that lies just beyond this one-time countrified suburb of *New South* aristocracy. One can sight cracks in the stairs leading up to Austin; but they are less noteworthy than the resolution that holds them fast, cracks and all. Fifty steps symbolize the golden anniversary of a city coming of age, it all done as a piece of the park's luminous dedication day on

*Confederate Memorial Day—April 26, 1898.* Documented for posterity upon a thick aluminum historical marker now stained and leaning, the memory of that day resides in concert with the hibernating hardwoods, the dozing walls of stone. The staircase opens on Austin through its resolute gate. Its squat pillars stand like a blockhouse, a contemporary Fort Necessity out on the frontier of this here urban 'hood. It projects squint-eye conviction, pride, honor, imploring its ragged soldiers to hold fast before the overwhelming odds....*They're in our front, they're on our flanks!....Hold fast, stalwart sons, hold fast! For country!*....And Cyrus blends with shadows as a shadow would.

The night consumes his trek. Alta and what is left of *The Ashlands* both pass. Cleburne is readying his (long overdue) profile for *The Weekly*, has already hammered out a first draft. Kel had been dead on. He has been dead set since. Central to the scene, out here, the enigmatic bard is still just that to most. And so, it is time to churn out column-inches, if for no other reason than to justify ten weeks of drinking on-the-clock. Those days are past, long uninterrupted treks through the city's slumber proving more fruitful. *The field parks* sit squat to starboard: a void of dreams past. The calm: a low drone. The pre-Winter sprinkles the land with frost. He could be the sole survivor of nuclear armageddon right then, the late-lateness complete.... And so, the gunshot jumps his heart! Another shot! A rifle?! The muzzle blast having lit up the firee....

"What—the—?!"

A third shot triggers self-assurance, Cyrus confirming he is not the target as he sights the rifleman deep in *the field parks*, one hundred yards off. Cyrus slips into deep shadows, watches the dude firing into....the sky?

CRACK-A! The soft recoil absorbed through upper torso.

"Damn, losin' my touch here," Goodspeed re-sighting the rifle on his target high up and evergreen in the moonlit canopy.

CRACK-A! The sharp pop reverberates, drawing the porchlamp inquisition of nearby pioneers / settlers.

"Damn, pathetic!" Goodspeed self-berating, his marksmanship a point of pride....

He'd discovered the M-1 and over 40 full clips, a bit mildewed but in working condition, hidden in the apartment behind what he'd previously thought was a hasty sheetrock repair.

CRACK-A! "God-dammit!"

Making his discovery known, Howard had told of a Korean War acquaintance that had rented the place in the '60s. Never right after the war, the guy had convinced himself that LBJ himself would personally order his call-up to Vietnam.

"Guy was so deep into the conspiracy thing, just warn't right. He'd been wounded up at Chosin early on, nearly froze to death; fucked him up all complete. Well, he was drifting, and when you drift inevitable that you gonna drift in and outta prison. So, we set him up down in the basement, tried to settle him a bit. Sure enough, 'Nam heats up and he goes and sets up a god-damn'd armory downstairs, gonna be ready for when the Feds come to get 'im. Just warn't right, ya know? I cleared out a damn'd arsenal after he up 'n split, must have overlooked the rifle. He left a note, said he's headin' up and out west for The Peg or Calgary where the Feds'd have no jurisdiction; course that note was pro'ly a ruse to throw 'em off his true intentions, figure they'd coerce it out of me, or something. The guy, Gustav his name, called him Gus—and he come from a well-respected family about the county too—well, he had conspiracy within conspiracy runnin' through his sick head. Late-30s and fifty pounds overweight? Only thing LBJ could've used him for was a boat anchor, poor guy," Howard had recalled, his laugh and head shake recognizing the commonality of human weirdness, nature or nurture....

CRACK-A! "Dammit!"

Howard had let Goodspeed keep the rifle: "Finders keepers there, Marv, been our best tenant to date."

Down to his final shot, Goodspeed aligns his sights with care. He throws his focus long and high, the hardwood parasite lit from under by pink florescence, atop by lunar silver.

"I got ya. Dead. To. Rights."

CRACK-A! PING! The empty clip ejects over his shoulder, a sizable bough of mistletoe cracking at its branch and falling to earth.

"More like it. For chrisesakes, gotta get back out to the range."

Goodspeed staggers over towards the fallen prize, pulls out, and is lighting a cigarette when a cruiser screeches to a halt along Alta. Two flashlight beams light him up.

"Drop it, now!" yells Trey.

"Wait, wait....oh, fuck! Is that you, Goodspeed?! You fucking asshole!" Stu, Trey's new partner sighting the familiar stoop of the Regular, 70 yards distant.

"You got to be kiddin' me. Marv, is that you, you fucking asshole?!" Trey now hot and jogging towards Goodspeed.

"It is! It is! Be cool! Be cool!" answers the Regular.

"Was 'bout to put a hole in ya, Marv!" yells Stu, livid and jogging across the grassy void towards Goodspeed and his prized bough.

"C'mon, calm down. Gettin' in the holiday spirit a bit early s'all. Just gatherin' up some mistletoe for the lady, y'know, the traditional way," Goodspeed stammering, a bourbon-slosh drawl, drawing on his cigarette.

"Got a good mind to clap you on the skull, throw ya in the tank, dumbass!"

"Why so hot?" Goodspeed pleading innocently, almost smugly: As if having had this all figured out ahead of time. As if having known all along that this here world and his little slice of it were immune to the contradictory evidence demonstrating that its logic, its nostalgia, was a deep—if treasured and visceral—fiction....

"C'mon, gents, them rounds fallin' south of the tracks; nothin' but old empty warehouses down there. I should know," taking a deep drag, cradling the rifle like an infant in his arm.

"Gimme that thing, asshole!" Trey grabbing the rifle from Goodspeed's grasp and shoving him forcefully with his free hand.

"Re—fucking—lax! Thing's registered!" Goodspeed slurring, having landed hard on his ass. He gets back up, wavering.

"Ya dumb drunk fucker! Got a mind to smack ya myself. Having to haul ass out here and respond to a 'shots fired' call only to come up on you, ya dumb drunk fuck!" adds Stu, the scene milling about, the lawful lashing of tongues.

And as the words fly, the group and scene are swallowed by the rhythms, out here. The nature of things, of people: *the day, the night, drinking, harmless fun with guns.* ("Shots reported off Alta in the Vale. 418, do you copy, over?" "10-4, we're on it.")....Cyrus, a spectator to our good Regular's theatre (in the rafters of *The Globe?*) keeps to shadows as he makes his way back up to *Candler Hills*. The early morning hours preside over this machined lull, arched tree limbs black against the blackness. He is swallowed by the rhythm, the blackness.


THE YEAR GROWS LONG. But it is of no mind. For time, that poster child of nefarious manipulation ("the epic swindle underwriting incorporated tyranny") has been rendered irrelevant with the manuscript's completion— THE BOMB *dropped!* He has done it again. He has written himself free. *Victory!*

Goodspeed's new work is to be called: *Within.* Dorothy—lover / lawyer / biker—is still in the process of pushing a revision of Goodspeed's contract on a reluctant publisher. She has her motivations. Goodspeed is glad she does, the acquisitions editor who originally signed our good Regular (to a decent deal it must be said, it being a small house out of the Twin Cities), not so much at the moment....

"A royalty schedule that begins at 20%? And this, from the first copy sold? Now D, darling, don't take this the wrong way, but are you—fucking—high?"

"Phil, don't call me darling and I'm dead serious."

"Then it would appear we may have a problem."

"Apparently so."

Despite the dog-eat-dog negotiations (D really is just testing waters, it being a top-shelf request), things seem on track to shake out, the in-house editor having already begun working with Goodspeed—'er, let us rephrase that— the in-house editor having already begun working on *Within* whether Goodspeed likes it or not. The editor marshals good sportsmanship. A low-key chap (originally from Sheffield), he tolerates liberal use of the nickname "fuckhead," it having been said / yelled by Goodspeed with such rabid frequency during editing on TSM that it has stuck. But considering this was the team that turned out an *underground sensation*, it could be seen as a term of endearment....

Goodspeed: "S'pose the Brit ain't so bad, when he ain't being a fuckhead."

The Brit: "Yes, our lively muse. A piece of work, that Goodspeed. And man o'mighty, can he put away pints."

A thick envelope containing the new manuscript had arrived on the solstice. Tagged with editorial revisions in red-ink, a note paper-clipped to the title page stating: "Suggestions for your consideration, sir" (got to frame it just so with Goodspeed, or in this case mash his buttons with a dry-wit squint-eyed glee), it had been delivered by Gid along with a folder-over and rubber-banded

*Newsweek* containing a fat eighth. Anger management being not so much his strong suit, he knew he would need all the help he could get. *(Thank you kindly, Mr. Marijuana!)* Goodspeed was with the manuscript all of yesterday, letting fly bold-faced strings of vitriol heard clearly by the lunch crowd upstairs. Martha: so proud, Howard shaking his head with a grin as he washed and dried his sinks full of glasses....

"Did he even read the whole fucking chapter? You must in order to get it. The context, the pacing, is like he didn't even read the whole thing. Did ya even bother to read the whole chapter, fuckhead?!....*Can lose this sentence entirely. You already made the point, just sounds like you are ranting....* What? Fuck that shit! I can't make the point loud enough. I should have added a third. In fact, maybe I will. Three stand-alone sentences all describing the same damn'd thing should do the trick. No, no fucking way that second sentence comes out, fuckhead!" Goodspeed having dutifully blown his top over a minor point and then dutifully re-worked, re-wrote, smoked, cussed some more....

Yes sir, the gears are in motion.... And to boot, when not working hard our good Regular has been hard-at-work restoring the natural balance, getting back in with his loves, his hates—giving 'em all he's got. He has had help. The thin truce has been blitzkrieg'd, nature's elite guard having rolled over the DMZ to lay bloody siege to the root of all that pains. Time is again in his crosshairs, all of those complicit in the first-degree murder of one's time (the most up-to-date list featuring: the "art as commodity cabal" and "all obnoxious assholes who just don't know when to shut the fuck up") in his crosshairs. As a proven marksman, they will surely fall. (C'mon people: mistletoe in a treetop, at night?!) Yes, he is making up for lost time, celebrating the season with abandon.

Goodspeed slumps over, hands on knees, head hanging like so much heavy meat between shoulders. He sits on bed-edge in D's bedroom, her house down on Dixie Way. He stews, this an opportune time to rekindle some old hatreds. His desire to out-sleep a vile hangover did not return the desired results. He was up early, staring at the ceiling, thinking over edits. An obstinate temper now clouds an otherwise sparkling Winter's day. He upwardly motivates, balled fists on bedside; up on his legs, three steps to bedroom bay window. He parts blinds, surveys it all; this bungalow residing atop a knoll, this city built atop the rolling piedmont. He is looking out over this forsaken quarter....well, once forsaken, that is. Lashed by the knotted-leather of *New South progress!*, *Springvale* has held fast. But then there's this new trend gaining steam. It has plans for these in-town 'hoods. Beneath an instinctual skepticism, Goodspeed sizes up the accelerating trend of gentrification. Is it natural progression, or *progress redux?*

"No one blows sunshine like the Sun Belt booster, a time-honored New South tradition."

For him, the jury's still out. Go ahead and call him cynical. (No really, go ahead.) But he just can't accept that the prevailing winds of gentrification blowing in under the guidons of *renovation and restoration* is a "moment" on the level.... Is it a rejection of that which drove a previous generation of whites to leave for the 'burbs? Is it a social moment breaking with the hot tribalist traditions of clan and race that in its own time opted for self-segregation once the once-unquestionable apparatus of apartheid had been torn asunder by the judge's gavel, the legislator's pen, the Nat'l Guard bayonet? Is it breaking in favor of diverse spectrum-wide participation?....Or, is it just the "hegemony of white-bred monomania" in boomerang? Having done its best locust impression on the 'burbs, is this here just a "progeny swarm of pre-programmed company 'n cultural automatons" looking to plunder the latest-greatest frontier, urban as it might be?....Love it, or hate it? There is but time for one or the other.

Goodspeed simmers. He wants to be convinced of an unforeseen, calculated angle. He reviews the evidence: the obese tract-housing that engulfs *The Beacon*, a belt of flab a dozen counties deep and extending to all horizons. He dredges up history: a generation of lily-whites recoiling from the concept of social equality across economic lines having fled for the "new company mill towns" on the outskirts (a migration, he is all too aware, having been prodded by a real-estate industry unafraid to fabricate racist lies in stoking white fears of black neighbors—all in pursuit of a half-century's worth of self-perpetuating profits). The post-war exodus to the outskirts proceeded under a cynical ruse, he'll claim....

"The American Dream? Just a marketing gimmick peddled by corporate shills to white suckers. Callin 'em out to the homogenous suburban hive where their loyalty would be measured by the yardstick of materialism, codified in social conventions designed to serve up the willing surrender of their time, their freedom, to the Big Mules. It was just the second coming of the New South lie that drove a generation of company slaves to the 'burbs, scapegoating blacks—*again*—to ensure the most profitable end-result. It makes ya wonder: Was racism pursued for its worth as social-capital to uptight ignorant lily-whites? Or 'cause it was worth real capital to the scheming robber-barons? Call me cynical, go ahead. But who's to say this here gentrification ain't just the latest attempt to dupe a new generation of suckers?"

Is it natural evolution: the living death of gridlock pushing a demographic coming-of-age to reject old *New South* prejudicial ticks and yardsticks and slip-the-noose of the corporate stranglehold? Or, is it just the latest land-grab being subtly engineered by the powers that be, and bringing its flab with it? Goodspeed stews over the hidden (imagined?) machinations of this gentrification trend. He is skeptical, can fall back on the tradition / the instinct of leeriness, at a whim. He'd prefer to lean on the tried-and-true eye wool of conspiracies and hidden agendas instead; like a good *Populist*, he is okay reducing complexity to simplistic explain-alls....

"The grim greed of these cabals is self-perpetuating, extracting all of a land's nutrients, leaving those sold-out in the process to contaminated pools and exhausted fields left in wake. Woodruff could sniff out bullshit like a bloodhound. He could've sensed where this was all heading."

Our man casts a squint-eye, honor-bound to defend this forsaken quarter: *Ferget Hell!* He must channel his man. A drink, or two (or six) will get him there....

\*       Not to belabor a point. Well, actually, to purposefully belabor this point, let's revisit the environment of our man as seen through the eyes of our man—the history *within*.... *Springvale Park,* the city's original suburb. Tapped into the vein of capitalist aristocracy, outings in horse-drawn barouche, highfalutin palaces run round by freedmen just as slave as they ever were, here was the material proof of the triumph of the *New South* V.1. A century ago, this annexed farmland on the outskirts was prized for its remoteness to the city, sold as the place to be for those on-the-make. Decades passed. It grew old and stale. And there came to be a newer *New South*, V.2. And the rich, and all those the company advertisers had hoodwinked into thinking they'd someday be rich, all up and moved to the NEW suburbs. Here they would be free to fantasize anew, free of old tired fads, an uppity black merchant class and the unsightly desperation of the urban poor. They could leave all of that behind, reckon (per the amnesia-inducing vapors of nostalgia) that it had never existed at all; that the cause, *the causes*, were always righteous—or at least, right.

And the transition was swift. Urban housing prices, having tanked in the toilet of the *Great Depression*, never really recovered. Old city wards were given up for dead. Urban was a lame fad of that OLD *New South*, suburbia now the deified (and codified) goal of those on-the-make. And yet, the ironic end result of this migration of caucasian wealth was to open up space for all those marginalized— by-design, or of their own volition—this *New South* V.2. *Springvale* pivoted from aristocratic status symbol to the capital of cast-offs inside a short generation. And for lack of anywhere else to go, the fringe flowed in: the artists, the beats, "the queers"—the musicians, the hippies, the yippies—*the regulars*. They all flowed in to settle alongside the poor, the blacks of all economic stations (with no suburbs of their own) and those free-spirit mansion dwellers (i.e. traitors to their class) who had never left. They all took to the discarded in-town 'hoods, the sagging Queen Annes, the buckling bungalows. They took to *Springvale* as one of their own: cast offs all....*Give me your tired, your poor, your huddled masses yearning to breath free. For the wretched refuse of your teeming shore will find refuge here. This place will fit them to a T....* This *old belle*, her club membership having been revoked, welcomed those who would have her: unreconstructed *New Southerners* all, by-design or by-choice.

So, that brings us up to speed.... But what to make of these *Go Go '90s?* Is it interested in spreading wealth, even out to society's fringe? Or simply pushing that fringe beyond view in its voracious hunger to reacquire urban-scapes made suddenly hip again? Benevolent or inclusive? Malevolent or exclusive? Love it or hate it? Either way, the urban centre is in business again. And either way, it is grand irony: *Springvale Park,* the spawning stream of suburban-sprawl. *Where it all began.* The contradictions, they run thick as thieves, out here.

And for more on this, we go back to our man....

Goodspeed, blinds parted, throws a look down Dixie. Across from where it ends at Euclid lies *The Long Acres:* a woodland preserve / park entrusted in perpetuity over a century ago. It is a forest in the city. It shocks the primacy of *progress!* It is nature holding its own. Naked branches stand guard, snap to attention in saluting the recent solstice. They are defiant, sight the growing forest of for-sale signs that put sagging bungalows up for a song. They are leery of stated intent. They have seen a lot. They do not expect benevolent urban pioneers (or so one might muse) but instead the bulldozers' wrath: tearing down so as to build up apartment blocs, dense tracts of pre-fab flab, more convenience plazas, more sprawling malls, ever more acres of asphalt plains and arterial roads blocked-up with materialistic plaque; and worse: even more homogenous defeated drones "doing the company's bidding." The esteemed historian Woodward himself claimed that the bulldozer would leave a far deeper scar on Dixie than the carpetbagger.... Goodspeed is with the trees on this one. There is ample historical evidence by which to fuel suspicion and cherry-pick a convenient explain-all....

"Automatic masses beaten into submission by the repetitive blows of the corporate mallet: less the carrot, more the stick; mindlessly gorging on the obesity of convenience as reward for accepting the shit-end of the deal. Are they lookin' to bring that shit intown?"

Goodspeed looks at Dorothy beneath the covers beside him. Something resembling deep affection stirs, peering up over their understood bond of mutual dependence. This is a team first-and-foremost, the end goal being: *freedom creation*. Warm, joking, loving and tender, even. But is that just packaging around the core element? However requisite love may be to their program, the core aim seems to settle on bringing home the bacon. And lest you go all cynical, dear reader (in that we have lately invited you to do just that), this here is no manipulative codependency type of deal. It is an agreement. It is contractual, 50 / 50. Though all troweling to date would have it as unsaid, simply understood, the obligation is no less clear, its fine-print summarized with bold / italicized concision: **live free or die!** So long as "this thing" they have got pays out, they're in. It is understood.... And yet, even the coldest most calculating entrepreneur could not resist the rush of emotion entirely. Obsessive / compulsive? You bet. Pathologic? Not our man, all the proof we need residing within the upswell of affection welling up from the gloom of a cotton-mouth queazy at that very moment harming his seconds and minutes. He steps over to bedside, strokes D's hair. It is done with loving care, knowing she was up all night with *Within* (yes, while he was out drinking hard). She stirs, rolls over, drops immediately back into deep sleep. He leaves without a word.

On exiting D's abode, our man is confronted. It is fork-to-face. The low roar of the not-so-distant parkway connector drools across this soundstage of his. It is the anthem of the corporate program. (A reconstitution of the *Gilded Age?*) His loathing rolls to a boil.

The red hand abruptly interrupts his steps. No go! Freedom denied. Goodspeed is held up where Dixie ends at Euclid across from *The Acres*. Traffic blows past as if the braying steam of a shift-whistle. It is the daily grind flying the standard of *its cause....Same as it ever was, same as it ever was....* "Benevolent, my ass." He knows this to be true. He will not turn his back on it. It is not to be trusted. Goodspeed faces the street, standing fast. *For duty!* As if one of the ubiquitous aging sentinels set atop town square memorials mythologizing the Confederacy, a memorial to be found in every Southern town large enough to host a post office, our man just so happens to be facing due north. If quite by coincidence, his simmering stare could have him cut of marble right then. For he is defiant, facing down this latest threat to Dixie right then speeding past the intersection with Dixie. He squints at this malignant, if innocent, army, this solemn anonymous horde rifling by; unwitting enablers of the despoilers of freedom....

"Exploitation. Everyone run ragged to satisfy someone else's agenda. Innocent fools conned of their time by rapacious crooks."

A passel of traffic passes under Goodspeed's squint-eye glare. This here, the exploitation, the calculated swindle of a rigged economic game, this was what the *Populist*, and the burdened *Allianceman* before him, this—right here—was what they were fighting against. Goodspeed faces the street, block-chinned. CAUTION: *Harangue Ahead!*....

> *In this age of ours, when we—the hardworking agrarians who choose to live and work as free men—are told instead to quiet down and take our place as a gear in the machine.... When those in* TOWN *tell us in* COUNTRY *what will be our meager take after they have had a chance to divide the lion's share, when those who have rigged the system to swell their own pockets tell us that our devalued crop, our foreclosed farm, our penury at the hands of arbitrary interest rates is* OUR *problem. And this, even though they are the ones who speculate on our hard-wrought crops—they are the ones recalculating and calling loans before due—they are the ones foreclosing so as to expand the land-holdings of the big monopolies—they are the ones who limit the circulation of currency so as to induce dependency.... This reptilian scourge creates a speculative cycle of inescapable debt and*

*then laughs at your penniless dismay.... Fellow men, it is when we have been sold a bill of goods under the assumption of free labor only to realize that we have been sold up the river instead that the truth of our age is unmasked for the oily lie that it is. This is not the design of a free-labor marketplace. This is but one thing: bondage! And so, we fight!*

Gordon Patrick Woodruff ~ *1894*

"An age-old strategy: induce loyalty by marketing it as freedom, when in fact it is all about selling submission to the cause of making others rich. This here? Just the latest version of the 1890s merchant lauding the virtue of private ownership while he arbitrarily hikes an interest-rate, calls the loan, and indentures a small farmer. This here today? All just heir to the Bourbon Democrat who went fist-to-palm on the stump over his commitment to individual rahts, while he quietly passes a poll tax that will disenfranchise a generation of Southrons, black and white. This here, nothing more than an up-to-date version of the great 'civic patriot' of a mill owner drawing in laid-off miners from Appalachia and giving them jobs, as the benevolent patron he is supposed to be, where naive and penniless they're turned into legal chattel through usury company store credit, the only place by-contract they're allowed to procure provisions. This here is the Klan laying claim to the blessing of God's supreme grace that ain't nothin' but cover for bloodthirsty fear and tribal hate. It's the segregationist governor claiming his actions are 'not because I dislike the coloreds, just that I'm duty bound to uphold law and order.' It is the manipulation of the honest by slick civic liars. It is the validation of violence run out from frail egos. It is as it has always been. Some things change. Some things are the same as they ever were."

He breathes. He is seething. He fires a parting shot: "And the average work-a-day dupe got stuck with the bill 'cause they bought this sales job every time, whoring themselves out for the promise of material crap, or moral superiority, or racial supremacy, or whatever the fuck. I got to give it to the demagogues: They can sell ice to the eskimo, peddle their slave patriotism while erecting legislative façades that allow the bastards to plunder at will. There's your New South, chump, Versions 1 and 2."

Which begs the question: What of V.3? How the coming trend of urban gentrification will set up under his harsh assessment is not yet clear. But the fact that all of it will filter through said assessment seems abundantly clear. In the end, it doesn't matter what form the perceived enemy *within* takes. If it invades Marvin Goodspeed's dear old *Springvale*, he will fight. He'll fight the invaders because they are down here....

Goodspeed crosses Euclid in a cloud of breath steam. He draws shoulders up tight, *The Long Acres* drawing up snug around his steps. The leafless hues age views into sepia-tone relics. It all slows down. Our man is allowed a different take. In here, time is not square-pegged into a commodity "abused for profit," but is returned to the weary (and leery) alike. Amongst the bare poles of sweetgum and poplar, of red oak and white, he is (we are) reunited with nature's patient intent. Its long game makes a mockery of our cursory tail-chasing ways. *Time is on our side and we are as old as the hills*, a grand magnolia seems to say. Nature, guardian of time "proper," is in this for the long haul. And whether we are zeroing in on nature "proper" or our own in this little digression here, the question seems obvious: Who in the hell are we to fight it? How is it that we cannot breath deep the mystic vapors and realize it is us, we—*ourselves*—with whom we have been waging this pitched battle all this time? And if only we could accept it's hot futility and call a truce we would be delivered to a peace otherwise unrealized, one revolving on the sure axis of acceptance: accepting the weirdness, bear-hugging the fucking shit out of that thing and doing it all the time with a squint-eyed grin.... Goodspeed breathes deep the frozen air, casting a long shadow as he makes his way to a bench, mid-*Acres*. He grins, as if getting an inside joke.

The clang-clash of I-beams being loaded onto a flatbed reverberates down from nearby Bremen Steel. It is superimposed atop the incessant rush of traffic streaming off the connector beyond it: the very caterwaul of *progress!* But it's of no mind, in here. The needled scalps of pine whistle relief, *The Acres* having become a required respite within our man's daily routine (re: the maintenance of *laissez-faire*). Word of his second full-length novel has hit the streets, the camps—pro / con—lining up. He is sought after, the daily battle having escalated sharply, up to about DEFCON 3 at the moment. (And yet, if our study may suspend objectivity and speculate for just a moment, we could hardly go wrong by stating that if he didn't have something to battle daily, would he even drag his ass out of bed each morning?) *The Acres* bring pause. The public buzz grates him. But he will stoke the coals. He will play the part. He must.... He stews with the thought of a freedom-inhibiting fame. It is tempered by thoughts of fortune.

A review in advance of Goodspeed's latest work quietly appeared in the previous week's *The Weekly*. When asked for comment on what was a fairly objective review, more advance excerpt than critique, the *Springvale* troubadour responded: "A review of what now?" It is a good act, soundly engineered. He will, however, respond heatedly on being asked about a more recent article that appeared in a cultural literary-arts publication of some renown, with whom, it must be noted, he has had a running feud. (Surprise, all: Goodspeed making easy hay of reciprocating pettiness when "the cabal's parasites" are involved.) More a time-bomb designed to derail, oozing of spite as if personal (we'll get to that in a moment), the tart sidebar in that magazine's culture file preemptively slammed any and all future publications based on what the review article's author argued was the trite failure of everything else Goodspeed has published to date: "unrealized sketches strewn along the trash-draped shoulders of our congested literary highway like so much paper waste," a line even Goodspeed admits appreciating for its descriptive heft, despite his squint-eye reaction; the article's conclusion going something like this:

> Beneath the symbolic verse lurks not ironic wit, as the blind-following bantams are so quick to advance; but an obtuse protest of materialism and the tired corporate conspiracy we all seem to be *suffering* just fine. (A noted drinker, it should be noted that Goodspeed seems not to rail on the

corporations that deliver the mass quarts of beer and bourbon he downs daily.) It seems the same rabbit-hole approached via different trailheads. Have we not all had enough of this rehashed dystopian paranoia? It is not *1984*, c. 1949. It is 1997 and we are wired into boom times. Subtle irony in skillful hands is a most authentic tool for incisive critique; but you'll not find it hiding amongst Goodspeed's thicket of adverbs. It is glaringly absent, beat instead by ham-fists. Goodspeed does not elevate, he pummels words that further wilt beneath the boozy vapors emanating from his real person. You would do best to prove leery, unless losing faith in fiction is your gig.

Sprinkled throughout were key details on Goodspeed's haunts ("Be it the diner where he nurses his daily hangover or the hole-in-the-wall where the damage is done," etc.) and physical descriptions to boot ("His not quite six-foot lank evokes that classic super-8 Sasquatch film, but for that sightings are as common as the homeless, within which he blends naturally," etc.) Low blows for sure, especially petty for a magazine of "some renown." But it should come as no surprise and is par for a squabble with a school-yard history, one of many—Goodspeed being unafraid to dangle the bait and jerk wildly when something bites. The article went unsigned, which our man, rightly, felt the act of a coward; the source a no-doubter....

Back in November, the article's author, his several phone calls having been ignored (we'll get to that after we get to this here), was passing through *The Beacon* and decided to invite himself down to the Regular's lair on Austin. The prior history of negative reviews would have been enough. But this, this here was an insult not just to Goodspeed, but more the brethren, their sanctuary, the order. For the guy brought a long list of confrontational questions and, you have to admit, courage enough to ask them. It was, of course, a bad idea, said courage met with a broken broom-handle.... But what surprised Goodspeed was not the guy's brazen confidence in coming to *Asa's*. (He thought that fucking moronic.) It was instead something foreign to our man, a feeling he couldn't quite place at the time. As he watched the guy retreat across the avenue to a rental car, bleeding from his nose and lip and wildly threatening a legal avalanche against the broom-handle-wielding madman of *Springvale*, our man had felt something he has since pegged as pity. "That poor fucker, a lackey like all the rest sent to do the Big Mules' dirty work." He was reminded that for the vast majority of "economic producers" *freedom* is painfully incremental, a thing achieved in small slivers over expanses of well-murdered time, if at all; and reliant on the whims and subject to the creative destruction of others—a life-choice Goodspeed had shit-canned many years ago....

"Compromise yer freedom for dollars and yer just one more poor sucker whose loyalty is used to benefit another. It's like gettin duped into fightin' the rich man's war."

This here Goodspeed, he has the ability to surprise us every so often. But in the main such irregular asides are momentary blips. For there is the *maintenance of the status quo* to consider: a duty to the order, in here....

Not surprisingly, Bid and Laverne, who responded to

the assault call—made by the guy from a cellular phone in the cabin of his locked rental car—threatened in turn to arrest the guy for disturbing the peace. Goodspeed claimed self-defense, a claim at least adjacent to accuracy in so far as protecting the brethren, his story corroborated by those present for *Asa's* roll call. It was a good show, Howard having stood by without a word, drying a sink-full of well-washed glasses and not about to get involved in potential litigation—his patented silent grin, shaking his head.... Ya, let's just say that smart money is on the bleeding-nose critic guy as the source....

And so, this all points to an interesting discovery. In meticulously scraping around sherd edges, our trowels have revealed what the unschooled might consider a simple character flaw as yet another vital tool. (Shall we just call it *asshole-d-ness?*) What is fascinating is that it may indeed be as important to our good Regular as those more mainstream tools—pen and pencil, OJ by the gallon, sweet sticky bud—previously identified. Stoking negative reactions seems a key trick in the public relations bag. Goodspeed will pull it out for reasons simple (garnering street cred) and more complex (sheer masochistic joy). Its application seems wide-ranging. As we have experienced, first-hand, he tends to start there: a caustic, demeaning *asshole-d-ness* as an entry-point, an acid test gauging the situation / character who dares disturb.

Back in the late '70s and early '80s, the band: *Ecstasy of Eunuchs* (often likened to a local equivalent of *The Velvet Underground*) employed a strategy that they called "the disease." When playing a room they felt was filled of poseurs (i.e. non-fans slumming an underground haunt to say they did), the band would break out "the disease," a free-form improv'd noise fest, that at points may have been interesting to an artist-type who'd ingested a strip of LSD tabs, but in the main non-linear and purposefully uncomfortable to those who only understood predictable melody. How long the cacophony was to last would be aligned solely to the metric of how lame a crowd seemed from the stage, the band continuing until they'd cleared the room of all but those looking for authenticity. A recent interview in *The Weekly* with the two surviving band-members (the other three members having been tragically killed in a car wreck a decade prior) confessed: "Oh, the disease never failed; cleared out the frat boys every time"....Goodspeed's tactic shares intent: call out the disingenuous poseur acting the role. But then, our man tends to take it one step (a baker's dozen?) further. For if an unwitting victim objects—or worse, fights back—it is the equivalent of *honor defamed*....and it is on.

Negative-print meets him in a satisfied way. It is proof that he is fighting. Whether the odds are in his favor, or not, is of no mind. A fight emanating from ideological resolution would have its defender carrying on long after thoughts of victory could, or should be rationally entertained, anyway. Even if *the cause* be lost, there would still be the body count by which to tally a total worthy of the yardstick of success: "How many of the bastards I can take down with me"....That said, such a pyrrhic stand, despite its deep regional roots (only the enslavement of others digs deeper, is even more appalling) seems holstered at the moment. It is there to be called up at a moment's notice. But for now, everyone—pro / con— seems to be ingesting nourishing sustenance from this fight, ballistic salvos that serve up a mutual benefit....

"If I'm not relevant then why the do the parasites put in the effort to hate my guts by the column-inch? Hate me with all you got, motherfuckers. I'm gonna do you the same."

It is the good ol' M.A.D. theory of the recently past Cold War, but turned on its head. It is a contradictory instant running on the plank of regional inexplicability: strange, if expected. For the more mega-tonnage deployed, the more bang for the buck.

And all this serves as an apt segue back to the contradictions running marrow-deep. It is a dead horse that we simply cannot kill enough (our flogging cudgel proving itself a tool equal to the trowel, our excavations uncovering more and more and even more shallow graves of memory).... So, if you would take a moment to consult your scorecards, dear readers: Our man = a revolutionary fighting to overthrow the establishment—and— entrenched defender of a *certain status quo*; an auto- biographical author reliant on the fiction of alcoholic mind-fuckery; seeking a tranquil peace, as he starts hot wars.... But be not fooled, though this cat seems aimed for a mountain-man style insularity, a mutual dependency is rooted snug. As deep as the tendrils of a fierce Scots-Irish independence may quarry into his fiber, there is an equal interdependence with those outside forces he so often slathers with shit. In the end, they raid and plunder his end goal: *doing with his time as he damned well pleases*. But he needs them. And they need him. And you get the idea that he knows that, even if they don't. This all smacks of a compromise. Anathema under any other conditions, it can be seen as strategy in this crystalline instance. So long as he gets the press—the good / the bad—then he gains the cred. Contradictory. Strange. Genius?

And the work of our good engineer proceeds....

The attention generated by the bleeding-nose guy's article has snapped on klieg floods. Not only is word out of Goodspeed's new work, but now any "automaton" discharged to gather info knows what the *Springvale Madman* looks like and where he drinks. His cover blown and a civil suit looming (D's restive annoyance on the latter: "bullshit bluster, would have it dismissed before the lunch break"), a steady dose of "parasites" have flooded the phone line down at the old *Buffet*. Culture-columnists mostly, a few reps pumping "big-house firms with big-time plans" thrown in (one even touting a movie offer), they have all tried to insist their way in—a few "morons" even attempting so in-person....

"Could never explain it in terms they'd understand, the what, the why that drives someone to write a book or build a solid house or blast an astronaut off into space, for that matter; and even if I could, would they care to hear it? I'll waste no time in it."

And though sudden fame alters the frame, it has changed nothing in so far as his duty is concerned. There is still the *maintenance of the routine* to consider. This here is an honorable defense. It is Goodspeed's nineteenth-century ancestors having signed up to defend whatever it was they thought they were defending and over 1400 days after-the-fact those that remained still manning lines stretching ever thinner to the west of Petersburg. It is an act of redemption against the perceived injuries of a reconstruction. It is the pursuit of grimly earned reparations against real injury (as in many centuries worth). But the parlance of sectional history aside, the aim of employing such metaphors is simply to snap into bold italics what is beyond question: ***it is about the maintenance of things as they are***. In here, one reckons camaraderie as—still—a pensive act, silent drinking the most noble of goals. It will inspire a spirited defense.

Out of duty to the brethren, Goodspeed has hired Omar as security-detail: "Just keep 'em from displaying their dumb courage and me out of broom-handle litigation 'n I'll take care of yer tab, O. We still have our business to take care of, in here. And that is a show that must go on."

Goodspeed also paid to have an answering machine wired-in to *Asa's* main line, it silently screening all incoming calls (Goodspeed himself tasked with the joyful duty of listening through and erasing parasitic inquiries). Omar, nothing if not thorough when it comes to threats, and the potential of ass-kicking for pay, has been on it. Disturbances have been reduced to zero. It all has allowed the business of *Asa's* to proceed unmolested. And it does, with a sincerity one might mistake for zeal....

Goodspeed sits down on the bench. Leaning back, he peers skyward. Behind a tree-limb lattice, the sun tracks a low arc across the day. The cold nips with a zeal of its own, our man slowing down a mind whose standard is to whirl as a pinwheel in a hurricane. His thoughts swirl about days past, days spent within the machine: "the sham covenant of the 50 story office tower, submerging the individual beneath mission statement mottoes that bait-and-switch loyalty into working a worker's hours, minutes, seconds, to death." It's a toxin called up (repeatedly) via memory. But it is still cured by 1000 daily milligrams of *The Acres*.... The night shift: that was Goodspeed's speed. He was in tune with the freaks, the hookers, the cops, and dead tired. Fakery dies late-at-night; honesty, often harsh, served up silver-platter-like regardless of it having been ordered or not. It is the M.O. And Goodspeed was in the audience for its nightly act. It was a classroom, an outpost blockhouse on the perimeter of humanity's slow-moving tragi-comedy—its leavening catastrophes indistinguishable from its apocryphal triumphs. The job demanded little for meager pay, a trade-off that allowed him to scribble at will: setting down the scenes and the better-than-fiction conversations overheard, while scratching out verse on the backs of used reservation tickets. He had built up a library's worth of material in but a few years. The more salient points teased out the shadow society subsisting and persisting regardless of how effective governing bodies and paternal social mores may think they are controlling *the mass status quo*. They also underwrote whole portions of TSM. But again, with buyout / corporate-restructuring, he'd found himself at the home office downtown, "promoted" into the belly of the beast. Wasted days flickered past with slot-machine vigor—*2 cherries, a lemon / 2 lemons, a cherry*—always the promise, always a bust. Goodspeed shudders with the recollection. Or is it the chill in the air? Thinking on the past smacks of a compromise of his (stress *his*) time. This is no time for compromise, his terms trending unconditional. He stops thinking.

Our man sits and stares. Solace does its thing. Even the most dedicated soldier needs a respite now and then, all and nothing zeroing out the moment right then and there.

He slips the noose of time's grasp. He will sit there for hours, breathing, thoughtless.... And he has sat there for about two hours. It is noon-ish, he figures: eleven-ish, actually. But we'll give it to him, for he has achieved the taming of the shrew, sorry (Shakespearean slip): the slipping of the noose. He has ejected time's tyrannical tendency from the equation, leaving only its submission to his unique orbit—revolving, in turn, as it does around his lair, his *captain's chair*. For in there, time (as in the murder of) is a rare patron. It knows that if it is found out, it is likely to be collared and roughly deposited to hexagonal stone out front. The haven is sacrosanct. It must, nay, it will be defended.

And so explained, there are times when *the status quo* can seem the most radical idea of all, when its reinvention of the very concept of time so upsets the Big Mules' moonlight and magnolias exploitation that it will draw heavy fire. And once crossed, once challenged, once defiled in so personal—such a kid-glove to face public humiliation—once that crossing of lines is so egregious to the chivalric instinct that code, duty—*honor!*—demand the unfurling of flags, the long roll of drums, a retaliatory response so devastating that the very ages will quake in their boots recalling the waste-laying perpetrated in the simple name of righting this perceived wrong, this—*this*— is the point that Bill Faulkner once claimed as the play-acting "raht" of every white boy in the South: To again imagine that it is 1 p.m. on July 3, 1863, the cannonade having just ceased....and it is on, motherfuckers! And with that, *The Asa Inman* awaits.

Goodspeed stands and stretches and makes his way down an adjunct to the main trail. The sun's rays pepper the preserve with gold pixels. It lights up the body laying half on its side in the trail ahead. Goodspeed shakes his head, this being not such a rarity out here. He rolls the body onto its back with boot heel (doing so with a highlander game log-rolling zeal). A hollow stare. All systems are down. It's a local addict that no one he knew knew by name. No bullet hole, no foul play. OD'd, choking to death on one's own vomit...."Je-ssus Martinez."

"Damned stupid. What a wretched way to go," Goodspeed scratching his head in honest disbelief over heroin's recent comeback, the appeal foreign to him. He leaves the deceased and continues down the trail towards Euclid. He exits *The Acres*. His steps plod the sidewalk, move him towards *Asa's*. What a welcome way to go.

The door swings open. It throws light on the cadre gathered about. It is time to set things right, to mastermind the potential of one's idiom. Goodspeed greets Boo and Gid, Ez and Victor, Chuck and Tench, Martha and Howard.

"H, can you call up whoever's on? Another smackhead od'd down there in the acres. Je-ssus Martinez, getting to be routine. I don't understand, stuff is pure poison. Bourbon neat when ya get a chance. In fact, make it a double. It is Christmas Eve eve, n'all. In fact, set us all up, H. This one's on me! Pick your poison, fellow patriots!"

They muster a cheer, despite the early hour. *Glad Tidings of Joy!*

THE ANNUAL YEAR END ISSUE of the *The Weekly* is a production the staff pines for (re: magnolia-scented nostalgia) and reviles (as with a squint-eye). Sleepless weeks deny all but the most meager of holiday vacations, yet delivers a yearly tradition: a popular, even award-winning, good / bad / ugly post-mortem on the year clocking out. It is good riddance, as in a rousing arm-linked tankard-spilling plea that *old acquaintances be forgot,* and bon voyage all in one big fat double-issue. But producing this printed catharsis has burned out the most hearty....

December 30, 1995: The day that year's edition hit stands, the original editor of the Frederickson-era *Weekly* walked out beneath an odd sombre adieu (that no one thought to question at the time) and disappeared for six weeks. Though staff was hard pressed to edit-by-committee in Lane's absence, when he finally did reappear to officially resign, no one—not even Gibbs—took him to task for it. It may have been water under the bridge, or just the discomfiting notion that *anyone's* indelible fissures can rupture should the volume of bullshit hop-scotch our personal containment fields (a fact now known to our good journalist in no uncertain hungover terms). For the subtle, yet relentless drain of "gumption attrition" knows not prince from peon in this industry. Like wit or addiction, it is but another of the dispassionate levelers whose lance will find your armor-chinks just as sure as the julep be mint.

Though responsible for three columns in this year's year-end opus (what was the boy thinking?!), Cyrus Cleburne has been burning the wick on one in particular: an offering from his "field research." He is crossing T's, dotting I's, scratching out notes in margins as he rifles through a short-stack of printouts.... Having started as a curiosity, a diversion from the gumption attrition of documenting social dystopia in our midst, our self-anointed scene-stalker has begun to view this story as his charge; his duty, even: shine light on a homegrown talent lighting things up. Yet what began as a quick foray to offset the underwhelming profiles on the *Springvale* bard that had achieved ink to date, this "chump" has opened up untamed wilds previously unknown. Significant discoveries lay just beneath the surface and the red dirt earth has been giving up her secrets hand-over-fist. A long piece wasn't his intent. 5,000 words at once seemed to be overkill. But Cyrus' deft turn-of-the-trowel has uncovered what not even a series of columns could do justice, *Goodspeed, the man,* having revealed even greater treasure: *Goodspeed, the myth.*

No single column could feign sufficiency. But this one will amplify the buzz created by the advance passage of *Within* printed in *The Weekly* a few weeks earlier, and do honor to the alt-rag's masthead mantra: *Down Home Defender of the Local Arts.* The core of Cleburne's piece? The visceral sense of duty rolling across the backdrop of Goodspeed's work....

> *To say that Marvin Goodspeed considers himself a tribune for all those oppressed by the stultifying routine of the dominant corporate workplace—and leaving it at that—is the descriptive equivalent of saying it is warm in July: a 'no shit' observation that fails for having not sprinted instantly into the weeds of "why"....*

It is also a not-so-subtle statement-of-purpose, a proposal in the creative non-fiction mold, and at the very least assurance of his "getting it." Should a certain local wordsmith—or more likely his lawyer / lover / biker companion—happen to be tuning in, it could pave the way for an offer our good Regular really should not refuse.

This column will stick close to the one salient point mentioned. But it does so implying a mother lode (the delusion of drunken timelessness scoring so complete a *Victory!*, for starters) to be rolled out at a time and date of our persistent troweler's choosing.... But let's not get ahead of ourselves: Cleburne will sketch *the man* first, then move onto *the myth*. Just let the record state: when the latter comes about, he'll be doing so whether our man blesses the effort or not....


"You kids still on for New Year's in New Orleans?" Anna asks Kelly, pulling out a plastic sword kabob of olives from a martini glass atop the bar.

"Cy?" Kelly inquires, drinking ale as she devours a heaping plate of frites (to the usual quiet amazement of her crew).

"Affirmative, confirmed with Grey; leave New Year's Eve eve. Tomorrow? Tomorrow. No offense, ladies. Lacy gave me two hours, like, an hour ago," Cyrus hand-signaling regrets, moving to an empty booth along the front wall.

The two continue over late-afternoon drinks at the popular office hangout. Having retrofit one of the two original filling stations in *The Points*, *Austin's Full Service* now serves fuel of a different, but no less essential, grade. We pick up with the ladies....

"He pulled it together," Anna says, the strong lilt of surprise (maybe, hopefully, not too surprised?).

"And without a moment to lose. I was done with it all, was done with him. I couldn't tell where the play-acting ended, neither could he. It was one long binge; was done with it," Kel summarizing, devouring.

"Research," Anna punctuating the point with all the authority a plastic sword air-jab can command.

"The morning after that night at the Point, that's when it clicked for me, that there might really be a problem," Kel attempting the same mid-air authority thrust with french fry.

"And he was on a tight deadline that week, which he did not make."

"Ya, I know. Lacy was not happy and let *Prez* know it too."

"Figured."

"Guess it should not surprise that it got so out of hand so quick; what happens when you think you are in control. He is a lucky kid, that he had people around him who gave a shit," Kel giving the no-brainer smirk she gives when there is only one obvious action in lieu of a *situation*.

"Well, he has poured obsession into something worthwhile," Anna drinking down a dirty martini. "He told me on the first that he'd really fucked up, was going dry for the month, would not drink again until New Year's. That he stuck to it, not usually how that goes."

"He had some motivation. He actually asked for my help, which I was skeptical to give at first. Just not gonna be played with. He took a dumb stunt *way* too far, actually thought it was something other than just being drunk—all—the—time."

"Isn't that the problem? Talking yourself into a myth?"

"Especially when it's someone else's myth."

"You screw up the wiring of your brain drinking like that. The science of it alone, you wind up drinking yourself into a new normal that is anything but. And the body, amazingly, adapts, just tries to survive. He needed a kick in the ass."

"I just pointed out the obvious. All anyone had to do. Just lucky there was someone there to do it; not always how that goes."

"You win saint of the month, not sure I would have had the patience," Anna owning a limitation.

"Don't know about the saint thing. I mean, we are spending New Year's in New Orleans. Just, I don't know," Kel twirling a french fry, wondering if the next thing needs to be said....

"About?" Anna, leaning towards *just say it, sister*.

"Is what you do when you care. That, plus, I believed in him. Everything was right there, right in front of him. The stories and all of the background material had been pouring out of him for months; even took a night-time course at the Center on how to identify alcoholism, just to understand the physiology of it all. He was dedicated and was fucking all that shit up —

"Wait, think I got this: 'cause he was shit-faced—*all— the—time*."

"I was not going to watch that happen to anyone else I knew."

"Workplace romance. That can be tricky."

"The two of us? That wouldn't even be news, right?"

"More like about time y'all copped to it, been dancin' around it all Summer."

"There was more than dancin' going down."

"Ya," Anna *as-if-ing*, "we all figured that too."

"Freelancer, so technically not a workplace romance."

"Would Gibbs even care?"

"Would probably want in on it."

"No, ug! Lane flashback. A little close to home," Anna's patented lip and face curl-up in wake of thought-revulsion.

"We were tight over the Summer. It was moving towards a real thing," Kelly: a satisfied grin, fry plate now empty (as in crumb-less), drinking ale.

"But then *the research* intervened?"

"Ummm, ya. And lest we make this conversation all about him, I was not ever gonna be taken for granted again."

"Damn straight, girl."

"I don't know. It does work....us....ya know?"

"If he doesn't screw it up," Anna picking a pimento from back tooth, a tongue-sweep and tooth-suck to be sure.

"So, your piece is done?"

"Lacy's final proofing it as we speak. Why I'm here, a bit nervous."

Anna's end-of-year is a long-form case for that other Olympia, Washington, band: *Bikini Kill*, setting them up as having written a new chapter when all thought punk was dead (if only by sticking its misogyny with a *Riot grrrl* shiv); and all while advancing a scorching brand of equal rights that not a million burned bras could have achieved. The core of the piece makes a case for band and lead singer / shrieker, Kathleen Hanna, as civil disobedience embedded in a roaring piece of performance art.

"It's great, it really is. Never realized she so tongue-in-cheek bad-ass. Lacy'll love it, or he's a shit head. It'll be the lead. Cy thinks so too."

"She's fearless. The more I got into it, the more I felt it was somehow my duty to do it up right."

"That is exactly what I told Cy, that he was blowing a serious dish; that if he was gonna be true to it, honest with it, then he needed to stop fucking around and do it."

"Wait, you talking about the story—or you?"

"Ha, *yes!*"

"You kids. Y'all are a dish. New Orleans with Grey, gonna be great. I miss him a ton."

"Where'd we all be without New Orleans?"

"Lost. Culturally, spiritually, lost."

"Can't fathom it."

"Let's not."

"Just hoping that the boys can bury the hatchet," Kelly a bit anxious actually, forecasting stormy relations. This will be the first meeting between Grey and Cyrus since a certain someone bailed on his responsibility....okay, alright (insert objective observation here)....since Grey left *The Beacon* for a new gig.

"If New Orleans can't cure it all, nothing can," Anna, a *beacon* in her own right, the two moving on to more serious matters—their celebrating, that is.

Meanwhile, down the road a piece (Austin Avenue, that is), the wallflower minions must certainly be heralding a night of cheer / good will. Pursued with an animation one might confuse for ardor, there'd be no reason to think otherwise....but despite the ardent attempts to keep it at arm's length, *otherwise* is no stranger in here. And for the moment, at least, good will has flown the coop: Henry having dropped George with a tooth-loosening uppercut before storming out. A violent door slam rebounds the front door to fully open. George flexes his jaw, stunned, a concussive jumble slowly settling. He gets up to his feet. He receives no helping hand, only squint-eye censure from all the other revelers then assembled. The breach of protocol hangs like an acrid stench, the smoke-filled room singing in the struck silent aftermath as if its own bell had been rung. Such a blatant disrespect for "the ways," the order. No, this will not stand.

George shakes it off and is charging after Henry when his malevolence is stunted by the human wall that is Sax. Boo steps up: the grand old regular. By the unspoken agreement of protocol alone, he is allowed the first accusation:

"Ye should know better, son. In here, we don't goad a man who's findin' himself down on his luck. Not in here."

"Fuck that, Boo! Had no raht to hit me like that! No raht! Gonna settle the score right now with that S.O.B.!" George adrenalized, erratic, working his jaw.

"You got it ass-backwards, son. Henry just did finish things. There ain't gonna be no more to it," Howard, the ultimate authority / referee in here, documenting the indictment, delivering the ruling: "Now, ya know his woman just did take up with that sack-of-shit fresh off the stint downstate, stole Henry's car, what little money he had and disappeared. He wasn't fibbin' through none of that. We know that boy well enough to know he don't kid about that kinda thing. Yet all ya can do is goad him like ya was. *That* is what ain't raht. And it won't stand in here. You started it, Henry finished it. Now we've all had enough of your irreverent bullshit, hear?" Howard's cool squint, something that would unnerve anyone concerned with self-preservation....

"No, no, no way! Had no raht!"

"He had all the raht in the world, asshole!" shouts Goodspeed from his usual seat, eyes locked on the disrespecter. "Johnny Cash is Henry's salvation, 'n all ya can do is spew crap 'bout Cash being nothing without his promoters? First, who the fuck cares what you think about things you, clearly, don't know a god-damned thing about? Second, even if ya did, why the fuck do you heap on a man clearly down on his luck? Do you have a mental deficiency? Are you fucking retarded? You are clearly suffering some kind of neglect syndrome, think the only way anyone'll pay attention is when you shoot your mouth off loud enough for everyone to hear. Johnny Cash has been the one reliable constant all on down a hard luck life for our friend, Henry; even come to play for him way back during his stretch at the federal pen out west. If you'd shut your god-damned hole and listen every so often, maybe you'd know all of this. But no, you're too busy running your god-damned mouth all the damned time. I woulda done the same, except I woulda made sure ya didn't get back up."

"Don't be sayin' no words ya can't back up thar, hot shot," George challenging with a sudden coolness.

"Alright, enough. Get out now and do not show your face in here again, George. That—is—final," H making a future full of hurt as clear as anyone can to someone who is, obviously, not paying attention.

"Sure, take the side of the big shot. Marv, the big-time hot shot, too good for the rest of us in here, always needin' someone to stands up for him! Must be right 'cause he's a famous big shot! Ass fuckin' faggot is what he is!"

"What d'you say?" the stoic, almost always silent Ez

getting up from her seat, standing alongside Sax, their shoulders broadening into a ridgeline.

"I call'd 'im what he is: a fucking queer-ass faggot!"

Ez, squint-eyes ablaze, steps forward. She is actually rolling up her sleeves when Victor troops out from the back room and gives the intruder a preemptory "who the fuck do you think you are?!" shove....

"Hey, what the—oh, you too? Well, you can fuck off too, Gutiérrez. Why not crawl back south-of-the-border, leave a job open for a real American, dirty brown fucker."

Victor, a roaring four-alarm blaze now firing his rage, closes in on the interloper. George takes a step back. Ez and Sax take a step forward.

"That's it! Sick of all y'all! Sit and spin, motherfuckers!" George, a one-finger salute.

"Yes, that is it!" Sax throttling George with the intent of tossing his ass through the front door and out onto the hard unforgiving hexagonal stone.

"Hands off, nigger!" George pulling free, violently....

Okay, so those with any amount of street smarts or brains at all will recognize unwritten codes of conduct as glowing red lines you don't cross unless you really just want your ass beat. No one's going to tell you, in here. There is no handbook. If you are such a dense dumbass as to not catch on, then you have it coming. The only fortunate circumstance for the loudmouth at the moment is that Omar is not on duty this evening. But no mind, all: Goodspeed is lighter-than-air in hurling himself at the defiler of "the ways." It is fight-dirty time in the old southern tradition. And Goodspeed does right by the custom, crashing into George and jabbing him in the eye. The two are a mass of wind-milling limbs. They plow into and through a booth bench. Goodspeed is kicking at the same time he machine-wheels a scythe of fists. George fights through and starts to gain a headlock, landing a punch. Goodspeed pulls free, sinks his teeth into trapezius just north of the shoulder, jerking as a ravenous cur trying to rip meat from the bone. George backhand-punches Goodspeed, a banshee scream, fails to dislodge him, the two stammering and careening into the back-door doorframe, violently. Stunned, they fall as separate bloody heaps. Sax jumps in, clamps George by the arms and literally hurls his scrawny frame 10 feet through the still open front door. The defiler, breathless and bleeding at half-a-dozen points from the neck up, scurries backwards on the sidewalk like an injured crab. There is shock in eyes, but no humanity. He is shaking all over, as he yells:

"Y-y-y-you—are—dead, Goodspeed! You are fucking dead!" pulling himself to his feet, reeling backwards with such force as to dent with his elbow a fifth-generation Cutlass sedan parked before *The Buffet* (no small feat, y'all); the defiler running off.

Goodspeed gets up, stumbles, finds his center, grabs the bar edge. He yells, red-faced, is running out the door in pursuit when Sax and Tench hold him up. Goodspeed turns and back-hands an empty glass on the bar top. It flips several times before smashing on the floor.

"Now just settle down, Marv! Just let it all drop!" Howard advises in light of needless property damage. Goodspeed is repentant, offers to pay for the glass and orders a round for the house. He grabs a wet cloth from Martha, wipes blood from his lip, having cracked a capped tooth.... And within minutes the situation has turned over a new leaf.

It is late December. Football on the television diffuses the need for in-bar violence. By the second quarter, the earlier drama is a distant memory. The cure of liquid elixir produces howls of camaraderie, glad tidings and joy....*Having fought for honor, having fought for the cause....* A battle won, there is still the war to consider. But all triumphs—large / small / middling—should be celebrated as the victories they are. For all such victories (as we are coming to understand them) are but temporary way-stations between the polar ends of a hard life, a hard truth that requires no air-time but is simply implied within the bowed-paneling of this modest place. Like the code, it is never more than inferred. It is simply understood....*It is constantly evolving. It is what it has always been....* And if you have to ask, maybe it is something that you might never come to understand. Having pulled up alongside so important a wayside, perhaps reflection on one's welcome should be mulled long and hard. To cross the line is to disrespect—to defile— the natural order. And if the regulars have one thing in this life, it is their nature. Respect "the way," or expect to pay through the nose.

DIXIE WHISTLES PAST WINDOWS. Two monster fronts are converging: a cold and calculated northern drift crashing into a fluid hot-blooded disturbance rising up from the South. They will slowly envelop the entire Southeast with heavy rains to fall. A respite has it spitting at the moment here on the road in *East Al-a-bam*. It is of no mind, the engine churning to the rhythms of the journey at the moment under glass. Music saturates the cabin....*I propose a toast, to my self-control. See it crawling helpless on the floor....* There comes a time to toss away the style-cramping fig leaf called "restraint." For these two, it nears.

Miles fall. The piedmont slowly flattening. Creeks, ravines, and cumberland scenes slide past as on a conveyor. Passion and lust fire this pilgrimage to the mothership, the cryptic capitol of revelry imploring the masses to come for the show—*to be a part of the show!* (Interactive revelry: so modern, so wired.) Cyrus glances at Kelly piloting this leg. Opting to make haste (and make it there, period), they had opted against Cy's '68 Westfalia for Kel's brand spanking new '98 Saturn coupe, a sporty dish boasting an attractive onboard package that includes, amongst other things, a slick new contemporary feature called: heat (unlike a certain beloved microbus). It is a choice he feels good about. For this, right here, could only be better if she were naked. ("And you're welcome for that mental snapshot there, sport," Kel so gracious in her telepathy.) The red sash of lust, so potent as to be visible, flies as a semaphore from car-radio antennae, announcing their intentions, that swelling flush of a new unexpected love blooming and the carnal carnival that is its most temporal benefit. Cyrus taps out the rhythm on dashboard. Kelly taps out the rhythm on steering wheel. They say not a word. Not a word need be said....*Come forth ye children! Let the rhythm of the moment be cast in the lust for life!*

And the heart of Dixie passes with hardly a notice.

Meanwhile, back at the ranch, the vanguard of the *blue* front has arrived, the *gray* front deploying to the south on its right-flank. The mixing of the two promises bloody meteorological conflict. But for now, it is a cold Winter rain falling. The clouds are in no hurry. A leaden ceiling rolls low over earth. It smothers the tops of buildings in the not-so-distant downtown. The spires of *progress!* slice open its grey underbelly. Guts pour out as rain. It could be viewed in a negative light: instigator of bad moods— despair, even. Yet the rain can hardly be taken to task. It is just doing its thing, proceeding without a care.... And Goodspeed walks down the avenue, as if unaware.

The rain is steady now; insistent, bitter, and raw, breath visible. But far from worsening, his mood is lightening with every step. He might as well be whistling a tune. Dixie? (No, dear reader, we could not resist.) Winter rain has been unable to penetrate his new coat. It is his first new anything in years. (The aforementioned desklamp and its short run can hardly count.) It is a waterproof trenchcoat, with a warm inner-liner. The well-oiled leather hat he's had forever. A water vein rolls off its brim and extinguishes the cigarette notched in lip-corner. He grumbles, spits out the butt, walks on through cold spit. He passes the old *Carriage House* at the outlet of Elizabeth, the equestrian depot's value to the neighborhood having been done in by Edison and Ford. As if to prove the point, this is the very road up which the *Eastside Trolley's* tracks strode from their downtown power-station before merging onto Memorial and continuing up to *The Points—the new* taunting and flaunting its arrival right under the nose of *the old*....

"Smell that, old-timer? It's the future, here and now! What are you gonna do about it?!"

*The old* closed-lip chuckles to itself in the face of the

taunt, thinking: "*The new,* that poor dumb kid; has no earthly idea of the beat down the past will dole out when crossed."

The trolley tracks were asphalted over in the '50s. But chunks of pavement still crack loose on occasion to reveal a sliver of rail. The past, it is still there.

*The Ashlands* and Alta pass. Goodspeed treks on through the swampy *field parks*. It is walking that clears his head. It resets his mood, so often soured by the daily trials. He lights another smoke, rubs a black-and-blue welt at the corner of his eye. His lip is cracked, his knuckles scraped and scabbing over; wrist tight with a sprain....

The preceding day had proceeded routinely: slow to wake up, bourbon for breakfast, a long long walk. But when Goodspeed returned to his hovel, there was George waiting in ambush in the alley. Looking to make good on his threats, George was out for blood. He had rushed our man, who was unawares, and knocked him down. George came on flailing, landing blows. But the wild and unfocused attacker mapped out his weaknesses like phrenology: swinging against his core, countering and raising his centre of gravity, exposing ribcage with wild swings, etc. And Goodspeed, though stunned, snapped to and read the faults like a bestseller. He held off a flurry of swings, one splitting his lip. A lucky shot. Goodspeed viewed the rules of street-fighting in open violation: stagger elbows to mimic your stance, forearms perpendicular to your center, *defend until the attacking's good*. The fucking moron, defying them all, left his ribcage wide open. *Bullseye!* Goodspeed kicked with both boot-heels, with everything he had, knocking the wind clean out of the antagonist. Stunned, George stumbled backward, coughing breathlessly. Goodspeed brought all he had, blows windmilling like a Gatling gun. George blackened Goodspeed's eye with a wild self-defense swing; but this was a footnote to the beating doled out. It was a one-sided thrashing. The day belonged to Goodspeed. Honor bound in defense of "the way," he had brought the house....

Post-pummeling, Goodspeed had deposited the semiconscious violator at the curb along with that day's trash. Howard, just then opening-up, happened across the aftermath, chuckling:

"Coulda seen that comin,' some kinda damned fool, that boy."

"Fuck 'im," Goodspeed wiping his bloody lip.

So it had gone down.... *The field parks* give way to Euclid past Austin, the sponge-like give of soaked moss and unkempt bermuda giving way to city sidewalk. Fooled by the absent sun, streetlamps light up. Goodspeed marches on, the precipitation soldiering on. They do what they must: the few, the proud. The Regular surveys the lay of his land: commitment, out here, a testament of one's faith. Invest yourself completely or move along without a word.

TORRENTS OF SIN-SOAKED WAVES wash down draws cobblestoned and lathed of enclaves filled of those full up on the spirit, a swirling whirling turbine of the dazed: *Jockomo Feena Nay!*....And we sight our crew through open wall-high casements: Cyrus and Kelly, Grey and fellow *Crescent* compatriots, Erin and Hari, cheering on the evening. It explodes in restless color. *One last hurrah!* A hot-blooded Gulf storm dumps rain. It pours off eaves, makes Venetian canals of las calles. The rain does not hinder. It is nature's absinthe doing what it does—what it must—the peal of lust a high thunder rolling.

Our good revelers cheer on a fellow reveler running / stumbling towards the overhang's shelter. He makes it, soaked for his effort. He gives the thumbs up. They toast him, their table strewn of Dixie lagers ringing a red-hot tin of crawfish. The boiled shells steam, a head-sucking promise goading the faithful out of their shell....*Come forth, ye! Come out for—nay—take your part in the show!*....A group of rhythm kings take to a delta-shaped stage angled into a corner. They wrangle the accordion, washboard percussion, upright bass; pour down Creole with a dash of Delta. Gas lanterns flicker at the sidewalk's edge, the dripping metal mesh of second-story balconies sure in their relaxed vanity, the downpour steady. It is all big, boisterous, easy. The year surges with a gusto (that one that could rightfully peg as verve) towards its final night.

Grey Stinson. *Weekly* alum and "In Case Anyone Cares" co-researcher—if not co-writer (which we'll address en un momento)—has recently left *The Beacon* to seek his calling amongst the coffee houses and tarot shacks of old NOLA. Actually, he'd just received a better offer than *Prez* was willing to counter. No one—not even Gibbs—had held his leaving against him, one being able to do MUCH worse than working as a staff-writer at a respected New Orleans arts-rag in the year-of-our-Lord, 1997. That said, at least one felt there had been unfinished business left in wake of a precipitous exit. (But with luck, the evening's planned charter will retain a civil course when the subject is broached. Fingers crossed.)

For the moment, the three former cohorts merrily dredge up ye olde days to the curiosity of the compatriots:

"Lane? No, no, he thought he was an in-house marauder," Kelly sizing up the fornication resume of *The Weekly's* recently mentioned ex-managing editor, calling it true: "but laying an intern and the intern's best friend, does not a lady-killer make."

"The magic was in that mustache. That was the irresistible element, got all you ladies a'tremblin," Grey with color-commentary.

"Hardly, voyeur."

"Voyeur? Hardly."

"The handlebar phase? That was bold. I will give him points for that," Cyrus' comment eliciting exactly two rumpled-lip head shakes indicating *aye*.

"Okay, but anyone else think '70s porn kind of ruined the mustache for, well, all time?" Kelly, elbows propped on table, palms ceiling-ward.

"Hmm, well, not a subject-matter expert. And you are since when?" Cyrus intrigued (in fact, just the slight bit engorged....)

"Ya, well, file it under: research I'd like to forget. Lane's idea—the pervert—wanted authentic fonts from title– and credit-reels to go with that piece on Midtown in the '70s."

"A New Southerner's Guide to Smut City," Grey's tone echoing the critical praise (and moral indignation) that met *The Weekly's* expose having led the end-of-year extravaganza, c. 1995.

"Of course, you had to sit through what came in between title and credits?"

"Literally."

"Ya, well, Lane literally couriered over a stack of VHS tapes to my apartment with a handwritten note, all matter-of-fact. Asshole."

"Still amazed that no one brought a suit during his time," Grey, an incredulous head shake.

"So, okay, I didn't 'have' to watch the tapes; but admit to some curiosity there."

"And?"

"And, after sitting through a dozen well-mustachioed *Lowenbrau Men* serving up money shots? Let's just say the details are kind of burned-in; for good, I fear."

"Great. I was unable to not see that in my mind. By what you're saying, there is no way I un-see that, right?" Erin's pinched look indicating a demonstrable mind's eye disturbance.

"Nope. In there for good, I fear."

"But now, it was '60s long hair evolving into the mustache once all the baby-boomers had to enter the work force; so, maybe a tip to past radicalism promoted a profusion of 'stache," Erin displaying a muscular command of *'stache* theory.

"My god, y'all. The '70s. It was 'stache a Go-Go."

"Was it only hetero-porn?" Grey, sounding surprised.

"Lane?" Kelly, sounding surprised.

"Well, ya. Dude made a drunken pass at me my first year: Christmas party, what, three years ago? Before your time."

"Really? Would not have pegged him for a switch-hitter."

"Mm-hmm, grabs my package during the proposition. I was like *man, you are not my type—and—being my kind-*

*of-boss makes not a fuck all o' difference."*

"Reeaaally?" Kelly punctuating with a quick violent laugh. "And nothing came of that?"

"Nope, fell into the 'we'll not speak of this again' moment; never did."

"Ya, well not actually too surprised. First thing Anna tells me when I started freelancing: sure as shit, he'll hit on you, *but just roll your eyes, walk away, will shut it all down; should be fucking harassment, but that it's so pathetic.* Sure enough, very first time we are all out, I am like no way, dude, and roll my eyes. He was wearing that freaking smoking jacket! Never tried it again, never came up. Great editor, but grade-A sleeze and cheese."

"Damn, now I'm feeling left out," Cyrus, a lover of the ladies, not really wanting his junk cupped by a dude; but still....

"Ain't a favorable portrait y'all painting," Hari, born outside of Delhi but raised in the American South (he even *fixes* to do things), giving voice to what the compatriots to this conversation are thinking,

"It was the package deal with Lane."

"Occasionally a grab-your-package deal?" Hari, catching on.

"Yes, occasionally. But for all his many often public faults, he understood storytelling, was serious about it as a vital cultural glue. It was innate," Grey echoing the others.

"It was a strange genius with Lane. He'd say: *Now, Cy, to tell it true, you need to unearth the fact and the myth, as the truth of an era will eventually congeal somewhere in-between the two,*" Cyrus the student, an uncarved block—*a sponge.*

"And, let us not forget, he would say all this deep touchstone shit while gripping an unlit pipe in his clenched-teeth?!" Kelly accentuating *the strange*.

"And all while wearing that damned smoking jacket," Grey with more echoing.

"And reeking of cologne!" Kelly with the volley, adding: "Lane's fact-myth theory, also true of particular characters set within our own time, eh?" winking at her beau, having straightened up and flying right, knowing his headspace.

"It was a kind of genius, that is right. He was able to digest the present for its long-term nutrients. That notion of journalism as the first draft of history? He was uncanny, could separate the wheat from the chaff in the present."

"All the while acting out the role of a walking talking '70s stereotype."

"Even his real seemed fake; and maybe it was. For all his unapologetic willingness to be a public embarrassment, he was close to the vest. Maybe just part of the act: create your own myth?"

"Sounds like the tag line for a 'build your own' burrito place."

"Ha!"

"Ya, despite all of Lane's fake and highly annoying *suave*—I mean, he drank brandy and modeled his moves on soap operas, all."

"Right, would stop what he was doing every afternoon to watch the *Young and the Restless*, claimed it as the modern lineage of Shakespeare."

"Case-in-point: grade-A cheese."

"No question, but he also had a finger on the pulse: could plant his audience in front of the prism through which he wanted to be viewed, would gain their trust."

"In the tradition of fables?" Hari digging for clarity amidst the praise-fest.

"Right, right, left you wondering where the real left off and the myth began. But you never held it against him because of the larger truth in the telling."

"And, again, the hitting-on-everything-with-a-heartbeat thing aside, he could be mentor-like. It was not a power trip. If you said no, that was it—as if he just needed that setting of boundaries; my experience, at least. The work was the thing. He was hard, but fair."

"Aside from requesting that you research hours of exploitative porn?" Erin reality-checking, persisting on behalf of the skeptical two.

"Right, mostly fair," Kelly applying an asterisk. "But even that, you had to know Lane. It never seemed misogynistic, so much as a dumb bad joke. Poor taste? Perverted? Hell yes, but it was just him enjoying a laugh off-stage."

"At your expense," Hari, adding a brushstroke.

"Always!" Kelly emphatic, Grey and Cyrus confirming in-unison: a head-shaking chorus of mmm-hmms....

"But hoo, lawd! Could he spin the outrageous yarn. He'd command an audience, in-person and in-print," Grey exploding with restless color.

"Each and every one of his stories was leavened with, let's call them favorable, edits."

"Which, like his eye-rolling attempts to seduce, you forgave."

"Right, like waking up in a Miami dumpster with those German sailors? The details never interfered. You never stopped to ask a question like: *Does Germany even have a navy?*"

"That storyteller's gift: weaving in exaggeration without tripping up the punch-line. Still wondering how I missed his *bi-tendencies*; did seem to have an inordinate amount of sailor stories."

"Or, how about his delivering the high school valedictory address?"

"A questionable reach right there," Kelly, again, palms ceiling-ward.

"Right, no doubt; but while peaking on, his words: a heaping handful of LSD tabs?" Cyrus, the amused skeptic.

"And the pièce de résistance: smoking crack at that Saudi prince's penthouse party, you know, because everyone else was; he didn't want to seem rude!" all three mimic the lines they had heard umpteen times from Lane himself, in-unison: "I ask of you this: what was I to do? When in Rome, right?"

A rolling peal of nostalgic laughter aligns with the distant thunder rolling, the rain continuing to drain down easy.

"Set as it was against all the corrupt assholes we were, still are, covering?! Those liars ooze sleazy manipulation for self-gain. Lane's embellishment was harmless fun."

"Ya, he gained nothing aside from an attentive audience."

"Which, of course, was a form of currency to Lane."

"For sure. He needed to be loved more than respected."

"A willing deception for the sake of others' enjoyment does seems an acceptable trait for cocktail parties. But, am I pointing out an obvious here? Seems a liability for the editor of a newspaper?" Erin the uninvested observer, positing fairly.

"For sure, and that is totally fair. But he employed it as an editorial strength, recognized the hues that trail off between fact and fiction, that they're often interchangeable in the present tense, all those little lies and half-truths we use to ease our minds, make what we're doing set up as legit, or at the very least: necessary to survive. Our perception of the world follows how we want to see ourselves in it. By default, that is part real and part what we want to think is real," Cyrus, the sponge exuding.

"Man, listen to Wittgenstein here. But true dat, Lane would tell me to *let it all work itself out, the fact and the fiction; a more complete picture will inevitably reveal itself*," Grey again with the giving of due.

"Hmm, also seem to recall him saying one should follow through on a piece to the bitter end." (Oh dear, it is what we had feared....)

"Okay, let's not start," Grey leaning back, folding arms.

"You walked away, is all."

"What could you be worried about? The piece is gonna win an award."

"Trust me, it isn't the praise that's the problem. It's the white-hot heat from the indicted, thank you; which I'm now taking on alone."

"Both Lacy and Gibbs gave you the chance to back out before it went to print."

"And they both have my back. Where are you?"

"Look, you know what, fuck that! We've been over this: it was always your thing, you were driving, you were the *investigative journalist*. I just got you in the door."

"I call bullshit. The ride-alongs? The scrutiny of stats?

Both critical ideas. Your ideas led to the break; would say that has you invested in the aftermath too."

"I got involved 'cause of what my brother and the others in the precinct were hintin' at; to both of us, by the way. Do you not recall that? They were clanging alarm bells, alerting us, lowly little alt-rag reporters, we, that this thing was bigger than we could imagine, went down a deeper hole and all the way up the chain. We were profiling gang violence. Trey was like: man, you two need to step back and take it all in; goes beyond just the gangs. And that was all he could say. They went to us, too afraid for their jobs to go to the corporate news-hacks. I was just elbowing you, man! I wanted you to corroborate what he was sayin' and then run with it so I could back away from it all. I wasn't gonna get Trey fired over that!"

"Okay, alright, you're right, they were sticking their necks out for us. Just that I wouldn't have gotten there without you and did not do it on my own. I'm just tryin' to give you some fucking credit."

"I don't want it. I backed out as soon as we made the connection. I'm no Woodward or Bernstein, friend. I just want to write about the music and art and all the crazy art fuckers. Fuck that whole nauseating universe of corrupt fuckheads fucking over everyone and then walking away with fortunes subsidized by taxpayers."

"No—fucking—shit! And thanks for proving my point: I know you wanted them rung up too! I know you wanted that story to hit and hit big. I know you wanted to nail those fuckers! You were in on it, can't deny it!"

"You wanted it. You cracked it. You needed to write it—alone!"

"Ya, okay, okay, I'm going to guess that this quarreling

is about as entertaining to us all right now as a zoning-board hearing, of which I have had the privilege of attending many, and yes, they are mostly mind-numbing, spiked with hot little moments of selfish ranting. So, how about less arguing the *hues of perception* and more *eat, drink, be merry,* ¿si?" Kelly, tiring of the argument (to which she's had a front-row seat for weeks now).

A taxi-driver skippers his hack down the cobbled canal outside open casements. Plunging past, he soaks a crew of pre-soaked revelers gliding up the sidewalk. The most inebriated of the crew runs after the perpetrator of the soaking, yelling, fists-in-air. The comic scene arbitrates a lightening of tensions, king rhythm lightening the gloom of gloaming. It is Delta-dashed Creole, less the stern stance that now stirs spirit and soul. It is as it should be. And it is honored as it should be: crawfish rattling down the gullet, calls for another round. *Encore!*

"Right. Okay, moving on. Here's what we do," Grey presenting the revelers with a plan: "there's a hole-in-the-wall up on Toulouse, we start there, work our way down, end up in the streets for the countdown?"

Affirmatives are confirmed in the glow of expressions. Glasses ring as they all toast the plan. They are all now laughing with each other, at each other, and with and at those passing by. The spirit is tangible. It pervades the torrent. It is the magic of New Orleans that they hold dear: the physical and the spiritual dirt. It calls on the senses, strokes them to climactic heights....*Oh, fuck! Oh, I'm coming! I'm coming! Don't stop! Do not stop!*

It is the verve of these days, these nights.

Grey bands layer up the sky, a furrowed forehead

skeptical of the sunset optimism then coursing through fine skeletal tears in the cloud field. It is a finale not to be denied, shoving through the clouds: *to go out with a bang!*

The year speeds towards a conclusion, the view before him one of the more familiar. Yet it rains down scenes surreal, a real subsidized by creative interpretation. (Or is it the joint that he smokes?) He traipses the perimeter of *Waverly Park:* the gingerbread hung under pitched roof dormers, the gaslit globes as sentinels. The coursing rays frame a squat late-Romanesque era mansion. Eyebrow dormers casting a leery eye. It is all not as it seems. A car motors past. (Or was it horse-drawn carriage?) A dog is barking. (A coyote howling?) The Tudor at the corner could very well be the walled fortress of Old Yorke, a widow's peak on the same block embattlements lined of trebuchet, archers, vats of hot oil at the ready. Besieged by a modernity it does not yet understand—or trust—*Springvale* holds fast. The uniformity of suburbanization, the bigotry behind the blight, gentrification. Modern day barbarians? It's all in the perspective. This old quarter, this *grande old belle....They're pressing our flanks! They're everywhere! Stand your ground, over. For honor, for country!....*And Goodspeed plods through.

Imagination / perspective supersedes a strict interpretation of reality out here, the rhythms of history influencing (fucking with?) the present. It is a thin membrane, but a thin layer of red dirt dusting the shallow burial of artifacts we'd so rather forget and / or deny. But then, those historical frequencies, erupting like sonic booms: cycling, whirling, building-up-speed....BOOM!

"He just couldn't hide forever. Finally caught 'im, poor bastard."

His thoughts are heavy. There is weight to the air itself. The past weighs heavy on this little quadrant of the world. It is never far: slow-blooming like mold in the gaps of flagstone curb, an occasional boiling over as ants in the cracks of hexagonal stone. Unremitting, relentless....

"Comes a time when you tire of running; was just no more run in 'im."

So much past we find irreconcilable with *what's next.* It will run scared, until overtaken: inevitable, a final dying ember. It will stand its ground: a pyrrhic stand before an irresistible tide, and fighting to the last. It will decay slowly without a word: back to the earth that gave it life.... Goodspeed stops before *The Woodruff House* just long enough to pay homage and light a smoke. He notices the growing blooms of mold fouling cornices, rotting siding. He looks to stand his ground. He promises without a word, moves on.

Christmas lights ring the *Heights.* Side streets are constellations. Passing through a maze of festive light on deliberate heavy steps, he turns on Dixie. Grey strands of sky are shot through to the west by one final rose-orange pulse: a sliver of finale, an eye relinquishing its final strobe of life to the grey nothingness. The horizon retracts the day, the year. It will soon belong to the ages. It is dusk.

He walks up the front path to D's front porch, opens screen-door, knocks on front door. He peers in over the dentil detail, opens the door and steps in....

"Babe, ya ready?"

"Ya, in here. Just looking for my wallet, lying 'round here somewhere," Dorothy responding from another room.

"I got tonight, babe; let's get on."

"Don't feel like it, stomach's all tight," D buttoning a sharp blue denim shirt.

"It's the raht thing to do."

"He was no angel, but that whole mess. Some uncalled for bullshit."

"It was bound to end this way. The inevitable always wins out, the bastard."

"Guess it's all we can do," D sighing, pulling back her long thick cinnamon braid, the few distinguished grey strands, donning fringed-leather jacket.

"We'll remember the man as we want to remember 'im."

"That's it, s'pose, what gets me about these things; knowing the parts that are a put-on just to ease the grief, the bullshit. Having to fake it some, y'know? And yet, knowing that's what needs to be done."

"A dose of nostalgia helps get you outta bed in the morning."

"Is that it, hon'? All this time was thinkin' it was my all-world cocksucking that got you up 'n at 'em each day," D's fiery glance, light-scratching his cheek with fingernail.

"Why yes: nostalgia, blowjob, coffee—healthy, wealthy, wise."

"It's the hard soul that can just take the bullshit life dumps at your door, as is; s'pose we can be allowed a little revision after the fact. In fact, think we're due," D straightening out and zipping jacket, looking tired but ready.

"One thing Henry knew all about was *the bullshit*; one too many times, s'all."

The two step onto the front porch. A drizzle has begun to fall, prefacing a return to cold rain. D leans to look up through the screen at the misty murk, pulls out an umbrella. She thinks back a few years to her Uncle John's funeral, how fact and fiction had floated up from the speakers until a thick revisionist cloud hung within the rafters of the church....

"Just thinking, driving pop home from Uncle John John's funeral a few years back, he leans in to tell me: think Uncle Johnny'd be right touched by all 'a that; but sure's hell he's up there shaking his head, snickerin' some over all that rosy stuff."

"It's what we do. A little harmless editing, just helps make for a better story."

"An easier pill to swallow, s'pose. Think we're due that, at least that."

"Nothing like nostalgia to help smooth out the rough spots past. Sometimes ya just want to remember it like ya want to remember it. Fuck all the real."

"Take out all the rough spots, is there anything even left of Henry's life?"

Goodspeed breathes deep and exhales: a silent concurrence. "Well, we'll cobble together something we can all raise glasses to and then can get on to the business at hand."

"It's the raht thing to do."

And they are off to pay homage and be overcome by emotion. They will rattle off *Auld Lang Syne* and toast to the memory of a fallen comrade: a poor sap who hid and then ran and ran and then hid until there was nowhere left to run, nowhere else to hide.... They will all move on, regulars continuing to hide, run, fight to the last. They are world wise. They will be looking over their shoulders with every step: leery, nostalgic. They will look out at the unspooling future ahead: leery, uncompromising. Tonight, the regulars will drown this year's bullshit in hard drink. They will proclaim *Victory!* in the face of the inevitable defeats. Battle tested, these two—arm-in-arm— are ready.

A trumpeter blows *ragged jass*, wailing in silhouette of hole-in-wall windows lit sweating and hot. The party swarms las calles: a head-dress trails to ass-less chaps; street dancing, group groping. It is 10p CST, 12/31/97 (11p EST for our *Beacon* friends). The scene is pleased with itself (pleasuring itself?), rhythmic strokes swelling collectively towards climactic heights. The group spins up *Calle d Borbon:* a whirling tapestry of metal railings, open shutters giving up the half-naked, thumping bass beats penetrating each step. Hari stumbles into Erin, who catches him in a tight embrace. They laugh. They start making out. It hardly attracts a notice from the former cohorts who stumble and laugh. Paint peels from stone foundations, a scene of epic writhing improvisation. *Wash the girl of your choice,* it says, the sin of lust a tangible scent....*Go for it. You know you want to....* It taunts them all. They drop it like a hurricane.

They tack, heading for the square. They pass the trumpeter, lofting loose change into open trumpet case. He sustains a note as they pass. Time, meanwhile, is losing its grip, seconds and minutes falling away. Reality and dream fall into each other, trading lovers' spit, hot and heavy, on this: the final night. Laughing, groping, passionate heat rings Cyrus and Kelly as a radiant glow. Hari and—well, wait now—Erin and Grey providing some tag-team action, Hari now making out with our man Grey; this here, a spicy indigenous dish. The rain has passed, dark wet cobbles warbling neon reflections. Every street corner is a new party. It is hopping. It is bound to get freaky, the lust all-pervasive—groping the aura of Cable, Faulkner, Bechet.

They all pass into the square: necking, groping, singing. The carnival swirls, the general regal and brave....*The Union Must and Shall Be Preserved*.... He wants her and she him. They veer for the spare bedroom at Grey's apartment.

"Hey, ah, meet you beauties back here for the countdown?" Grey locked arm-in-arm with his beaming necking compatriots.

"See ya," Cyrus explaining without explanation.

"Happy New Year!" Kelly confirming, a double arm-wave.

And they are off to do it in tune with the year's end: to come in-unison @ 12:00:00 a.m., 1/1/98, the goal. It will be too much to ask, logistically; a wild orgasmic passion not respectful of on-the-clock efficiency. In the throes they will forget all of the timing. They will let *it* come when it may. They will fall asleep wrapped in each other—in the afterglow—will miss the countdown altogether: *going out with a bang!*

And we are back on Austin, in *Asa's* front room. Plastic flutes of champagne are being hoisted: an extolling—*what should be done, what is right*—a final send-off to one of their own having reasoned his way out with a revolver.... It was the day after Christmas when news came down that Henry had shot himself. His apartment up Washita had been ransacked on Christmas Day, gleaned of everything pawnable—including the title to his car, about the only thing he owned—by his old lady and some half-her-age ex-con she had since run off with. But having been cleaned out of his few material possessions paled to the vindictive shard-pile of the only other thing he owned and truly cared about: the smashed remnants of Henry's complete Johnny Cash collection. This, on discovery, prompting the broken regular to shove a .38 into his mouth and author a conclusion to the only thing he still held control over: a life he was done with.

"Poor bastard. He always said it: she'll be my end; just a matter of which *she* it was gonna be," Goodspeed absolving suicide through the vexed vernacular of a life as trying as Henry's had been: having labored for minimal pay down at South Atlantic Rail off and on for the twenty years that he hadn't been in prison, always hooking up with troubled women who grew increasingly more troubled as the years progressed.

A few cobbled together words from the grand ol' Boo leads to flutes tipped and emptied of their elixir in-memoriam. The resolution of grief proves a resolute thing on this night, in this modest place—bowed paneling showcasing the mold of mis-care, not a lack of love. Sentiment for the brethren is a tangible thing, in here. And so is the cryptic unsolved mystery of hard living. And when they collide, when the fault-lines rupture and consume, it is all they can do to raise a toast and move on.... *Que sera.*

And like that this gala of the gangrel gets underway, drifters all, but for the security of *Asa's* warm hearth. *Home Sweet Home.* A festive gusto (that one might could readily mistake for gumption) powers up. Flutes are emptied and refilled to be emptied again. This is a night like few others. The regulars will give all they have got; for those past, for those present. Mantras are amplified through the sheer act of taking it to excess, heavy thoughts and heavy hearts leaning hard upon the panacea of heavy drink....

The iron grip falls away before the iron will of the new year. It is coming on *Asa's* like a freight train; but will be treated like all others: with indifference, lackadaisical contempt at best. Champagne, domestic lager, and lit cigarettes summon the reveling regulars to hands-on-shoulders, a few tears shed—which summarily break into laughter fits, wrestling matches, liquor shots. Boo and Chuck lead *Auld Lang Syne*, Paul's slurred chorus more akin to *row, row your boat*. The cool Ez and Jude, arm-in-arm, cracking grins, killing off George Dickel. Omar and Marjorie have found a motel room less than spontaneous, doing the deed in a back-room booth. Victor doesn't even notice, wheeling and dealing the pinball machine's bells and bumpers and whistles. A hard ker'chunking showcases his devotion, his desire for high score—doing all he can do. A stool falls over. Gid dumps a beer on Paul's head, its attempt to drown out his singing unsuccessful. Dorothy is biting Goodspeed's ear: tangible tough love. The seconds count down, Howard and Martha and Olivia wheeling out elixirs as magicians producing coins in empty palms. Catcalls and caterwauls, the joy of reckless excess. And the line at the bar stands and sways as one: *eat, drink, be merry, for tomorrow we—ah, to hell with tomorrow!* Huzzahs! Rebel yells! The reflections of regulars melting into the line of bottlefronts along bar back wall, a canonical aura ladled over the room like a preservative. This moment, one for the ages....

And the front door opens. And in steps George. And he calls out Goodspeed's name. And heads turn. Goodspeed turns his head, sights the invader: *down here! in here!* Blood rushes his eyeballs. George draws a stolen Glock and fires at Goodspeed through the crowd. Three shots. Paul goes down. Goodspeed is knocked clean off the stool, crashing against the back wall. Seconds are an eternity.... And George is swallowed in a swarm of fists.

Dorothy's maniacal curse slices the freeze-frame moment. Howard vaults the bar, palms at his forehead. Regulars are beating George into an unrecognizable pulp, the gun having been quickly torn from his grasp and in Pete's hand, his own revolver drawn. Omar, pants half-off, stumbles in from the backroom, hands out, triage-ing Goodspeed....

"Son of a—fuck! Alright! Okay! Outta my way, let me see this. Collarbone is broke, but it's a clean-through. Alright, okay, just got to control the bleedin'—uh—Sax c'mere, right here and immobilize his shoulders, collarbone's all fucked up. Marge, help, uh, okay, just help me lay him out," Omar, having been a medic (with the 173rd Airborne @ fucking *Dak To*, y'all), kicking in muscle memory. "Marv! Can ya hear me? Just look at me. Focus on my face. Do—not—black out. Marge, talk to him for me; get him to talking, if ya can."

Marge, skirt half-off, is imploring Goodspeed to focus on her hand, which she holds up before his face. Omar is now at Paul's side, inspects the bullet having grazed the right side of his head; an actual bloody groove, the same bullet having ripped through Goodspeed's upper-torso.

Amazingly, the other two shots hit no one: one puncturing Martha's favorite stew pot resting on a shelf in the kitchen, the other having defiled Daisy Duke's denim-clad left tit: a neat clean hole in the moldering *Dukes of Hazzard* calendar hanging at bar's end—there, where it has hung since 1981, as if it still were....

Dorothy is primal screaming as she kicks George's limp body. No one in the swarm has backed off the vicious beating. His face is unrecognizable. It is bloody meat. His name will not be mentioned within these walls again. It will be law. Howard will declare it so.

Pete is finally able to muscle through and drag the unconscious defiler off through the front-door by his feet, regulars getting in final kicks—Ez and Jude both required to hold back the wrathful D. On the sidewalk, Pete rolls the perp onto his front (doing so with highlander game log-rolling zeal), handcuffs the defiler with shoulder-separating disregard. Bid and Laverne are 30 seconds out, the paramedics only a few minutes behind. And it is a good thing: Goodspeed is coming-to through the diffusion of shock, the first pangs like a red-hot poker. A long low demonic scream....

And like that, the night has turned. But oddly, this unexpected twist doesn't seem entirely out of place. Sure, *the unforeseen* is rarely a welcome guest, in here. But then, in a place where the maintenance of things as they are is so very prized, why would it be?....And yet, here it is, not to be denied, its shoving-through-crowds demeanor indicating that *the unforeseen* is here whether they like it or not. *It* has fought to be noticed, recognized, as out of a sense a duty, of self-determination, clawing at the right to its own unique permanence and place. In that light, *it* could even be seen as a natural fit. Fighting for the sake of honor and duty? Fighting like demons though the odds be long against you? How does this not sound like *it* belongs? How is this incendiary scene anything but another of the roaring patrons stunned into hot blank stares, hands-on-heads-shaking, their wild vile vitriolic strings of fearful loathing hate being heaped atop the now (per Howard's law) nameless motherfucker who dared desecrate the order?

No....no....this here is different. It points at another way: the eventual necessity to leave certain traditions behind. As difficult (as in moral-fibre-like) as that may seem, such a radical departure from *the norm* seems more and more, well....the norm. This here fades towards an unconsidered alternative. What could have been considered crazy talk but a few moments before now seems to have legs as a general theory, that being: the harder you cling to the past in the present, the harder *the unforeseen future* will leech your ability to maintain any such thing.

And so, to accept the new, the evolving, the different? To simply accept what is, whatever what is....*is?* Such foreign ideas will be held in the crosshairs of a squint-eye or two, for sure. But then, in keeping an eye on the regular's prize, such strategies as: 1) holding pat out of inertia, 2) fighting to the last to hold on to ways well past their sell-by date, 3) ignoring nature's resolute, if indifferent, flanking maneuvers until it is too late....in lieu of our unfolding portrait of this here *New—Newer—South*, all such time-honored traditions would seem an epic waste of one's own time. In the end, these customs—passed down through generations to this generation as things that were unquestionable truths simply because an elder era claimed they were so—all that any of these customs, traditions, ways, banal and antiquated and appalling alike, can now promise is the onset of slow sure oblivion regardless of how righteous the claim.

And that is when we catch a whiff, or more accurately huff deep into our lungs the fumes of irony that our aforementioned trowels have so painstakingly excavated rising up like an olfactory phoenix as from the ash heap of history itself, in that having allowed someone, something—*anything*—other than one's own damned self to dictate how one might waste one's own time? Well, that's like losing *the cause* all over again....

11:59:57 — 11:59:58 — 11:59:59 — 12:00:00 —

*Happy New Year!* ~

ROMANTICS OF THE APPALLING

KEEN RAYS BURN FOG, *a gold orange steam. The tree limb lattice overhead grates the sky beyond, mid-Winter steel-laced of drifting vapor trails jet-setting, their regrets to a past fretting over a future it does not care to understand. But then, that is its tired song to sing, the day's more aspiring tints serving a summons to Spring....And while some things will change, some things will remain as they ever were.... The hard light sears the frost and is in-carom off bus windows, the distant glass of skyscraping towers. Beneath the gleam of this new day rising, one might claim to perceive a contemptible grin glaring down as it will from behind said high-story walls, glowering upon the late twentieth-century sharecroppers then scuttling along city avenue and parkway connector. One might look to see these temples of glass and steel—the prosaic pagodas of progress!—towering in the distance and scanning, with voracity, their metro fiefdom. For each dawn the mill-whistles bray, goading the various villages forth. 'Deliverance through the salve of work-a-day devotion,' they say. 'To betray our benevolence an affront that will require a waving of the bloody shirt!'....Dour banal defeated: the drones of the prophets of profit. Ragged brusque defiant, the Regular growls: 'Don't tread on me.' Middle fingers unfurl within gridlock, our man's unfurled as a crest. Herein lay his test.*

*Let's put this thing to rest.*

HE SHIFTS, HE WINCES, Goodspeed's new year having begun with an operation to pin his shattered clavicle. *(Oh, be joyful!)* He simmers with the thought of it all: upper-body and right arm in a binding sling, having to sleep bolt upright in a chair to deter side-to-side movement. Mornings are the worst, a test interrupting all attempts at rest.

"Fuck you," he mutters through a grimace, stewing over the unwelcome return of his persistent reviled nemesis: *Mr. Electric Pain.*

"Ain't got the best of me, fucker," despite strong evidence to the contrary, re: the wincing—*and*—trace hints of uncertainty about a defiant instinct perhaps less convinced of its own supremacy than it once was....

The year-of-our-Lord, 1998, had settled into its new digs. It had brought with it that 'not so welcome' change. Hand-in-hand with the mentioned nemesis (having updated his list of heart-felt hates for '98), it set to strutting about in full view of the squint-eye glares falling upon it. And though our man was able to fend off the invaders for a piece, this thanks to a previously unconsidered ally in the fight: *Mr. Morphine Tablet*, the masterful strokes and sheer audacity of the flanking maneuvers that typified this alliance proved short-lived, proved subject to a reality overwhelming audacity via vast innate resources. Goodspeed had gone for quick-strike victories in what proved a long total war, exhausting two months of pills (and the ability to withstand pain's war of attrition) by January 17....

"Damn, could go for one of those triple dose days 'bout now."

Dorothy made it clear to the prescribing doctor the imperative of supervised ingestion of medications, to which the Doc had responded: "Yes, I understand just by looking at him." D'd taken over the once Pez®-like dispensing of narcotics since January 17, having eased the tough love by taking Goodspeed to Saint Augustine to recuperate: warm Winter sun, seafood buffets, drive-on beaches. It was a solid plan—but for an interminable f-ing drought.... The seasonal rains that had drained with normalcy across the Deep South had skipped north of Florida. The state's pitch-soaked pine forests stood as thousand-acre matchbooks, a lit butt all an aspiring brushfire would need to become a monster (the odds of such careless flicking a gambling man's bet, billboards hawking the *Sunshine State's* cigarette outlets starting 50 miles north of its border). The suspected culprit was making a mess of paradise.

D and Goodspeed had arrived in town under what set up as your run-of-the-mill overcast skies. Thinking nothing of it, they'd settled into a façade-burdened

Spanish Renaissance just down from the old fort. The next day, the sky smeared to charcoal and they were made wise to several massive forest fires then tearing across state and national forests mid-north state. At first, it was just another novelty: one more eyebrow cocked in a town flaunting historical authenticity and low-brow kitsch as if nature itself could divine no more pure a pairing. But by day three, the smoke clouds were so complete that it all had the feel of a storm brewing dusk at mid-day. You could taste the ash on the air. With rain chances nil and the fires spreading, they gave up and headed north for the coastal islands.

"What bullshit; of all the luck."

"Bullshit's on my trail, babe. It's a package deal. Didn't ya scan the fine-print before hitching your wagon to this here star?"

"I wrote the fine-print there, super star. We'll just head up the coast till we get sun, rent a beach house," Dorothy improvising Plan B, the headlights of the *7 Series* BMW Goodspeed had recently bought her struggling to penetrate the ash-murk.

"Super star. That's a good one."

Following the mis-start, the islands proved just the thing. The low white noise of crashing waves and sharp salt air helped kill worry, time. They weren't necessarily a replacement for *Mr.* unregulated *Morphine Tablet.* ("I'm gonna miss ya, friend.") But *Mr. domestic-in-a-bottle* and the scene had stepped up to subsidize the physical and mental repair: midnights under moonlight, the smear of galaxy daubs, pelicans caught in updrafts. What was this tempting thing called *peace?* One buxom painted mistress, for sure....

"You beautiful whore, you."

Sunrise they had rarely missed: crimson, blue, cool with the season. For days and then weeks, Goodspeed sat on the beach (bolt upright, of course) and stared out to sea. Sailboats, cutters, trawlers. He watched the giant freighters inch their way out the shipping lane: slow, deliberate, rusted monsters of salt-stained metal, containers by the cord on deck. The scene set his mind at ease. (Or was it the pot that he smoked?) Making peace with past, present, future, such an odd, irritating, yet somehow possible outcome. He had watched the freighters shrink, fade and fall off the edge of the earth, would ruminate on a mariner's life, the delirious repetition: the weeks and months of the same pitching sea, the tedium. *Rum, sodomy and the lash* had been Churchill's take....

"I'll take the rum, can keep yer S&M," Goodspeed divining the true oceanic purpose of the lash.

But then, sand-in-shorts philosophy was only to get him so far. His own sense of tedium began to wear the scene thin. Within the staccato bursts of peace he sensed a ruse, some unstated disingenuous contrivance curled up in the dimples of its wry sidling grin. It was a nice peaceful drive in the country, till a meet-up with the muscle produced Tommy Guns and the nice neat disposal of your little rebellion. Yes, there was a hidden agenda here—and certainly not of one's own creation / delusion. He found himself increasingly simmering away bursts of peace: leery, needing to get back in the game. It was duty calling, a benchmark for this coastal rejuvenation; for he'd begun to crave *home* again. D, working our man's emotional status with aplomb....

"I know my man can only sit for so long; and that is a good thing. Get him edgy, keep him there. I need him to get back on it. Got a franchise to see to here."

Time was re-setting the old collarbone, the mesmerizing mass of waves having re-set the mental buttress girding devotion, duty. It was time to look homeward: *for the cause!* And though Wolfe claimed that you can't go home again, perhaps that is not always the case. Especially if you never truly left the place....

Vaulted rays bend. They cast this new day in a new light. It is his first morning back. He is gearing up, is back in the saddle. Having done the preparatory work (having updated *the list*) he is working to regain his stamina, bootstrapping back up to fighting strength. He must apply himself, regain his searing focus—give his all. He is not there yet, is feeling soft. *Buck up!* He must reconstruct the frame, drop into that bloody breach between those being screwed and those doing the screwing. He will redeem the dreams and the dignity of those long downtrodden souls living simply because they are not yet dead, living because others have affixed a price to their toss-away lives. Those bastards, they short-sell the living and breathing for exclusive *Gilded* returns. And he knows (*oh, he does!*) that he is in their crosshairs, that they are conspiring to crush him. For they can see—beady-eyed plutocrats, all—that our man's one-man rebellion, his reconstructing and redeeming, could yet bloom into a brandishing of pitchforks, a storming of the Bastilles of *progress!*....It is a daunting task, this reconstructing, this storming; if only in words. Is Goodspeed up to said task? It is mid-Winter, early February; he thinks. He is not entirely sure. He has not known nor cared enough to know the date since being shot, having realized after the fact, to his giddy satisfaction, that without even trying he'd given time the slip....*Take that, time, you dick!*

Goodspeed observes the "mad doings" from his restive cockpit: *Delta Point Park* empty but for Goodspeed. *Mr. Electric Pain* and the homespun exploitative masque of *moonlight and magnolias* are just two of the bullet points right then firing his boilers. Building up steam. Hard be this freedom work. He must regain focus, stamina, strength. He is not there yet. *Focus, focus!* He applies himself: takes a healthy drag from a cigarette and unscrews the top to his bourbon breakfast. (*Take that, dick!*) The mandarin rays in-carom off the windows of a passing bus blind the lazy observer to its true intent. Belching black-blue exhaust, shuttling off those interred within to the modern-day mills—the newest of the *New South* lies. The machine's whistles bray, calling the chattel forth. He watches it all unfold from park bench: his command-and-control centre in the field. He shakes his head in honest pity, this slow-moving disaster, sighting the scampering along city avenue through squint-eye slits. He projects solemn misery on all of this seething "responsible-ness," all of this time wasting on behalf of the schemes and the treachery of others who would just as soon sell-out their own bloodkin for one dollar more as they would breath the villainous air....

And as the modern-day horde of lint-heads pile out to build up the fortunes of others, his slow boil—208° / 209° / 210° / 211°—spit-whistles its own shrill cry. A battlecry? *A Rebel Yell?* Vibrating every fibre of his being, here is our caustic foot soldier of *the cause*. Another drag, another shot.... *He is back, baby!*

"All these poor suckers. Look at 'em, doing what they's told is right; the starring role in their own sad demise."

> In this strange and savage hunger....spoken of as a better life, a greater city, in this delirium of intoxication which drove them on, there was really a fatal and desperate quality, as if what they hungered for was ruin and death.

> Thomas Wolfe ~ *Boom Town*

Though distant, rush-hour can still be heard stewing along the connector. Traffic-copters eddy overhead, hovering as flies atop roadkill. They broadcast the mayhem that breadwinning has driven us to....*Folks, you thought yesterday's commute was bad? Sad to say it will prove a cakewalk compared to the mess we have on the parkway connector this morning. We have an accident involving a tanker truck that is currently blocking up everything; all inbound traffic is being diverted onto the shoulder. Every surface road and exit ramp from here to the horizon looks like an exodus. You can put a fork in this rush-hour, folks. It is done....*

Goodspeed sits a whole neighborhood away, but can still sense the idle angst of gridlock. It prods his smoldering contempt. He sights a distant traffic-copter: index finger a barrel, thumb the hammer, he shoots it out of the sky with his *hand gun*.... His thoughts spin round the alkaline distaste of recollections fused to his days spent mired within *the machine:* plodding through the stifled hours, the in-box's mountain, the out-box's molehill—the damned *man*.... But the past has its place, Goodspeed conveniently filing his under *inconsequence*. (Or so he'd have us think.)

A sharp shoulder spasm and a wave of dull pain in its wake reminds him of all the fun that he'd had on New Year's Eve. "In lieu of a hole in the ground, s'pose"....

"Was lookin' to kill ya, Marv. It was pre-meditated. Glock was reported stolen the night before New Years by that dude's employer, was workin' at some frame alignment shop down on the southside. He must of thought it out, knew he could nab that piece; convicted felon, couldn't just buy a gun," Trey had said while getting the Regular's statement in-hospital.

"Uptight asshole, couldn't take his beating like a man."

"Two inches to your left, Marv, that bullet catches you in the carotid, woulda' bled ya out in a minute."

"Thanks for the elaboration, son. Ya can leave the flowers by the door," Goodspeed thinking back on the bullshit recently remedied by sand-in-shoes, marijuana....*peace?*

Outlook rectified, suffering his updated honor roll of hates just fine, such leaden thoughts are rendered as foreign to him as Afghanistan or Sierra Leone. The sun sears frost. Home again. *Duty* calling.

And it should be mentioned, a deal was finally sealed on *Within*. It should be out by the Summer: a 50K hardcover run. Dorothy had spent the bulk of the "Goodspeed beach party" on the phone with editors, publishers, other lawyers. The deal had gone down, the two (as incentive) having worked out their own deal: a brand spanking new BM'er, D's choice. She had picked the *Silver 7*. He finds it a middle-of-the-road deal, what with her handling the bullshit business end of things Goodspeed so "manfully" avoids. It's a tag-team effort, they are in it to win it—or else. (Or, so they'd like us to think, re: the love evident.) They have their roles. He is back to doing what he does: *fighting for—defending—freedom.*

He scowls at the surface-road rush hour on Edgewood before him. Two cars try to beat each other through a four-way: brakes biting the road, horns cursing, both speeding off.

"Just look what it's driving 'em to? Slavery by another name."

The scattered irritants, the trials of this *freedom defender.* He must regain his focus. For the bastards are regrouping. The work of revolution, it begins anew each day....and yet, there is a wrinkle: the unsettling sense that all which was once set-in-stone, lofted atop marble obelisks that will come down in time as will all myths past and present, that all of this may be no more than a parchment pact subject to the torch. That even *the status quo* could go up in flames? He unscrews the cap to his personal vaccine, the swig washing down his throat with a burn. Taking one last drag, he flicks the butt, recaps the flask, stands and aims steps for *The Ashlands* (what's left of it). It's a perfect morning, he thinks. It is, at the very least, another morning.

Having powered his way up to *The Points* and having deposited his quarterly check into the "freedom fund," Goodspeed has reversed course and made haste. *The*

*Ashlands* and Alta pass. *The field parks* sparkle, fired glaze under rays long with Winter. He cannot resist, veers into the plot of a past erased. The frosted grass and vines crunch beneath his feet, the easy hues. This, this here he'd missed, this here home of his. And yet, the *peace* it has to offer: the weight of a haunted past, discomfited and ashamed, though not yet provisioned with the collective nutrients required for a regional confession of sins. It is not yet ready to starve out the past's disproportionate hold on the present, continuing its blockade-running exploits on behalf of besieged anachronisms that still, to this day, harass the present and repress the future with history: the exclusive economic distortions that resulted of a *Gilded progress!*, the lynchings, the slavery legislated through the criminal code, the actual slavery, our fucked-up bullshit Civil War. ("Now, peace? Don't you mess with me, hear?")

No thought. Vacate the mind of worry. No worry, not on this morning. Goodspeed loops up through *the field parks* to Austin Avenue, turns, aims steps for Elizabeth Street. Always a lady, the street will not disappoint Squirrels scatter before his steps: random, spastic. A shoulder spasm. He winces, the occasional encore from *Mr. Electric Pain....*

"Asshole!"

Goodspeed, with his free hand, unscrews the flask cap and takes a slug of *Mr. Morning Breakfast*. (Tastes like *freedom!*) He is already making his way down Elizabeth and is turning on Euclid in heading for *The Long Acres*, mandarin rays....*peace?*....Goodspeed thinks back on the first hours of New Year's Day, laying prone and staring at the overhead lights in the back of the ambulance as it whisked him off to the ER. He thinks back on how strangely satisfied he'd felt with the whole situation: his view clustered of IV racks, a pinging monitor, paramedics checking vitals and encouraging our good Regular...."We're doing good, guy, doing good; just hang in there, hear?" He remembers flashing them the V in response. Everything would sway as the ambulance rounded curves; a satisfying surreality to it all. It was, oddly, warm and comfortable: a mood, a sense without contradiction, without conflict. He is not sure that he's ever felt more *free*. Maybe it was just the loss of blood, but he thinks that maybe—*just maybe*—what he felt was *peace*.

He pulls out a cigarette and lights it, all with his free hand. A shoulder spasm. An electric strike. He winces, curses, simmers. But enough with all that peace business. For there is a war to fight, a war for and against *the status quo*. It is a contradictory friction that produces its own strain of high-test fuel, a tradition of self-fighting-self that spins turbines enough to light this fight for years to come. And though you would think that you can't have it both ways, there it is: the deafening roar that sets up as the backdrop to his daily war. No man's land awaits. The whistle blows. Our man goes over the top.

FROM KELLY'S KITCHEN WINDOW, Cyrus sights a rankled horde of the responsible stewing along DeKalb Avenue. It seems more irked than usual. The second-floor apartment of this c. 1920s duplex serves up a sidling view of the main *Candler Hills* intersection: DeKalb and Highland. A cold morning comes to, the rush-hour fuming. It is a mad angry dash going nowhere fast: carhorns, the hurry, the wait, a collective caffeinated blood pressure boiling over in the push to beat out yellow lights. A parkway wreck is always the culprit, commuters pouring out onto surface streets. Cyrus slugs coffee, satisfied to watch the mess from a distance.

"The responsible hordes, look what it's driving 'em to. The Beats: unemployed, poor, free of the machine—were they onto something?" Cyrus, plumbing his first deep thought of the day. "Of course, being a slave to your junk, dying depressed, bloated, and drunk. Hey, that was pretty good!" Pulling out his well-worn D6C (gifted to him by Lacy out of the flotsam left behind by Lane), Cyrus records the morning's first *brilliant* stroke.

Cloudlines edge buildingtops, a cold fluid day lighting up the mess below. He takes another slug, peers out at the seething mob. An expression like that of smelling a fart not your own crowds his face. A motorist tries to squeeze out one more car-length from a red light, is hit by another gunning the first hint of green: a fender-bending mash-up. Fists shake, middle-fingers. Cyrus shakes his head.

"Goodspeed: gainfully self-employed, momentarily loaded, free of the machine—is he onto something?" Perhaps; and if only in leveraging the staying power (and ironic capitalist profit model) of a robust populist rancor put to use. Cleburne strokes the rudimentary van dyke he is taking for a test-drive. "Of course, there's the whole slave to your junk, and all."

For there are always the contradictions to consider, out here. And sure, dropping such common sense in the midst of so rigorous a scholarly pursuit, and calling it *wise*, may be akin to taking a victory lap after an uncontested layup. (To which, dear reader, we could riposte: since when did celebrating an easy victory become a crime, eh?)

But no matter. We can agree that if a human is in the mix there is likely to be such a reckoning, if only as a matter of course. Okay, noted.... However, if the course of our study has shown us one thing it is this: predictable fronts cloud over out here—*down here*—with a shade more urgency. The cycling banshee scream of tornado sirens betrays an instinct: the parallax of lying to ourselves and all those within earshot while, oblivious, the b-roll of a brute cultural honesty scrolls across the backdrop. One could call out hypocrisy, but that would imply conscious manipulation, which in turn lays planks for an even more mysterious explanation. For there is a well-worn phrase that goes something like this: "It's just how things have always been done." Mysterious, strange, the untouchable honor of tradition saving present and future from *the puny inadequacies of fact*.... And all of this could suffice as a nice neat cultural op-ed, but for a few dissonant notes ringing in the backdrop distant: 1) how to reconcile all those who failed to benefit a lick from lily-white tradition (were in fact, in the crosshairs of *tradition*), and, of course, this head-scratcher: 2) the conscious engineering of tradition's irreconcilables to one's advantage. The latter may yet prove a kind of genius lurking within the cackling weeds of all of this deep-fried weirdness: a romantic trafficking in narcotic lies.... Gumption at the ready, does Cyrus have what it takes to punch this thing home?

Kelly emerges, pours coffee: milk + sugar. She shuffles over and sits down on the couch. Consciousness @ 50%, she smiles automatically.

"Maybe we forget all this responsible work-a-day stuff, Kel. Go *On The Road*—'er better, form a band—and hit the road!" Cyrus spot-scheming, caffeine raising a cloud of enthusiasm more geared for a time better later than early.

"You don't have a musical bone in your body," Kelly yawning, real world dosing.

"True, but all we need is a stoked go-for-the-throat marketing team to score a hit these days, right?"

"Okay. Can I wake up first, before the world tour?" stretching, folding legs up under seat, coffee regular.

"Right, best stick to the task at hand. And look at the time; got to get on with my research."

"Still not sold on the beard thing, by the way."

Cyrus strokes his thin-whiskered chin with a grin, absorbs the critique. Recorder returned to inner coat pocket, backpack full of gear, metal thermal to-go cup, he is off to get on with *his* thing. He lays on a deep kiss, a quick morning make-out on his way out. Still electric: firefly eyes. These two, getting on with *their* thing

It is ten minutes later. Cyrus stands in the square of *The Points* out front of *The Weekly's* office. The drum circles and whirling girls have moved on with the season. The alleyway drug deals continue. He is alone, but for the world whistling past. Add'l poetic license could include: wind rustling dead leaves / discarded sheets of newspaper scratching past. (And please, feel free to add your own, dear reader....*j'ine the fun!*) The gridlocked peak of rush hour sans-connector-accident has started to ease. Still, a busyness circles him: fleet vans delivering, buses unloading, uploading, the responsible out in force. Delving deep into a particular populist disdain for all this "senseless scampering," Cyrus has scraped and brushed with respectful care about the potsherd edges of character having revealed themselves. But it is painstaking work.

Does he have what it takes? He takes regular slugs from the to-go mug. (Coffee regular, hold the bourbon. Observation and evaluation, less the hangover.) Can he pull this thing off? He is hard at work processing, scanning for the clues that he's been told—again and again—are all around: lying about like *lazy popes* within plain view of the eyes and the imagination that cares to critically question "what is really going on here?!" He looks at his watch: 8:54 a.m. He performs a thorough dutiful scan of the scene. It looks like rush-hour to him. And so, it seems fair to ask: Does he have the ability to think outside-the-box? Does he have the stones? The fight, he's been told—again and again—begins anew each and every morning. And yet it looks like just another morning, which would seem to indicate the need for a tactical shift. To break this stalemate of imagination, perhaps it is time to widen the aperture, consider more fully that core reality: *What of the myth?*

"Yes, what of it, chump?"

The lights turn green. Traffic races up the avenue on this Winter's day, smoking nerves interred within the fray.

*Stand before the prophet of big enterprise, make it your idol and pray, watching from deep in the bowels of utility as the duped all drown in the day.*

*For it is another day and another dollar's worth of cheap lives to be bled, all in the name "freedom" and "progress!" and the poor suckers' toiling dread.*

*To the work-a-day folk this work-a-day ruse alleged the liberty they crave, yet the fine-print reveals the simple padding of rolls: big bossmen, overseers and slaves.*

*And yet, each morning those indebted and duped shove off to survive the commute; their dreams of freedom draining despair, a morose mass falling mute.*

*But then from within a lone voice calls out: "the homicide of time, s'all," these captains of industry and their redolent lies driving them all to the wall....*

*Driving them to the wall, y'all.*

Marvin Goodspeed  ~  *Within*


CROWS CACKLE AND CAW, a murder of two. *(For joy!)* Cyrus Cleburne is sitting on a bench in *Waverly Park*, lakeside. He is replaying the recent past, dilating on a refractory future still laying about his head in pieces-parts. He is revising his plan of attack, sending up flares in an attempt to see what should be in "plain view." He aims to drop a few long-tailed sparks—*zig-zag-flicker-sizzle*—into the fireworks factory of possibilities. Is he about to ignite a wondrous show? An expensive fuck-it-all flame out?

"Got to square the myth with the man—hmmm."

A warm afternoon infers the equinox but a month distant. It looks like Winter. It does not at the moment feel like Winter. It is and is not what it seems.... Cyrus is right then sensing that he has exhausted the usefulness of field research. His trowel he has worn to a nub. Having amassed a *Lookout Mountain's* worth of notes and dozens of cassettes strewn of thoughts and bad field-recordings documenting *the man* in the flesh, he has come to see that he was documenting much more.... A dearth of imagination, was all; for it was all in plain view. This here a subject not so much to be studied, as an attitude to be felt, its visceral blows absorbed. He was standing up to his neck in it the whole time.

Cyrus has put in the miles, having exhumed enough shallow graves to verify the violent ends that a dutiful defense of *the status quo* can induce. Be it a collective commitment *(for country!)* or an individual doing one's duty *(for honor!)*, its smoking—if proud—wreckage has come to color our study's impressionist take on what IS worth fighting for.... No, our good journalist did not need the inebriated miles strode (stumbled?) in the duct-taped shoes of his subject to see all of this; but only the harvesting of a single kernel of counsel from our good Regular. "See through to things as they *really* are," he'd said.... Indeed.

But a curiosity is still rattling about the ol' brain case (let us call it *sober* reflection), that being: Did the Regular scatter just enough breadcrumbs to mark a trail? "Do the legwork," he'd said....

"You are free to do your own thing, chump, just s'long as you and everyone else stays the hell out of the way of me doin' mine, hear?"

For the Regular's thing is his own thing: a right (a birth-right, even) that no high-flying moral certitude, or governmental decree, or yellow dog culture and arts rag is gonna impinge upon. Besides, there is no way to fully know the carnage of a mental combat not your own. There was no insight to be gained by play-acting *the drunk*, only the loss of self (a capital offense, out here, lest we forget).

Cyrus had not been prepared for the masochism, the violence to body and mind. It was in the process of stringing up a living corpse when he wisely, with aid of a right-square kick in the ass, quit it. ("His thing, not your thing. And until you get that, there is no *our* thing!") Cyrus had no business trying to leverage the physical defeat of addiction in duty to some larger symbolic victory. No, Goodspeed's commitment—*his thing*—is all his own. Cyrus Cleburne's is to be something else entire....

"An authenticity test," he is now convinced. And in review, a single piece of evidence seems to make the case: He did escape that first meeting sans violence to the head-and-neck area, hadn't he? (C'mon, people, that is certainly reserved for a higher degree of chump, eh?) In an instant, Goodspeed had sussed out the scene and the fresh-faced dupe in his midst as potentially useful, offering him a single out. In this frame: "do the legwork / do your worst, chump" actually comes off as some kind of challenge.... And so (revisiting that recent past), if our good journalist was to lace up the concrete shoes and drown the originality, ergo the authenticity of his own idea, in the bottom of a bottle, then our good Regular had his answer: an unoriginal bottom-feeder copping someone else's lick. If this Cleburne cat was anything but all in on *his own cause*, then "good riddance, scalawag."....But suppose for an instant that this interloper with a spot-specific line of inquiry was setting out on his own course, then maybe— *maybe*—it was something Goodspeed could work to his advantage. "Do the legwork"....

"Indeed."

Which brings us back to this urban park on an unseasonably warm Winter's day and this here bench upon which the mentioned dilating is straining to wrangle and coax and forge rebar enough to support this wobbly tower of speculation. It is no small task, residing as it does atop the swampy DMZ spread out between real and *myth*, and knowing the ardent squint-eye conviction by which honor, pride, *tradition,* will lay claim to the former....

"Yes sir, this dog'll hunt."

A WEEK HAS PASSED. Cyrus Cleburne is sitting on a bench in *Waverly Park*, lakeside. He gathers the collar of pea coat up around his neck. Winter's bitter return is just like that old thespian: zigging when thee doth expect a zag. It is of no matter, this lakeside bench-sitting not about comfort, but about stitching together pieces-parts, working this dog up to hunting shape. Such minor inconveniences as it being stupid fucking cold exactly one week to the day from mid-Winter's Spring-tease irrelevant to the task at hand: *the cause, his cause....*

And on that, the latest: Our good journalist has honed in on *the myth*, realizing that this might be, in fact, the bulk of what he has documented to date. For what is the chief ingredient of our public-facing mug but *the myth* of ourselves we wish to project (foist?) on the world at large? Yes, it yields a significant haul; hand-over-fist, at points. Still, as a *good* journalist he must turn over the mythic runes and see what slithers out; and if only to substantiate suspicions plucked from the shadows of observations of the man. For the flares are revealing several cause-and-effects still unaccounted for. And methinks within the substrate of *myth* lies *the man.*

Cyrus is not yet sure if all of this is leading towards a

simple recalibration of his study, or a hard re-boot. Is it time to run it all through once again? And if so, perhaps now is the time to revisit *the environment* hosting both *man* and *myth?*

"Indeed."

Water oaks hook gnarled limbs over his seat, arthritic hands espousing the hard wisdom of this place: *Springvale*, this *grand old belle* holding fast, having seen it all first-hand. Cyrus stands and exits the park. He makes his way up to Elizabeth. He turns south, heads for the tracks. The mansions of Elizabeth give way to its old servant district: a tract of shotguns lined up along Memorial Avenue just north of the railroad. Having once housed the freed slaves of the *New South* aristocracy—hovel-ing as north of the tracks as the "redeemed" white folk would allow—these symbols of surviving in the face of brutal institutional defeat are now being sold as niche renovations for "creative folks." Change is in the air, not so much seasonal at the moment as demographic. What of these forays into gentrification? Pioneers yield settlers, if the land allows. Will it? Or more to the point of our study: will those pioneers having dropped roots, out here, and deep within the urban frontier, have any say? Cyrus pushes a swift pace through *Shotgun Row*, attempting to combat outside chill with inner-warmth; and this, as outside forces idle just off-stage. For better or worse, they are set to define the future of this stoic 'hood. A few of these simple shacks have already given up the ghost, porches and moss-laden roofs caving beneath the undertow of feral ivy and kudzu. The guidons of *renovation + restoration = renewal* have been hauled down, the hurricane flags sent up in their place warning of gale forces hovering at the gates....

"I don't want to see nothin' of the suburban fat roll reversing course, in-fillin' prime lots with their cheap-crap hip condos and McMansions," a certain Regular has said.

What will the bulldozer have to say about all of this? What of the successful pioneering, the initial forays of said "creative folk" into this down—but by no means out—urban 'hood? There is change in the air. (Is there ever not?) Is it a recalibration, or a hard re-boot?

"Each and every morning it begins again," like a CD on repeat. Cyrus starts here with each park-bench mull over, every stroll about re-examination. Sifting the evidence: the soul-robbed wraiths of suburban vanilla v. a tradition confounding urban diversity. *(Southerners all, y'all.)* Is this multi-hued *Newest New South* a certainty, or just preceding the latest re-stratification of white wealth gentrification? (Again, with the impressive descriptors ending in *-tion!*) If this here be a *Gilded Age* reprise, is the best counter-strategy really fist to palm *Populism?* This, keeping in mind that the 1890s version was crushed by the goon squads of *the status quo.* (Oh, and let us not forget the racism, the howling, tick-tight racism.... ) Yes, the CD—skip-skip-skipping. But what drove *our man* so relentlessly to *this myth?*

*Progress!* hangs along the rim, spiraling up, hovering triumphantly over downtown. Yes, okay, he gets all that: relentlessly beating the air with the theories and the vitriol and all of that "booster-based barking of the chambers of commerce having camouflaged the flotsam spreading about in its shadows." But then Goodspeed seems one not inclined to instinctually give a shit about much. So then, why did he ever take it on himself to give a shit about this?

*Myths:* often enough born of a reaction to a reality not living up to the expectations of a previously considered present and future. *This myth:* a symptom of the ills of the man?

"Hmmmm...."

All of which brings us back to *Springvale.* Out here, where the outsiders and mavericks and the "not whites" kept the home fires burning amidst the rigor mortis of sanctioned legislated societal failure. An island of independence having separated itself from the *normal* urban present (re: dilapidated ring of blight), while having told the future (re: a burgeoning suburbia) to go fuck itself. For out here on the urban fringe, time is hailed only in its defeat. "Normal" will founder in this reservoir of the offbeat, enticing all: *You're one of us at heart....* But for how much longer? What of the Regular's squint-eye forecast? Is it to be a future driven by future, or the lead edge of the next great whitewash? What of this gentrification? Hmmmm....

WITH WINTER'S WANE comes the refrains of rebirth: *Sing! Sing! Sing!* The northerly invasion of hard seasonal terms has retreated, is tail between its legs—a warm southerly charm having redeemed its dominion. Pregnant winds stroke swelling branch-ends; neon green shoots: a landed lime mist. Skies so recently soaked of taupe-drear pour a tumbling warmth. Songbirds let fly: *I'm in the mood for love, simply because you're near me*—i.e. let's get busy! The rollicking restlessness of *Spring! Spring! Spring!*

March marches through this district of the strange, a

heady anticipation the order of the day....*Order up!*....Anticipation is right then propelling steps up this sidewalk of hexagonal stone. Cracked, uprooted, but functioning without complaint, we could learn much from such devotion in the face of an unrelenting disinterested nature. Goodspeed lays tracks up this corridor of the strange, navigating uprooted blocks, a tectonic run of sidewalk peaks displaced by old growth roots doing their thing—doing what they must. Our man trips on an uprooted block, barely missing a step; for breakfast awaits. It is time to refuel the duty and devotion powering re-taped / re-shoe-goo'd heels, Goodspeed already feeding on its motivational succor, its down-home charm.

Meanwhile, our good journalist stirs coffee. Stir, stirring, awaiting Goodspeed's arrival at the diner: each and every Wednesday @ 9 a.m. A balance-wheel precision. The door jangling, Goodspeed entering and taking his usual seat. Alice, the waitress, slides out a smoking cup of coffee....

"Usual, Marv?"

"Y'know, I don't know, feelin' it may be time for a change. It's all up in the air, n'all, should probably follow nature's lead, huh?"

"Great. What's it gonna be, Marv? Got a full-house here," Alice's counter-lean, hand-on-hip directness somewhere between a specific ennui with this cat (again, too real a character in these parts to be given special treatment) and a general *over it.*

"Hmm, well, guess we'll get to know that Tex-Mex omelette; uh, wheat toast, with those hashed-browned taters Frank makes? Ya, time for something new," Goodspeed stirring in cream and sugar, stirring up coffee to regular. "Oh, but toast to blackened," a parting instruction driven by the need to keep some things as they have always been.

Goodspeed taps out the spoon, casts a glance down the counter. A look at once hard, yet curious (and if by comparison to past encounters, even amiable). "What d'ya want?"

"Got something to talk about."

"No more excerpts. I do 'preciate the one, got all the vultures stirring; and thought that profile inventive too: imaginative. But that's it; under contract, book's out this Summer."

"I don't want to talk about your work."

Goodspeed mulls that some, scratches his chin, curls up a grin, drinks coffee. He gives in to curiosity. "Ya, okay. *Asa's*, four o'clock."

The door jangles open, Gid entering. An early riser, first one to hit his route each day, this here his first stop Monday-Saturday (got a long failing thing for Alice)....

"Morning, all. And now, good morning to you, Miss Alice. Your mail, madam," Gid slapping down a parcel packet, rubber-banded and heavy.

"Don't s'pose there's a million-dollar check for me in one of those envelopes?"

"Doubt it; wouldn't mind taking a gander at yer riches, though."

"Not a chance, mailman," Alice moving down the line, coffee pot in-hand.

"Smooth, Gid, smooth. It's the persistence that's impressive; sticking to yer guns despite the overwhelming odds," Goodspeed blow-cooling coffee, freshly warmed.

"One of these days. Never can tell when a change

might take root," Gid alluding to the stubborn predictability of the unpredictable and unfamiliar, if unfailing in his own desire to eventually bring things back to how they have always been.

"And a special delivery for you too, Mr. Goodspeed," Gid handing the Regular a thicker than usual and dual rubber-banded *Newsweek*. It is quickly accepted, tucked into inside-coat pocket.

"Where'd we be without the routine? Come by Asa's later, Gid. My treat."

"Sure thang. See y'all," Gid leaving without a trace suspicion of the transaction. Not that it would be frowned upon, or even noticed; for the petty deals continue unabated, with renewed vigor come the Spring. Gid breaks into beautiful song on exiting. What a voice.

"Got to step out, Alice, get my creative on. Will be back in time for order up."

Cyrus follows the Regular out the front-door jangling. Their business transacted, the two part without a word, just a parting glance; our good journalist correctly deducing that even parting words would be viewed as a drain-circling waste of that most precious commodity. No one wants to be a freedom impinger, not out here. Cyrus is too deep in the challenge to give it a second thought, anyway. The balancing out of *man v. myth*. Where the one ends is where this story begins....*Follow your dreams, young son. Hitch your wagon to its czar!*

The sun spreads vernal rays. Cyrus heading for *Candler Hills*, Goodspeed to the alley to wake-and-bake.


A CARHORN CRIES FOUL out at the intersection of

avenues, the indicted motorist taking umbrage—*the soiled honor!*—responding with gusto. It devolves into a good old-fashioned horn-off. The sonic clutter rustles up Goodspeed from pass-out sleep, eyes pried open by the incivility of punch-clock chattel. Hard blinks attempt to clear the blur, his prone-on-bed loathing. "Ruin and death, nothing but."

Goodspeed's rousing proceeds laboriously. He stares up at a ceiling board sheetrock repair looking to rend itself loose with one good stomp on *Asa's* backroom floor overhead. He sits up and surveys: the fridge, the collapsing bookshelves and old new desk, the mid-morning light pouring through window must. This will all soon be a memory, for it is time. He shakes out the blur. It is a somewhat momentous moment. But he is reticent, not willing to grant a watershed its due. It's an instinctual hostility in the face of that unwelcome missionary: *change.* And yet, what is this welling up, this tightening of muscular tissue creeping in along cheekbone and jaw, climbing up into the rear of eye sockets; and, wait, why are those....tears? He deep-snuffs at the sudden emotion, as if to suck it down: down, down into that place deep within where things that cause unease are sentenced to their solitary confinement, buried in the recesses of "that which we need not talk about." He turns back on his dear old comrade in arms: focused hostility, wiping away tears as if they had never been.

Goodspeed breathes deeps, swings legs to bedside and with aid of balled fists, motivates through all the expected creaking to an upright position. He shuffles to the door, opens it up: the patched screen, the weed strewn gravel of the alleyway, even the occasional stiff found stashed in a trunk out back, all of this—*the routine, the known*—it will all soon fade from his day-to-day. For it is time to move on....*Hello, Mr. Goodspeed? Collect call from your calling, sir. Do you accept?*

It is hours later, optimism in the air, surging through capillaries, winding the watch, the land having awoken. The tempo of nature is forcing its will. (Of course it is.) Crowns of cherry line the square in white nimbus, its *15 minutes* coated in pine pollen. The yellow-green allergen covers everything, everywhere. Cyrus, one of those rare blokes that could snort the stuff without so much as a sniffle, wiping a dusting off tabletop and seat on the porch of *East Line Pizza*. Cyrus hasn't worked here for years, but had figured he could still scam a free beer....

"Hey man, so Gibbs and I go way back."

"Cool. 6 bucks," says unimpressed hip employee #16 (damned unimpressed hipsters, they being inter-changeable, after all).

The order placed, Cyrus sits down with a full-priced pint to wait for his full-price slice. There are some things he cannot do. Other things now seem within his grasp. He runs through the check-list:

> The impact of time / place....Environment mixing with genetic predisposition....Past, present, future diving headlong into the scrum....*Check.*

Cyrus has stepped lightly, having adhered to *the ways* in order to get on "the in." Just a little respect for the nature of its constituency. ("Take your hat off when you're talking to a lady, son.") Lessons are learned and retained, or a hard unforgiving nature will rightly follow. And Cyrus, having earned his degree, having come to understand (if not wholly respect) *it—it* being self-sustaining, self-regulating, and self-policing all at once, and all due to the devotion, the dedication, *the commitment.* It is a sacred codex, in there, at once all-or-nothing and all-consuming. It is the regular creed, what keeps *it* real. For without the hard-earned respect of one's peers, the title would be as meaningless as titling oneself *Esquire* or *Colonel....*

*Regular*, it is an earned throne.

Goodspeed, meanwhile, is passing time: his own, as he deems fit. (Of course he is.) He does a loop of the lake at the center of *Waverly Park*, sights out of the corner of his eye every ripple that the breezy idealism shakes loose. A thick skim of pollen atop watertop keeps it real. Observing, making note of every new shoot, every dead leaf; yet not even noticed by a couple on a bench holding hands, gazing, hoping. It is just like him: an anonymity honed to perfection. "Young fools," his highly refined cynicism castigating hope as a delusional tonic. But then the argument is ready-made: he being not so hard a cat as he'd have us believe. The case could be made on nostalgia alone: an emotional attachment to things and ideas and (yes) people as much a shield in the daily goings-on of this war as anything. No, his loves may not be immediately apparent. But, like air, they are omnipresent. He does prefer to lead with his hates....

\*       And so, it seems an opportune (overdue?) time / place to grout in a significant gap.... The question on

Cyrus' mind had been why *this cause?* Well, having hard-earned the respect of a certain barkeep (willing to play both sides in keeping an eye on the future of his investment, no doubt), he'd recently been provided a look behind the curtain. Prior to the *History of repeated Injuries and Usurpations* of the mentioned / reviled hotelier, there were laid even deeper strata of past commercial failures, those having informed, well, pretty much everything. In Howard's words:

"The Populists? No, I never did hear of 'em prior. But, what now? What of Marv's thing? Well, son, fairly sure all that Populist talk of his starts with one incident in particular. See now Marv took over his father's transmission shop after the old man dropped dead; heart-attack, sudden, back in '85? '86? Now he and his pop never got on. But he loved his Ma some'm fierce. His folks had planned to sell out that shop when his pop turned 65, gonna be their retirement money. But that was still 6-7 years off when Marv's dad keeled. So, Marv boot-strapped up 'n took it over—as I heard him put it: loved his Ma more than he hated his old man, which is sayin' something, 'cause he loathed that old bigot....

"How'd it do? Well, word is, and I have heard it from others, that the place did well. He had a big fleet-vehicle contract with the city, bread 'n butter, y'know? But I don't see Marv being too solid a business-type; does not suffer bullshit. You know some'm about Marv's stand-off approach....

"What's that now? Well, for sure. Is just his way of clearing out his space, does not want just anyone takin' up his time. So, ya, he runs 'em all through that abuse routine, been watching him do it for a decade now. And it does get rid of most of 'em, aside from the most dogged, eh? Just show a little respect on his ways and days, is all it comes down to. Get under his skin 'n he'll go at ya, but otherwise a fairly reserved guy if you just let him be....

"But ya, right: the transmission shop. So I can say this: when Marv is at something, he's as intense as it comes. Fact, he told me that he'd once committed to memory the torque specs of the Big 3 from 1960 up through the end of hydraulic-only. Any one other'n Marv says that, I call bullshit. But that guy? Damn, son. Now, I've met a lot of smart folks down through the years, both the book and the street type. But Marv? Well, he's the only one I'd go on record sayin' was a bonafide genius. Boy's got quicksilver smarts; wouldn't surprise me if he could step through a tranny-rebuild with a blind fold on....

"What happened? Well, what happened goes to explain a lot about the man. See he's only at the helm of that business for maybe a year or so, when this big chain— 'n they're still around, see 'em everywhere, ads pop up on the TV all the time—well they tried to sneak one past him. But he proved equal to the sleight-of-hand, could see their buy-out package was a screw job; 'n going to what I was sayin', Marv doesn't exactly have tact down to a science. My guess is he went and told 'em off....

"Yep, figured you'd catch the drift here. No more'n month later that fleet-service contract just goes away, just like that. Disappeared. Someone knew somebody up the chain of the city's gov'ment and that was that. Marv is screwed without that bread 'n butter, said it was certain bankruptcy in short order....

"The what now? Okay. No, no. You must've only heard what happened last. All of that proceeded the final straw, when, like you just said, he tried to recoup some by franchising. But that was with a competitor chain, a whole other big chain entire. Again, he is not the business-type, wound up screwed all complete as that other chain fucked him over too. Only play was to sue, which he tried, but was losing what little he had left for his Ma in doin' it. So, he got it comin' and goin'....

"You got that right, all that would make a man downright bitter. So, he's a self-taught everything, readin' all the time. At some point, he comes on that Populist thing from last-century and it struck a nerve: a fellow-traveler type of connection, y'know? Marv felt that he knew what they'd gone through, had it happen to him in his own life: the trivial brutality of life that can make a man hard and irreverent. He felt like one of 'em, was some'm he once told me. He knew that brand of disappointment, the type that sidles up alongside desperation. We all got our chinks in the armor, son. Might just be that our man, Marv, that his are a little less obvious to suss out. But then, ya just got to know where to look....

"Dorothy? D? Oh, for sure. I mean there is a deep love 'tween those two, no doubt. But Marv, he won't go into nothin' no more without a lawyer by his side; 'n she's all of the kick your ass first and take your name later type too: dogged, tough. She saved our bacon here back when the damn'd city tried to ride roughshod over us with that eminent domain. You all up at that paper seem to be calling it pretty straight on the change in property values, and that uh, what d'ya call it?—gentrification, right; mouthful, that word. Well, yes: I do too; think it just a matter of time before it hits here, already seems it has some; could be this'll all be prime in a way it ain't been for most of a century now. But we'll see how it plays. Things gotta way of ziggin' just when you're expectin' a zag....

"Hmm, curious question; but I guess not. Not how I see it, not at all. I ain't betrayin' any type of privilege by doin' this here. I figure you have earned a little bit of credit, having come to respecting things and the ways of these folks; 'n since my guess is you gonna write on him somehow, somewhere, just want to make sure you get your facts right, hear?"

Having been heard, clearly, Cyrus had given Howard his word. He understood the all of what had been said and what needed only be said with a parting wink, an unsaid: "I hear ya," in the process of squaring up the *man* and *myth* with the barkeep that's had a front-row seat since the time of $1 gasoline.

Goodspeed ascends the staircase at park's end. Austin now before him, standing hands at side on the sidewalk, deep breaths: fifty steps having winded him as thoroughly as a decade of mining his *thing*—his *art*—from a bottle.

"I'm only drinking to be drunk, these days," he'll tell you.... Right, as if that was ever the case: change, and the fear of change, having thrown a hitherto unconsidered light on the subject. His stand, his conviction a little less sure of itself these days, the abatis and breastwork defenses thrown up and perfected over time not as invulnerable as he once thought. *Buck up! Stick them tarheels in line, son!*

He gets his wind, lays tracks down Austin Avenue. Wind wraps his face. The cleansing seasonal opiates spiral and swirl. It is working: the afternoon walk, the routine. It is helping to erase the minute rivulets of doubt. For the optimism of his gait could suggest peace. So tall an order, he will settle for nonchalance. That he can control, pulling up before the old *Woodruff House*. The front door: a sullen gate. Bay window: the bulb of an old truck-cab rusting to dust in the corner of a backlot. A breeze moves a half-hinged shutter. It creaks, groans. Goodspeed can sense the aged pain of his old friend (even if unable to put the pieces together on his own thing). He reaches into shirt pocket for a cigarette. His shoulder creaks. He lights up, walks up front path onto front porch. The weather-beaten floorboards, cornice soffits exhibiting the rot of mis-care, mis-love. Goodspeed winces with a collarbone pang. ("Asshole!") He takes a drag, sights the *For Sale* sign in front yard. The post leans, sign hanging limp as if a flag of surrender. Goodspeed stomps down, unhooks the sign and tosses it atop a pile of decade-old tear-out refuse moldering alongside the drive.... His advance cleared yesterday. He will close on the *Gordon Patrick Woodruff* house tomorrow.

"It is time, old friend," he says, staring up into the turret mounted to the house's southeast-face. "I take care of you and you do the same, hear?"

Brother Jim, meanwhile, has joined Cyrus....

"Does seems this place was more cool when it wasn't tryin' to be so cool," Brother Jim, lamenting change; or at least, this one particular change.

"Commercialize the perceived cool, leverage hip and sell it to slumming suburbanites. That is a strategy as old as the hills, or at least as old as the suburbs," Cyrus, as he sees it.

"You really think corporate marketers are that good?"

"Henry Grady was that good, good enough to sell this here *New South* as a place where black and white laborers alike know their place and would smile through a grueling 12-hour workday. Dude knew the trick: sell white people with money on what they want to hear."

"Damn, a touch more Old Testament on that tone and you could give Parn a few days off," the two glancing out at a mad bout of proselytism underway, in mid-throe....

The preacher is mid-square doling out an imminent apocalyptic hellfire for all sinners; which, of course, encompasses anyone within view. *(No one is immune.)* Handwritten leaflets scatter in his wake as end times confetti, the old mad servant letting fly on two well-dressed slummers who look to be comically overwhelmed.

"Well, Parn seems to be doing his part to keep things real," Brother Jim, a second of sensing there may yet be hope for an "authentic" future.

"You wonder, on the right cocktail of meds could Parn just be your average white-collar middle manager? Is the veil that thin?"

"Been here as long as I have. Any idea how long he's been out there?"

"You had to have read Lane's article on the homeless of *The Points?*"

"Kinda remember that, something about the state hospitals all being defunded?"

"Yes, mid-late '80s, the core of the crew you see out here, even today. But it started even earlier for Parnish: late '70s. He's getting serviced by a hooker in the back-room of some dumpy lounge that used to be up Highland: *The Sliver of Gold*, something like that?"

"Right, man, that place—where that new taqueria just

went in. But it was called: *The Gentleman's Club* and its slogan was: *where we'll turn your silver to gold*, 'cept it was mis-spelled: *sliver to gold!*"

"Right, that's right!"

"Was that way for like 20 years, would have taken someone two minutes to swap the letters. Wow, and a total shit-hole."

"Right, right. So, ya, Parn's gettin' serviced when she stops mid-hummer to warn him of a conspiracy afoot. It's a classic, if mad tale, which Lane could never get enough of; got all of this direct from Parn. The hooker looks up at him and tells him that the local Knights of Pythias were plotting right then to cut off his fingers and toes, one-by-one, if he didn't save twenty souls in twenty days: one digit per soul."

"Hmmmm—so, he claims that's why he's missin' that finger?"

"This is Parn talkin' here, claims he fell one soul short and that is why the missing index finger. Lane actually tracked down the last full-time job Parnish had—oh, and his real name? Ready for this? Clement Parnish Worcester—the IV!"

"Wow! That, that is like Kentucky Colonel awesome, right there."

"Right? So, the last full-time job was as a cabinet-maker; lobbed off that index-finger using a table-saw," Cyrus taking a deep draught from his pint. "But to Lane's credit, he withheld that part, wasn't out to humiliate him, just shine light on how the street people in and around *The Points* were turned out by the Feds and states de-funding all their state-run mental hospitals. They closed the *Candler* mental hospital in 1986. And yet this crew survives."

"Was a series of columns, right? I do remember the one on, uh, Eusty? The guy with the hip-length dreadlock, always arguing with himself about physics?"

"Actually, Lane got that wrong. Eustace cops all that from Sheba. He hears it from her and spouts off, and everyone thinks it's his thing; were supposedly friends until she stole his winter-coat; what Eustace claims, at least."

"Old Parn, 20 years. Now there's an institution."

"Tragic, to live that much of your life on the street, homeless?" Cyrus drinking ale, a look at the street preacher out there, out here. "And yet so committed, despite whatever is going on upstairs. It's hard not to be impressed with the resilience, at least. We're all posers next to Old Parn. He's in to win it."


It is hours later. Goodspeed is standing on the sidewalk in front of *Asa's*. Out here, where a certain perspective can be achieved, where one can smoke, can recuse one's self of the languid din and recharge in sight of the promise within. Out here, where one can rejuvenate the drive of devotion, or—if your pleasure—just stand and stare at the street.

"Seems thinkin' too much is either a freeway to genius 'er the other way clear to insanity; and since I ain't inclined to neither, I'll leave it to those so inclined and just take my drink," Boo once told Goodspeed.

"Amen, ol' salt," Goodspeed thinks.

For done right, at all points attentive to *the craft,* the drinking done inside will consume all thoughts of fear and isolation like a street-wise rat devouring rat-trap cheese.

There is the ever present unknown and knowing it could all turn in an instant. *(Sssssnap!)* But if done right, the payoff is nothing short of *Victory!* Each and every day steps off with such promise, in there. And that alone seems enough to offset the risk, the inherent peril. It is, at the very least, enough to curb any foul whiff of change.

Goodspeed smokes. He stares at the street, thinking.

> *Alongside a man's open course there moves a mystery, to him dark and shining at once. The mystery here is change.*
>
> Stark Young ~ *I'll Take My Stand*

ONE WEEK HAS PASSED. Goodspeed extinguishes cigarette in outdoor ashcan and enters *The Asa Inman*. The day is in its work-a-day stride, but that does not curb the restorative reservoir raining from taps. Its amber torrents drown trial and tribulation alike, scotching any and all attempt by all the little S.O.B.s out there attempting, incessantly, to hijack your time. It is pure predictable deliverance of which we speak. "In here" is there when you need it to be there. It is where worries drift off into the edgeless narrative of a mythic real, where cares are floated to insignificance like loosed balloons. It is there—*for you*—day and night. It is there when you need it, there when you don't.

Goodspeed breathes in its healing sanctity. Chuck, Sax, Tench, Omar and Marge, Howard and Martha attending. A pair of dice rattles in the back room, the reaction less than *hush-hush*. A general lack of luck elicits a collective groan but for one sole celebrant; sounds like Bid:

"That's raht, that's how the dice rolls, you sad sacks! Pay up, girls. High-rollin,' tonight!" (Though, again, it is mid-day.)

The pinball machine's cycling of orange, red, and red-orange lights light up the backroom jamb. They pulse as if an extension of the dice-roller's fortune....rattle, rattle, clatter....the mocking triumphalism "oh yah!" lording over the pained groans and lo-fi death march of alien pixels thrown from the burned-in screen of an arcade video game. There are the pennants, the bottles and posters. There is the mute brightness, the air's unseen tincture. *He breaths deep.*

Reveling in modest greetings, Goodspeed takes his seat, adjusts, settles in for the hours of work ahead: the worldly transgressions to drown, the corporate conspiracies to efficiently subvert. Martha delivers a pint and a shot, a motherly wink as she serves up his tools of the trade. There is some banter down the line, the low volume tick of the *Cable News Network*. But for the most part, the front room sets up as business-like: machinists of a métier that churns out product with precision. Drinks are tipped, emptied and refilled. It is done with a scientific industrial efficiency. Devotion scrim-lights the must, the shellac of mis-care foreshadowing a blessed lacquered daze.

"How's the wing these days, Marv?" Omar inquiring, eyes front and still upset over what he views to be a failure to do his duty on that night. Goodspeed will, of course, not permit such down talk, dismissing it outright and considering a shattered clavicle a square-deal to rid the brethren of an invader.

"Fine, O. Getting some mobility back," Goodspeed dropping the shot like a coin down a slot. "And hey, got these nice new scars to impress the ladies, right?" a group head-bob rippling down the line.

"H, isn't it openin' day? How do y'all think the million-dollar bums are gonna let us down this year?"

Howard, faithful H, flipping the channel, adjusting volume. Baseball takes center stage. The outlook is grim despite patriotic bunting and the buzz of opening day: the home team down 7 – 1, bottom of the sixth....*If they don't win it's a shame*....and yet there is no call for blame. For it is nature's prerogative. What will be, will be. To argue with the inevitable—a home-team's losing ways, nature's curt cutting off of an established oxbow in plotting a new course—well, we have established the useless waste of such an inexplicable act. Save it for the real fight. Save it for the spleen-venting to be hard-tossed at those who would injure and, or usurp your *freedoms*—all while (of course) saving back enough vitriol for all the bastards who do their bidding.... And Goodspeed gets down to business: an ambition that one could even dub resolution.

Strike three called. On with the seventh (chapter, that is).

Strike three swinging. Game. And so the season begins: optimism, tempered by the hard humbling real. Drinks are tipped nonetheless, perhaps with greater determination; stepping up resolve in the face of overwhelming odds, a trait with well-established regional roots. And the worries such as they are perish, the neon light of beer signs garish in the afternoon daze.

Cyrus, accompanied by Brother Jim, enters. They take

up stools along the short L of the bar closest the door and closest to the wall, a zone less prized by the regulars. It's a deliberate strategy: *respectful of the ways.* Their appearance, if noticed at all, saunters around the inert ease they have done their best not to upset; the cycling hum of neon sharing thin air with George Jones and Bill Monroe.

Direct daylight falls away from the south-facing entrance, obscuring the room's tenants (and they are nothing if not) even more than the benevolent reign of anonymity. A passing glance could tag the place as unapproachable, a man-made cave emitting such severe functionality as to attract none but the most extreme anthropomorphic spelunker—or, as is more likely, those lost and yearning for a cure to society's otherwise cold shoulder. And it is to that ilk that this hole-in-the-wall reaches out like Mother's loving arms. Drinks are served and drinks are drained. And if done right, time will slip, will disappear completely, the countless "carefully conceived" methods meant to scotch *freedom* beyond these walls rendered unto one vast collusion damned with each raising of the wrist. Done with flair, it's the unsung fight song of this lair.

Cyrus is working (kind of), Brother Jim, ever the scene-ster, here to revel in the oddity of it all. To blend in they drink. Howard presumes their purpose, serves up two pints.

"How are ya, boys?" Howard, having long hoped for a way lure in some of "these kids today," warming to the regular-like newcomers.

"Well enough, Howard. How 'bout a round for our friends here," Cyrus' largesse coaxing grunts of approval.

Olivia and Martha dole out shots down the line, Martha announcing: "compliments of our smah't young friends here, people." *Her people.*

Omar tips cap bill. Cyrus nods affirmative. The homeland defender knocks back the shot, resumes his straight-ahead penetrating stare. An acknowledgement not lost. *Understand. Participate with respect. Blend with the patterns on the wall.*

"Tryin' to buy us off now?" Goodspeed raising and dropping a shot of bourbon.

"Is it working?"

"Ain't hurting."

"Assuring y'all are oiled up seems to help get me through my visits," some closed-lip laughs down the line, a truth undeniable.

But the joke is lost on one. Sax adjusts his mountainous frame upon the stool at the very end of the long L of the bar, his rough appearance made rougher by a twenty-year tenure under the sun of southern steelyards.

"You tryin' to be funny? Awful lack of respect there, johnny-come-lately," Sax sliding the shot glass from in front of him, crossing his arms, glaring.

Cyrus, giving at least 100 lbs in the match-up, drains the pint before him. He sets down and slides pint glass out onto the bar, the understood request for a refill. (How very *regular!*)

"Sorry, man. Just a dumb bad joke; don't mean a thing."

"For chrisesakes, boy's right!" Chuck's voice deeper, appearance rougher, his tenure at the steelyards and *Asa's* even longer. "That white boy is right on, makes it all the easier to deal with yer sorry ass if I've have a tie-on or two.

With you, some days, helps to have three!" Chuck sucking wind from sails, complete with a sidling back-of-head-slap.

"Now ol' man, just get off me," Sax waving at the hand-that-slaps as one would a lazy fly in August. "Don't know what in hell you're talking 'bout...."

"Awww just drink up yer free booze, son. No need to be such a hard ass on that johnny-come-lately white boy."

"Damn old slap-happy nigg'r. Sun must be gettin to ya, Pops."

"It's all gettin' to me these days, Saxby, 'n it'll get to you too, son; attitude like that, shit. It'll get you sooner rather 'n later."

"Keep yer ol' man griping to yourself, always stickin' me with your down talk; feel like a damn'd voodoo doll," Sax stewing, slightly. "Now I don't forget, there, whatever your name is, johnny-come-skinny-white-boy. You watch your step, in here."

Point made, accepted. Cyrus nods affirmative, pledging careful steps without a word—all in the course of wordless drinking.

Sax downs the shot. "There, happy ol' geezer?! Sun must be gettin to ya," Sax seeking out the comfortable and predictable, dropping a request for Otis Redding. "No personal thing, H; just need some'n aside from white-bred and hillbilly at the moment. Those damn'd janglin' banjos, sounding like Deliverance all up in here."

"Again with the *Deliverance* thing," Goodspeed keeping his rankled thought to himself, understanding his cohort's desire for the predictable and comfortable.

Howard, having been seen corner-mouth grinning all the while, understands and respects the peculiar rituals—

the inner-workings of *in here*—through an agnostic eye. Howard is here to serve, *freedom of choice* (regardless of the physical, clearly devastating side-effects of his craft) being sacrosanct. He is a businessman plying a trade in high demand, this all an unspoken pact extended to all-comers. That is, so long as you ease your way in, respect the long tail of tradition. And Howard, dutiful servant of patrons, having already punched up *Otis @ Monterrey* on the compact-disc jukebox. The look on Sax's face, having hovered somewhere between sneer and chest-pain, eases in having been done right. Sax hums along to *Shake*, emitting the glow of *Respect*.

It is an hour later. Cyrus has gladly yielded his seat to Ez, she and Brother Jim—birds-of-a-feather—having set to conversing (commiserating?). Meanwhile, Cyrus has moved to take up a stool in the space behind Goodspeed and away from the bar. It is a front row seat, but respectful; the Regular's conversation smacking of convulsion. Firewater is right then fueling this firebrand. He is doing his best Custer: channeling the élan of reckless courage. Cyrus has not added a single word to said "conversing," observation of the subject in his environment—his element—all that is required of this moment. For the harangue has hit stride. A bottle resting restlessly atop bartop before Goodspeed is steadily being drained into a tirade so animated even Omar has moved along. It is on, pouring like a streetside storm rush:

"You must see it clearly now, Cleburne, now that you have gained a bit of perspective? Raht here is where we make our stand, in this very room. This is our Petersburg, the rear guard in the breach. All those poor bastards out there every morning, duped into thinking they're doin' the responsible thing, as if it grants 'em some special privilege, some benevolent baron's accolades, some manner of control over the ferocity of nature's course...."

Goodspeed pours then drops a shot. It is so fluid as to be completed in a single motion. "But all of that is a grand delusion, the grandest of them all; and of course the bastards fan the flames 'cause they make out standing on the backs of this slaughter of innocents. They plant the lie in the ads and the public relations 'n tend to 'em with ruthless care, convincing the mass that surrendering your time is the best thing—for you! The Agrarians were keen to all this bullshit, could see the New South for what it was: a ruse benefiting the few who'd figured out how to capitalize on the idea of selling cultural improvement via personal improvement. 'Get a job in our mills, improve your life, and honor the hard fought sacrifice made by your forebears in the process'....this when in fact the whole notion was cynically designed to raise clueless brigades of Gilded Age cannon fodder, capitalizing on the tradition of innocent loyalty that is our way down here, a method employed time-and-again by the economic aristocrats since 1607. That is the very core of this tragedy: a society of individuals shoveled in as the anthracite of pure greed; no less tragic than the plantation owners whooping up and marching off an army of poor-white crackers to die in defense of their 'property'—course, didn't even need the boosterism to then re-enslave all the freed blacks, jus' left it to the merchants, the courts, 'n the Klan. Personal improvement, my ass: the New South was as intent on constrictin' freedom for profit as was the Old South. But being nominally free, they had to sell it twice as hard to make it stick. The Agrarians illustrate the point: *We receive the illusion of having power over nature, and lose the sense of nature as something mysterious and contingent.* The contingency they're talking 'bout there? Nothin' short of the innate birthright freedom of the individual, of nature running its course. No marketing strategy can profit on a contingency, the quirks of an individual down in it rolling around in the nature of their nature. Best kill it in the crib in the time-honored way: call up the violent repression of tradition 'n let it police the state."

The beguiling spirit drains, stoking a thundering ministry ingrained in the mash bill of history, environment, and personal experience...."A heritage defined by the business end of a billyclub, fucking assholes," this here being his testament, his performance art....

"We were mirandized long ago, Cleburne, by the oligarchs, the zealots, the racists and their politicians. And here we stand still, new oligarchs, new zealots, old racists and their politicians filing in to bind their 'beloved countrymen' to the dustbin of a poverty-wracked ignorant past. Where is the duty and the deference to the people and their future in an alabaster lost cause that can't comprehend the South as it is, and always has been: colorful. I may not live to see the victory, but can only hope to take plenty of the bastards down with me before I go."

And there we have it: the reason he gets up in the morning, a mission statement if ever one existed. Goodspeed is so focused and has become so rapidly shit-faced, Cyrus is beginning to think he could walk away without our good man even noticing. For the input of, even the very presence of others, is no longer necessary. Here is the dividing line. Here is where *myth* takes the reins and aims for the heart of the matter. Here is where the ever-smoldering hate of having been crossed pulses and beats as a glowing pit of coals just waiting on the bellows' stoke of squint-eye devotion (and bourbon) to once again fire a roaring blaze. It is a cycle sure to continue until each and every ember has stepped up to give its last full measure of devotion, as (at this rate) they surely must—and that right soon.

It is hours later and it is all working: worry in orbit, this modest place serving its patrons a timeless vacancy.... Bright mute conversation is punctuated by random boisterous bellowing: a toast raised, the mold of one thousand such nights clinging to ceiling-fan blades, the cobwebs, the understood decay.... Cruiser lights careen down the avenue beyond front window: red, blue, white lights smeared across sight as a burned-in video game screen.... Last call: orders in, orders up, triumph spattering the scene with flung-brush fury—with *Victory!*....The low light, mute and orange. The whirling light. The tin ceiling whirling as he slips from his stool. Head striking floor. Vacant, black, peace but a fantastical rumor scrawled on a bathroom wall: *For a good time call on unconsciousness. It will love you long time!*

IT IS APRIL FIFTEENTH. *(Cough it up, chumps!)* The azalea lights up red and white, the conical lilac curtains of wisteria and still-green honeysuckle surging yeoman-like over fences and up pine stands and guy wires. The skeletal groves unroll leaves as umbrellas would answer April rain, every view full of bullish intent. It is a day to be lived full, nature's restless scrawl dropping this new chapter with precision....our man guzzling it like cheap wine.

Marvin Goodspeed surveys his *new* house with a careful eye, coffee and many aspirin masking pangs that simmer from head to toe.... He'd woken up that morning in the slope-down alleyway alongside *The Asa Inman*, habit and instinct having pointed his steps towards the now vacant basement apartment—the smear of being stupid fucked-up having dropped him before he had made it. And that's where he'd woken up, slouched against *Asa's* outer wall, a slight chill in the air. No less disorienting than usual; like waking up in Mother's arms, in fact.

He lights a cigarette, reaches across chest to deposit pack and lighter into left-front shirt pocket. A twinge lights up his right shoulder: a lightning-pop in a distant thunderhead, a worry now distant. For he is healed (sort of). He smokes.

The sun nears meridian as he makes his way up front walk onto front porch. He carries with him a crowbar, a sledgehammer, a regular hammer, gloves. A look of determination elbows its way through the mauve of sunken eyes. Goodspeed is looking to make some changes, to renovate and renew. If it's going to come to this neighborhood—this place—he's going to have his say *(in amongst the den of thieves)*. And here is where it starts: the *Gordon Patrick Woodruff House*, his *new* house.

He opens the door. It creaks. He walks in, knees creaking. He steps on through the foyer and into the parlor. The chandelier is all that's been left, dust clots clinging to the must having claimed it. Neglect embeds its patient resolve in the terrene odor of rot, water stains seeping in under warped moulding along a far wall otherwise cracked; broad sheets of flaking paint, pane chards from a broken window vandalized not recently. Nature has had its way. Yet Goodspeed proceeds unfazed. He is motivated by the challenge, dedicated to the duty at hand, going with the new indomitable forces of nature: *renovation, restoration, renewal.* He wonders what all this change will bring, keeping a squint-eye fixed squarely on the hype, the boosters and their promises. He holds the sledgehammer fast. He will stand fast for all the reasons he must: pride, tradition, etc. He will reverse time's dickish chinks in the old *Woodruff House.* It will take all he's got. And as you may have already surmised, dear reader, despite the outward signs of imminent defeat he still has plenty of will to give. He will give it his white-hot all. Against time he will war, opening hostilities with a swing and a splintering smash. With the crowbar he peels back broken wainscoting and the plaster / lath it fronts. Room by room, swing by yeoman swing, he will gut the place. He will build up the new over top of the old. It will be a masterpiece of contradictions, old and new; such an effort falling square within Goodspeed's wheelhouse, and all.

Meanwhile, Cleburne has turned the act of gleaning meaning, subject, and theme from the Regular's own words into a meditative routine. It goes with him everywhere he goes these days. It is with him now as he stands in an aisle, pondering. For he is onto something, gaining an answer inhabiting his skin like an itch. And despite a recent questioning of conclusions he'd thought settled, at least one thread has displayed staying power:

*Goodspeed, the engineer.* It is not just holding its own under cross-examination. It is evolving into something that may just settle the whole question on this cat....

Cyrus Cleburne is deep in a ponder at the moment, reviewing again how this whole thing of Goodspeed's seems plotted as on a map-room floor....*We will strike them here, here, and here, cut them off here, and destroy them here....* There is a cohesion that escapes the shit-faced fog looking an awful lot like a pattern. And from there, one does not have far to go on faith to this all being a calculated venture, a conscious plan. Odd. Strange....

But something about that take seems too nice and neat. Can we really be let off the hook so easily? That is the question needling Cyrus so.... Here he is in Aisle 3 of a small local grocer gazing deep beyond the shelves of goods, forgetting all of the reason why he is there for the moment, stirring instead the red-hot coals of this break-out thought: levitating above the diatribes and otherwise tedious *maintenance of the routine* there seems to be an equal, if not greater force than conscious will guiding this Goodspeed. Is it his loves? His hates? Without question. But this here is something more vague and chaotic (if wholly predictable), a level deeper than the subconscious even (if in tango with it). There are the designs of man and the designs of nature: the former conscious, the latter not so much; but both proving serviceable plans in a pinch. So it goes to figure that if one were adept at channeling that gurgling magma layers-of-strata deeper than the subconscious even, one's nature could, over time, harden into so involuntary and so unquestionable a driver of the daily routine as to supersede conscious effort. It is that great unknown, the one we all know far too well....

"Okay, so people plug along on unconscious instinct more than we may all think is the case—wait, what was I looking for?"

Okay, so people plug along on unconscious instinct more than we may all think is the case. *Check....* Cyrus scratches his second meager attempt at a beard this year. It is meeting the skepticism of conscious ventures that are tried only to fail time-and-again. Luckily, the other pursuit spinning up from his conscious energies has been coming around, beard skeptics be damned....

Okay, nature + instinct—got it. But why is that more so relevant here than anywhere? How about: as much as it is a universal trait, it is one whose regional roots dig deeper than most. And as with this dude and all things down here—universal, regional—it is seen to with, perhaps, a bit more veracity; what the careful and observant might rightfully label 'verve.' For this is a place that understands how *a high held cause* can come crashing down in the crush of humiliating poverty—and—how *a high held cause* can rise from the same smoldering blood-clotted clods of beaten-down dirt to deliver a freedom long and actively denied. This here is a land that understands how the authority of institutions can be purposed to exact the violent work of tribal / clan supremacy—and—how violence can be repurposed as its own Achilles' heel. It is a place that understands, beyond a shadow of a doubt, how fucking cruel we can be to each other; and yet, oddly, exudes a warmth seen nowhere else....all of that.

But then there is perhaps the most irresistible detail: that this here place has never lost its fight regardless of how very right or very very wrong *a cause* has been. And it continues to fight, as if it still has something to prove. Of course, it could simply be that it just likes to fight—the conscious and the not-so-much doing the mentioned tango. (Maybe, even, the nasty?) But acting without a second thought on what you think or have been taught to think *right* regardless of whether it is, could make the case for instinct being a bit more lauded down here than elsewhere. For that *is* a trait with deep regional roots. Which is not to poke the tired trope of a region without a thought in its head, but to indict the guilty-as-fuck pull of tradition and its use as a fig leaf cloaking the worst base shit down through the years....

Aisle 4? Must be Aisle 4.... But stereotypes aside, how dumb fuck is it to fix a reliance on instinct to the heart of regional tradition? As if that isn't pleading for the worst base shit to find itself worked up into a tradition.

Aisle 4. *Check*.... So, yes, giving instinct a larger role than is probably wise and passing that old chestnut down the generations as tradition? *(Thanks for nothing, past!)* That could all by its lonesome explain the excessive need (as in "enough already, people") for all the mad-grasping at moral certainty, that need for a source temporal or heavenly beyond our own breathing bundle of blood and bone to assure us, with authority, that we are good—or at the very least *right*. It's an instinct as pervasive as that nag of nags: the plunging fear that we might (gulp) be *wrong*. But then, that seems to point at what is certainly the most regional thing of all: repressing the hard-boiled effect of hard times and hard attitudes and hard violence within the fizzing bubbles of an all-purpose bromide—having pride enough to simply carry yourself well, despite it all.... And talking for instinctual fatalists everywhere, the saturnine Alabamian, Clarence Cason:

*He must have learned in some way that composure of the human spirit is all that really matters.*

~ *90° in the Shade*

"In the nature of your own bein' resides every answer you'll ever need. Well, that and all the god-damned heartache you can handle," Goodspeed had said, a nugget flung as debris from the roaring cyclone of the binge rant but a chapter back....

Now, if Cyrus can only document the valley of this strange habitation before the dude drinks himself to death, he'll be in business.... Standing blankly, Aisle 4 of Harold Wu's grocery store up off DeKalb. Right. It is April and the time had come to fire up the grill. And they were about to grill up some righteous April dogs. But hot dogs without mustard? That is un-American. That will not stand. Kelly could have cared less, being more a ketchup gal (and more concerned with stanching a creeping ravenous hunger), the two having stared blankly at the fridge's longing emptiness before Cyrus declared independence from such gastronomic lacking. He would not stand for it: *liberty or death!*

And so, here he is, declaring an independence of sorts. But where the hell is the mustard? Cyrus asks Harold's slacker son, working the shift:

"Hey, uh, where's the condiments?"

"Stud man needs condoms? That's what I'm talkin' about. Up here behind the register, got smooth rib to rough rider, enough to please her plenty, man," Steve Wu, quite out of character with the customer service.

"Condiments, Steve. Where's the mustard and ketchup?"

"Mustard? Really?" Steve Wu folding his arms, tossing a 'that is weak, man' look Cyrus' way. "Aisle 3. One over, Captain Buzzkill," customer service dissolving back into this month's *Hard Rider* on the side-counter.

Aisle 3. Mustard. Ketchup. Cyrus at the register, standing, waiting....waiting....Steve Wu unfolding, studying the centerfold.

"Hot angle. I think I can actually see her uterus. A little help here?"

"What, no condoms with the condiments, stud man?"

"Just ring it up, Steve."

"Okay, man. You're too tense. You do need to get laid. 5 bucks."

"Even? 5 bucks, for mustard and ketchup. What are you skimmin' the drawer?" Cyrus not able to hold back incredulous laughter.

"What? No, no, man; just messin'—3.89."

"Here's 4, keep the change; need to fine-tune your scam."

"Hey man, just tryin' to earn an honest buck."

"So noble. Don't get the pages stuck together," Cyrus gathering up the vital toppings and exiting, a dismissive wave from Steve Wu who tosses a softball rank at the parting customer's (admittedly) weak beard before opening and chawing down a stick of counter-side jerky.

Out at the intersection the light turns. Cyrus and a woman begin to cross the street as a beat up '70s era Camaro runs the red-light at full speed. Squealing-and-screeching slashes open the moment like a machete. Horns blowing, it all Doppler'd into a slow-motion flash: frame-by-metal-crunching frame. Glass shatters, a tire puncturing like a gunshot. The sounds of skidding carom into the dull-thud of a door buckling against telephone pole. The pole fractures, held limp by the wires it supports: the high-tension ripple of singing wires. Cyrus has lunged out of the way of an old metal bumper that tumbled free. The woman was not so lucky, it having taken her legs out from under her, having fallen hard. Steam is spouting, glass bits sprinkling to a rest.... And though the screeching has stopped, the screaming has just begun. The perpetrator of impatience emerges from the wrecked Camaro. A cut on his forehead, rivulet of blood. Before he has both feet on the ground, a big dude is pulling him out and dishing it out. His co-pilot, another big dude, joins in the instinctual pummeling. It's a four-car wreck. What we are driven to....

The woman has only been stunned, though thinks her leg is broken. Cyrus, with the help of another, helps her onto the sidewalk. Trey emerges, running from Budd's Burger Shack across the street, Stu right behind him. The motorists and passengers involved in the crash—but not the brawl—stand back, hands running through hair, "what the fuck" looks on faces; the bodily scrapes, car body dents, and smashed headlights. Debris, yelling, everywhere.

Cyrus turns around just in time to see a meth-head who'd recently turned up on the streets (and already losing teeth, though no more than 20), sprinting off with the injured woman's purse. Cyrus takes up the pursuit, gives up two blocks later. The lost kid's head start and instinctual elusiveness have him long gone. He'll likely never be seen again. Cyrus gulps a deep breath, doubles-back for mustard and ketchup still mid-street where he'd dropped them. Sirens crowd up  the distance in all directions. A cruiser races up Highland Avenue past him. He sights Kelly out on porch and looking down, hands out, a drawn-up incredulous look: "what the fuck?!" without words. Forget all of this, Cyrus shaking his head, waving off explanation without a word—the fatal, desperate quality of it all....*as if what they hungered for was ruin and death....*

"Okay, so maybe more than colorful hyperbole," he mutters, downlooking, head shaking. For there are the persistent waters of madness that, by their very nature, overflow all levees of responsible-ness purposefully placed to keep them at bay—and often doing so with smug glee (it being what they do, and all). So yes, one can see how this could drive a certain Regular to seek his solace by any means necessary. In this particular moment, *it* is all crystal clear.

But to forget all of this for the moment, Cyrus falls back on holding fast to simple things. It is an instinct, a tried-and-true tradition at the moment coming on with verve. Kelly buzzes him in through front door. He trudges through foyer, upstairs to second-story hallway, clinging tight to his condiment cache, holding close what is dear. The making of sense will just have to wait. He'll settle for the first grill-out of the year.

DARE NOT RESIST TEMPTATION, a loaded phrase rising to the level of credo, out here. For resisting a tidal heritage, turning instead towards things untested, not traditional, not "from around these parts," is sure to draw a squint-eye or two. It is an act that demands sober reflection on the scope of ramifications sure to spool off in its wake. There is no turning back. It is the point of no return, a Rubicon that runs blood red. Think carefully. Act deliberately. Be *absolutely sure.* For this, this here is the point when resisting the temptations of heritage and tradition could lead to questioning a way of life etched as ardently and viciously as a monument to the past is cut from stone—such monuments, themselves, more of a warning to present and future than having anything to do with history.... Perhaps another line from Woodward's *Origins* would be of assistance here, a passage referring to another lost cause—one noticeably lacking monuments and myths to its memory. Woodward, our sage guide, spotlit the agonizing decision awaiting all those who wanted change but were still on the fence in the early 1890s, all of those proto-*Populists* who, having been double-crossed in their alliance with the ruling Southern Democrats (strange new aims having been co-opted and buried in shallow graves), were right then (as in way back when) threatening to bolt this—*the party of their fathers*—for a nascent upstart coalition—*The People's Party*—a new party, *a new way*, openly and brazenly opposed to old ways. But, as Woodward deftly surmised: *Changing one's party, involved more than changing one's mind....*

"Progress, we hear you have been hanging around with some questionable folks, of late. Perhaps it is time to introduce you to an old friend of ours. Now, he may seem severe in his ways, but it is for your own good. Progress, meet the crushing weight of the past."

"Nice to meet you there, son. Yes, yes, we are gonna

have a fine ol' time."

To turn your back on those things that hold us back, that we know in our heart of hearts has and will continue to do damage, has injured us outright—but—are nonetheless a part of us, as hard (barbed?) wired into the program as DNA itself? Well, for some that would be the equivalent of un-etching credos carved in stone....

For the past three days, Goodspeed has been tearing out the negligent decay, tearing out the *old* from the *The Woodruff House*—his *new* house. It is a brand of labor his body has not seen in years. And the years, the damned scroll of years. Sidling up to forty, he could well be pushing fifty. Aches layer up strata of pain that score their way to the bone. Time has been hard. Actually, time is innocent here. (Wait, what—?!) His use of time, now....

Goodspeed can recall memories of youthful vigor, sort of; more so the indifference of "youthful," back when pain and fear and hate were mere inconveniences, not inescapable facets of life to war with each and every day. He can recall those days but will spend no time there. He tends not to fix nostalgic claims on events of a contemporary vintage, instead letting the reel of his rearward glance run out far, far back—way farther back— longing, as do many, for times that never really existed as framed in the mythic present (to which he'd surely admit, if pressed). But, regardless of failing the factual sniff-test, there they are....still. And there they are still driving things, directing things and aims and conduct, if subconscious, or a layer deeper even. And this, in light of *the all* that has happened and has become known and has since been tagged as absurd and grotesque and appalling about those times way far back. Still, there they are, living off inertia until the day finally comes when they all, finally, just roll over and die.

Goodspeed is tearing out the old as much as he is tending to the roots left behind. He may take a radical step forward, but in doing so does not seem capable of slamming the door behind him. A regional thing? For sure. A universal thing? Without question.

And though the days of late have been split between the coming of the *new* and a repeat of the *old*, we'll concern ourselves with the windless coves of the latter for the moment....

"Another'n, H, just as you have a chance."

And on that, almost anyone else would call what we have here a problem (and perhaps all others should). Yet, in this place it is presented as "solution." A solution to work and life and *the all* still out there waiting to hit. In fact, raising the "problem" word may just find the truth-teller guided out front door to be tossed roughly to hexagonal stone. For in here, one must tread lightly and suspend outsider-metrics that could peg common traditions and practices as wasteful, destructive—sad, even. *In here* is not *out there*. In here, worries dissolve as salt in liquid, all the god-damned heartache and regret and boredom, all of it washed down the throat with a burn. In here, Marvin Goodspeed drinks himself irritant free. He is drinking his way to a better understanding of things. It is *his* thing. It is 1 p.m.

At least some of the recent pain / irritation, would be due to the advance excerpt of *Within* having appeared in the Spring volume of *Word*. A well-respected lit-journal that still manages to drum up underground cred, Goodspeed nonetheless protested going there. His publisher timed the publication to the first wide-cast PR push touting the novel's upcoming release....

"It drumrolls in the spirit of the thing without giving it away," he'd told Goodspeed.

"Drumrolls, that's creative. But this thing doesn't work in parts. But then it doesn't really matter either way. It's gonna get hammered," was Goodspeed's response.

The publisher had waved off Goodspeed's cynicism, a property he would otherwise stoke (serving as a coaling-station of this whole endeavor, and all). The formula had been to fire the anticipation boilers for pre-order prior to the book's proper release that Summer....

"It'll be fine, Marv. This is no fly by night 'zine. It's where you want to be. Besides, who cares about the reviews? This all about creating some buzz."

"Great, a load of damned boosterism; swell. I can hear the bastards sharpenin' their pencils right now."

"Just stop. It's a great work. It'll be fine, trust me."

"It's gonna get slammed."

Yup, the excerpt was ripped pretty good. But as with so much of the shade thrown Goodspeed's way, it was hard to tell through the sloppy pile-on *what* of his actual work was so objectionable. In the end, most conceded to the quality of the work. But in an age when the distance between the character behind a creative work and the creative work steadily erodes, it seems therein lay your answer: Those who have enjoyed only topical interaction with the caustic word wrangler of *Springvale* (and the strains of his own peculiar spin on *the disease*) tend to run reviews through the spin-cycle of their own loathing prior to churning out column inches.... If anything, it was the publisher who felt the burn of the spurns, even apologizing after the fact. Goodspeed, a sly grin, told him not to worry an ounce....

"Actually, I'd say it worked out according to plan."

The excerpt—Chapter 5—was especially hammered within the culture pages of several large print outlets, trying (too hard, really) to counter Goodspeed's raw portrayal of a world (in the not so distant future?) in which big publishing, big broadcasting, big culture, big insurance, big oil, big agriculture, big banks, big retail, the faceless rapacious nature of *big everything* has become so enmeshed in the daily *everything* that the automaton populace it has trained to output and ingest its product would not even consider there having been a time before that had been all there ever was; but, of course, for the lead character in Goodspeed's second full-length and that character's swarthy band of do-it-yourself bomb throwers. Specious is the adjective that comes to mind, stock reviews that reeked so thoroughly of hidden agendas they could be read as press releases in defense of commercial patrons.

Of course, much of this can also be traced to the ongoing efforts amongst such "culture shills" to salvage credibility, this having become something of a sport after *The Weekly* published a short list in June 1996 (that later found national syndication) of big publishers who'd rejected *The Satellite Man* (250,000 copies moved to date on a small press budget). *The Weekly's* purpose had been to simply appreciate / celebrate the stick-to-it success of a local dude done good. But the publicity had left a lot of salt to burn in the public relations wounds of those who spend much treasure and employ whole departments devoted to caring about such things. Redemption now seemed to undercut these late negative reviews of Chapter 5. Several seemed vaguely personal. Of course, this hasn't stopped the steady stream of big publishing firms tossing out offers....

"The proof is in between the boards, Marv. The work is timeless. Any review is dated the moment it hits air," the publisher had told him, having come down to *The Beacon* and *Asa's*, to personally reassure his biggest star.

"Whatever. Two more, H; just as you have a chance," it all an irritant to Goodspeed, at best; akin to the occasional pang that still lights up his shoulder.

But the predictable mainstream reviews aside, the underground press had (predictably) lit up, buzzing over this little taste. The incandescent *Village* predicted the work could set the pace for evaluating modern American letters....*Milquetoast:* "Getting us hooked, then making us wait until Summer? The jones-ing cruelty of waiting for your man"....*Garden Variety:* "The creative-art-as-commodity horde vomits lip synch formula onto mainstream communication vehicles marketed like potato chips: the more you eat, the more we'll make. But then, from the servile depths, a voice all its own"....Grey Stinson's *Vieux Carré*: "A hell-bomb of diction. Incinerate the feckless industry of art, dear Goodspeed. A little *creative destruction* is precisely what we all need right now."

And yet the point of all this discussion seems to have been lost on Goodspeed, all the words, all the push and pull, all the heat little more than a phone off the hook, that mid-range background hummmmmmmmm...."So long as there's buzz, it don't matter the make or model," he'd say.

True 'dat. And so, to the business at hand....

Whether in spite of the spotlit glare or just this toper's nature, our man's only noticeable response has been an epic bender. The one adjustment has him honing in on his new home base: stumbling as far as the front porch of the half-gutted *Woodruff House*, passing out on its stoop like curling up in Mother's arms. The spike has sterilized the progress of *renovation + renewal*, his drinking so often pissing all over any / all attempts at moderation. One could be forgiven to think it something he cannot resist, the schoolyard bully who bloodies your nose because he can; and that might yet prove to be the case, but for the documented purpose, drive, duty. Debatable, yes. But what we know for certain at present is the past few days have been a roaring jambalaya of morning, afternoon, and night. The distinct boundaries of time have dissolved, flickers of lucidity that scramble to deploy token stabs at health: orange juice by the gallon, B12 pills by the handful, sleeping "it" off—all of these just inklings of self-preservation that surface only to be swallowed in the muddled and confused throes of self-destruction. For he has been coming apart at the seams on a nightly basis. But then, there he is: every day, every night. Marvin Goodspeed: critically-acclaimed, critically-criticized, an ironclad commitment swinging up that slope towards the bristling breastworks of eventuality—a drive that smacks of resolution.

Goodspeed has lacked the wavering recently alluded to, as if having doubled-down: marching directly into the artillery's maw, staring down eventuality's double-shotted load of canister. As the addict smacking up the vein, he sees to the routine. It can be said he has not wavered an ounce. The *freedom* to do what one.... must?.... hummmmmmmmm.

THOUGH IT IS CLEAR that "drinking his way to a better understanding" of his subject was an idiotic waste of time *(the transgression of transgressions!)*, Cyrus Cleburne must still risk it as an occupational hazard in order to put in the legwork. For if not his thing, it still is *very much* his subject's thing. And one must do what one must.

It is the final afternoon in April. Cyrus has dutifully dragged himself out to *Asa's* for Day 2 of a conversation that'd kicked off the previous afternoon at *Los Alamos* and went something like this....

At Goodspeed's request, they had met up for a late-lunch. The Regular was popping with an electricity out of the usual for the dude. Cleburne hadn't even sat down before our man had launched into "the why"....During tear-out of the second-story, Goodspeed had demolition-ed his way through to an alcove cabinet of a dormer-window. All of it, window and all, had been systematically walled over. That was oddly compelling enough. But inside the cabinet, he'd found a bundle of letters that had been written to Woodruff's wife: Eliza. Pristine, he would eventually hand them over to the university housing the expansive *Gordon Patrick Woodruff Papers*. But Goodspeed was hesitant about handing them over just yet, needing to savor them a bit. 57 letters in all, Goodspeed had read them all in one sitting. Dates ranged over half-a-century and from the pens of nine writers, including Gordon. The oldest letters were from Eliza's oldest brother, Micah, and describe "soldiering with Lee." The letters drop scant mention of brutality and hardship, aside from "spirited fighting," a scathing indictment of an officer found out to be drunk during battle and Micah's longing for home cooking over the starvation rations of *cush* and chicory. Contents proved more the gloss over one would expect a protective older sibling to jot: reassuring of his "well-being" and "maintenance of good spirits." The last letter is dated September 2, 1862.

"I figure he gets that out just before they cross into Maryland, as Micah is shot dead at Sharpsburg, a meat-grinder to beat all," Goodspeed, crackling in the telling.

The latest letter dates to 1918. Eliza, known in her own right as a persuasive orator for the *Alliance* back in those early proto-*Populist* days, a solid partner to the fiery Woodruff (in an era when a wife was just as often considered property as an individual), she would die in the influenza pandemic that roared through the city that Fall. How did Goodspeed know all this? He had rolled himself a half-dozen blunts and spent an afternoon down at the county historical society.

Goodspeed, downing his second silver over rocks, had moved to his own lineage. There were two great-great-grandfathers and great-great-uncles, one each from paternal and maternal sides that had fought under Robert E. Lee: "They were old North-staters, all." One of the great x2 grandfathers had been killed on his twenty-third birthday: September 1, 1862 @ Chantilly, Virginia.

"A rear-guard fight that meant nothin' to nobody 'cept those killed 'n maimed; fought in a roaring thunderstorm, odd for then. Keep yer' powder dry, boys," Goodspeed ordering a refill before continuing. "Lucky for me, s'pose, my great grandmum's already been born. The younger brother has his hand blown clean off but for his thumb while storming Cemetery Hill, second night at Gettysburg; actually marched with the retreat back to Virginia 'stead of being left behind. Thought he was a goner as the wound got infected: gangrene, dysentery. He was a mess when they sent him home. Tough coot, made it through. And then there's the Goodspeeds," Marvin Goodspeed taking a moment to shake his head, scratch at the rough cut of pepper-grey crowding his angular jawline, that intense gleam. "Both of 'em make it through the whole god-damned turkey shoot without a scratch—not a one! Been sayin' it for years: lucky bastards, we Goodspeeds. Dumb lucky."

"There's bound to be a Confederate in the gene pool of any white Southerner of a certain vintage."

"A good deal of black Southerners too."

"Right on that. Former cohort at *the Weekly* grew up hearing about how the son of a plantation owner was in the mix on his mother's side. As best he could piece together, it came down that he'd raped who was likely a great-great-grandmother. The guy, now it was easy to find background on him: celebrated war veteran who wound up being a senator after Reconstruction. A respected lion of the community, dude even has a plaque. Pretty sure rape would disqualify you from the senate today. D'know, was never motivated to think over my lineage much."

"Really? Generational thing, 'spose. Shit, we still got Lee's birthday and Confederate Memorial Day off from school when I was growin' up, just like it was any other national holiday; 'course they were back then. Schools had all been integrated here in the city by then too. Got to wonder what the black kids must have thought of all that, the whites going off to lament over the thing designed to beat them down. Pro'ly were just glad to skip for a day. Last gasp of the white supremacist construct underwriting the whole damned thang, that was. Assholes couldn't hate in public anymore; which of course just made 'em hate all the more—banging away on that *lost cause* all the more."

Goodspeed had gotten to work on his third silver, just then delivered, Cleburne, having for some reason opted against the recorder (given the blur he knew was coming), sprinting to make mental notes—all the while in some surprise at the progressive declarations of this unreconstructed defender of *the status quo*.

"You realize even today a lot of white people would 'disagree' with your analysis, what the war was 'really' about?" (The air quotes Cleburne's.)

"Course they would. The sweet addictive nectar of myth is just too tempting, especially when it inverts the narrative, bathes the appalling in glory, duty."

Cleburne had soaked in the fine ironic distillation of that for a second, before continuing with the conversation Goodspeed thought they were having: "So, let me get this straight: you can go there on the war's root causes, yet still believe that the poor farmer in the ranks was just doin' his duty—and—that there's something to be said for that, if not celebrated outright?"

"Ya, well. It's complicated, ain't it?"

"Uh, ya, especially if you are heaping on the claim that the last gasp of white supremacy in this county was the 1960s?! You don't actually believe that the race thing was solved in the '60s? We're not even at a reconciliation point today, with thirty years in the rearview."

"But compared to how things were? A no-doubter."

"I—have to admit to some doubt. Public behavior may have improved. But all of the system still stands on the foundation of violent prejudice that built it. All the bricks are still there."

"But compared to how things were? No-doubter that it's all come a long way. Shit, man, ya couldn't even come up alongside the 'racial thing' (the air quotes Goodspeed's) when I was growing up lest you get an uncomfortable call from a 'concerned citizen' of the council."

"Okay, sure. But how much does it mean for white people to congratulate themselves on how much progress has been made?" Cleburne having tightened the screws and braced himself for a fiery rebuttal prompted, if anything, by a perceived lack of respect. But then came a funny thing: he received but a stale glance from Goodspeed, our man having become more invested in his third silver than a line of argument eroding as rapidly as the inebriated afternoon minutes. In a region historically informed by a tendency to fight on when the odds run long, Goodspeed seemed quite at ease with letting this one go....

"Well, maybe it's something, if just a little something, for the once guilty party to come around?"

"D'know about that. Slow plodding temperamental steps towards progress, at best. And I guess here is the point: Is that good enough, considering the all of what's gone down?" Cleburne having kept the foot on the gas, pressing on as to see where that line of going too far lay— ready and willing to cross it, you know: *for the cause....*"I'll give on the fact that there's generally less violence. But what of the institutions, the systemic violence? Rodney King was not all that long ago. South-central L.A. in '92 looked a lot like Watts in '65."

"Instinct, Cleburne. That's what the fight is against," Goodspeed, ever the elusive cat, tacking towards solid ground. "The very concept of supremacy of one race over another is only a short step removed from a tribalism even more primitive, even more unquestionable; the concept of painting 'the other' as bestial scum not worthy of human dignity? That there is a leery trait tracking back to our days in the cave. It's no wonder at all it is taking centuries to root it out. We can't change who we are on a dime, if at all. Curbin' instinct, society-wide? Hmmmm, might as well be moving a mountain with pick-and-shovel. It just is not gonna happen with some, just gotta wait 'em out, wait for the die off."

"Some people can't be changed, I get that. But systems can be."

"Right, but what are systems if not designed and implemented by people, people with  prejudices known and unknown, even to themselves. And on top of that, there's all those who'd rather just look the other way, let the tough stuff be someone else's problem. Often enough that makes up the majority. There's a reason a lie so grand and fallible as the *lost cause* continues to hold sway. Tradition is a powerful narcotic, champ; and most of its addicts don't even know they're hooked."

The two had ordered and the orders had been delivered and they had both dove headlong into plates of *atomic tamales*. Casting aside the husk, Goodspeed is shoveling it in as words continue to pour out....

"So, unless they were one of those who decided to skip the slaughter, head out west like Sam Clemens; or worse: a rich dude hiring up a poor farmer to die in his stead, every white male got sucked up into that clusterfuck of a civil war, down here. Naive kids most of 'em, had no larger frame on what the economic aristocracy had gotten 'em all into, what that fight was really about; just simply defendin' the all of down here," Goodspeed seeing to the hot work of this signature hot dish: masa wrapped shredded pork going down, words coming out....

"And shoot-hell, it was gonna be a big time! Get away from the drudgery of the farm, go kill some bluebellies! A tragic waste: duty and honor unto death. Right, and forgot the one: the youngest brother of my great-great-grandfather killed up in Virginia? He enlists the Fall after he heard his older bro'd been killed; only seventeen, lies about his age, wants to go serve under Lee, avenge his brother's death. But they sent him out to the west instead, serves in the same army as Woodruff—is killed near Shy's Hill, or what would be named Shy's Hill, out front of Nashville on, and I am not making this up, his twentieth birthday. The reason I'm not for celebrating my birthday: don't want to draw attention to myself, the powers that be and their dark humor."

"Your birthday isn't New Year's Eve, is it? If so, seems you may have side-stepped that curse."

"Hmmmm, too bad that is not the case. Would be nice to put that superstition to bed," our good Regular knocking back a final swallow of silver and throwing a V to the waitress. "Two Cuervos, straight-shots; just as you have a chance."

Cleburne had taken the brief spell to carry on with his

thing:

"Finishing that thought, the folks split early, never really took to the family lineage thing. The old man didn't get a lot of ringing endorsements. Besides, would probably have killed the inspiration to know what I'd find. He died on my fourth birthday, chance would have it; blind drunk, drove a '71 Impala into an abutment."

"Damn'd dreadnoughts, those things; surprised it didn't take out the entire bridge. Not to make light of it, didn't mean nothin' by it," Goodspeed momentarily unsteadied by his unintended discomfiting, a knee-jerk courteousness—reserved as it is for the "acceptable" members of the clan. (Dare we say we are in, dear reader?!)

"No worries. I never knew him. He was an only child and my grandparents, well, they didn't have much grandparenting in 'em. Only met them twice and both times were weird strained meet-ups. Somehow, they blamed my mother for the whole thing. Both of 'em died in my teens," Cyrus dropping the shot just delivered, setting sights on a final tamale.

"Ya, my pop? Asshole was a bigot of the highest order. Product of his generation, my ass. It oozed out of him too natural to be nurture-only. I never found anything, but sure he had to be in the Klan. Pret'sure he never had one conversation in his entire life with a black or a Mexican that went anything more than: 'boy, just ring me up,' or 'you seem to have wandered into the wrong neighborhood there, poncho,' entitled in his god-blessed whiteness to condemn them all. He would get on his hyphenated-American rants, all them 'unacceptable-Americans.' Always thought it ironic that he actually did call 'em

Americans. Just one more dick swallowed by history."

"Honestly, I'm a little scared at what I might find in our family tree; will stick to digging up the fossils of other's hastily buried faults."

"Not a bad strategy. It can all get pretty ugly on further review. Aubrey Williams said it straight: *we are deep in conflict with ourselves*. History don't have to judge kind; it just records truth and myth alike, let's the future weigh out the good and the bad."

"Ya, and that's gone really well. We're nothing in our blessed modernity if not experts at knowing between the good and the bad."

"Sayin' it like it is," Goodspeed knocking back the shot and twisting a toothpick up under an incisor. "The problem's that there's too many folks would rather a convenient revision shines it all up to a sheen; gives 'em a pass, sweeps out that gnawing guilt like a receding tide."

Goodspeed leans back, post-tamale (and four fucking tequilas!). He reaches across to pull out a cigarette pack and lighter from left-front shirt pocket, a noticeable wince within what seems an otherwise involuntary act. He lights up a smoke, exhales.

"Still can remember the day like it was yesterday. Got a black friend of mine to drop me off after football practice, senior in high school, knew my pop'd be where he always was after work: front porch with his rye, smoking, reading the paper. Man, did that get nexta' pop; thought the old man was gonna shit himself. We didn't say more than a dozen words to each other rest of that year; moved out day after graduation. Thought I was rid of that asshole for good."

At this point, Cleburne found himself foundering

around a stupor as much derived from deep-diving into the background of so violently anonymous a dude, as from the swimming swirl of that virile ol' conquistador: *tequila!* But given what he'd just heard, he felt compelled to rewind a bit and take an inquiring toothpick to one particular craw-caught tidbit....

"So got to ask, with a story like that, the veracity of bigotry —

"Veracity? There's a big word to toss about, champ. Ya must be feelin' that tequila courage."

"Pro'ly right on that; but d'you really believe that it'll just blow itself out? The systems are all still in place, trust me."

"Well, what the hell do I know? I'm not even convinced I'm beyond it in my own thing. All I know is I took the long slog down 'reconciliation boulevard' (again, the air quotes his own) and it was easier than I figured it would be; just had to call up my asshole nigger-this / nigger-that old man whenever I felt a twinge of tradition guilt holdin' sway. But y'know, it's also about realizing that you may never be able to change yourself. To a degree, you are: period. That's it: unchangeable. You can try, and some can manage the lie that that is. But then, as I see it might as well save the trouble and own it; for that is a most liberating thing. And if it is all about freedom—*and it is* (the author's italics)—it could even be viewed as a patriotic thing. History is gonna sort it all out in spite of anything you do, anyway," Goodspeed having rocked back in his chair, the inhaling and exhaling of his smoking a cigarette almost lyrical.

"I don't have the answers and not sure anyone does. Could be the whole racist thing never does work itself out. It does seem hard-wired into the human animal, most tha' time. That piece you wrote paints it fairly stark in our own time, and right here in our own fair city; says it with both barrels: the economics, still racist as fuck."

"You read it?" Cleburne having been honestly surprised. (And, well, honored?)

"All of it. Also read that this year's report confirmed y'all's suspicion: southside gangs having drifted with the tide of poor folks the city fathers suckered to the outer 'burbs."

"You did read all of it. Ya, how the gang shootouts are now spiking a county over from the one we profiled? Nice, huh?"

"And still, city's carting 'em off by the busload; article didn't slow it at all. Tradin' bodies for prime real estate, some hard-hearted motherfuckers, right there. My D's been dealin' with the city's eminent domain forays down *Old Fifth Ward* and *Springvale* way for years now, saying this year's report is probably what got you all nominated. She thinks y'all will get that award too."

"I'll be damned, who's stalking who here?"

And though the easy, if high-gravity, volley had continued a little while longer, it was just inevitable (because it is always so) that that swarthy ol' buccaneer: *tequila!* would come to drain the bottom out of the afternoon, a back-and-forth that was soon enough being slathered in a crude salsa of misogyny and mano-a-mano threats implying extirpation—but not before Goodspeed dropped this nugget:

"Always wondered, what if Lee had listened to Longstreet prior to making that charge, had prepared all of us southerners to come for a new way of thinking? Dunno, might of set a precedent: lookin' to the future for inspiration, not just the past."

Of course, this apologist-seeming head-scratcher was followed by what could only be pegged as the usual outcome of his late-lunch visits: Goodspeed soon after challenging the entire kitchen staff to step outside and see if they could man up to *his* tequila courage. Standard stuff, the revolving staff at *Los Alamos* never taking the bait—an entertaining side dish to *bacadillos y chile con carnes*. That cavalier *Old South* passion still lights up this Goodspeed no matter how much he may slather it with shit. A true confederate.

> *Over time, he began to think on his position within this cult of society, the very monolith he lived his life to upset. He grew glum in light of an irony, that being: He had grown so used to it—even as his foil— that he could no longer imagine life without it.*

Marvin Goodspeed  ~  *Within*

And so, here we are: Day 2. Cleburne putting in the blood, cold sweat, and tears, having dragged himself out to pick up on yesterday's fevered themes—again, by invitation.... It is oddly empty but for the two, Howard, Martha, and a newcomer: Sang. Guessing late-40s, Vietnamese, word is he was a translator that got out in May 1975; the supposition: that he's been homeless ever since. Perhaps no longer: drinking, silent and content, along the short L of the bar.

The resumption of Goodspeed and Cleburne's discussion lumbers about the bulwarks of this modest hovel: in here, where the sheer tonnage of the weight of the world is checked at the door, where life's needling irritants are pissed down the drain. It is *Asa's* guarantee. All those who buy-in deloused on entry of the time-homicide epidemic to these days. In lieu of *all* the defeats out there, the gauzy blur of nonchalance may yet secure *Victory!* in here. At the very least, it is likely to yield a draw: fighting all the bastards who would just as well enslave you—*as they did all those past*—to a breathless bloody stalemate. For though the hate runs deep, the hottest war must die down to pulsing coals every so often....right?

And yet here he is, his blood up, our good Regular in his element and playing the long game. He is expert at a few things, perhaps the most important being his maintaining the heat that fires the smoldering squint subsidizing purpose, duty, *raison d'etre*. Again, would he even drag his ass out of bed, or up off the cracked hexagonal sidewalk each morning without the prod of perceived wrongs and the interchangeable real / manufactured hate they induce? Despite the general tenor of nonchalance, the occasional "stand" will testify to the intense heat to be found when one pokes about the mentioned coals: a conviction, an ardor playing out (with aid of our intrepid journalist / stoker) along the length of *Asa's* bar....

"If you accept freedom as the baseline, then you just have to accept the nihilistic fools it empowers," Goodspeed loosening the restraint on vocal chords with a resolute gulp down from his domestic-in-a-bottle, the dead soldier placed respectfully atop bar top, having given its last full measure of devotion.

"We allow the sons-of-bitches to think the world

revolves around 'em, allow bastards the opportunity to exploit their workers, run the risk of violent fuck-ups getting their hands on a gun, we do all this rather than trust to restrictive laws and autocrats and nobles 'cause the very concept of curbing our freedom hits on the abstract as much as it does the reality; is why opinion and dissent is a duty."

It is an equal ratio: the more drinks that pour in, the more character that pours out. And more importantly, the more *man* and *myth* become one. It is to this outlier in the rigging of his theory that Cyrus has now turned an acetylene focus. Having scaled the walls designed to keep things out, he is now working *it* out from within. He is giving his all. In fact, it's taking his all just to keep from sliding off the stool....

"Wait, did you just diss the Second Amendment?" Cyrus, in an impetuous moment, prodding.

Goodspeed half-clucks a laugh, spreading his arms, resting palms on bar-edge—his temper immediately reduced to gauzy nonchalance, if not outright boredom. Cyrus immediately takes note. *(Tread lightly, young son.)*

"Context. It is all in the context. What is an argument, be it social, political, economic, religious, or other, without the context of all that has led to that particular moment? It is context not conviction that determines the relevance of points of view. An opinion is just the damned booster and his advertiser automatons without the peripheral substance of worth that comes with knowing how history has brought us to this point. Without the full sweep, it is just about the loudest megaphone and the clout it can buy."

Goodspeed picks up a fresh domestic having been

placed with diligent care before him by Howard, who moves on without a word, dutifully wiping down a clean bar top; eyebrow raised, slight smirk in evaluating the rare access given this one-time interloper....

"I can only see it for the dark comedy of it all, in that our first two amendments stack up a guarantee that those fuck'd in the head get a voice 'n a gun, which is made all the more absurd in that it guarantees your own raht to take 'em down with ya. The long and short? If someone's lookin' to kill, they'll find a way. Trust me. Hodding Carter, look 'im up; here was a man who sat with a loaded pistol in his desk drawer 'cause he knew, his words: *Southerners will generally treat you politely until they make up their minds to kill you.* We still have our guns and absorb the collateral violence it brings 'cause no one has yet figured out how to reconcile the heat of human emotion with the freedom to act on it."

"What about removing guns from the equation? Second Amendment was designed for a frontier nation. We can at least agree we're beyond a frontier state?" Cleburne, gamely, what "some" might call intrepidly, going for it, pushing when laying back would seem the more advisable course.

"You sure about that, son?"

"I'd say, yes. We're past the open frontier."

"Okay, so a hundred years from now yer tellin' me that folks won't look back at this point in time right now and think: Those poor ignorant saps, they were at the frontier of knowin' all of what the brain is and how very much the subconscious is working it?"

"I'm lookin' a hundred years back, not forward," Cleburne making a mental note of the jiu-jitsu of Goodspeed's rolling evasion of the question: how our good Regular actually invoked the future, not the past; that is, before pivoting swiftly back on that pesky past....

"Okay, so you need history to get down on your point? How about this: No one ever thought it a good idea to ban rope back 'round early part of this century, though it played a somewhat significant role in all the damned lynchings."

"But, uh, correct me if I'm wrong here: rope was designed to tie up boats and horses and shimmy flags up poles, right. Pretty sure white mob lynching was not its intended purpose?" Cleburne's volley sharp, despite the buzzzzzzzz....

"Alright, so I'll leave you with this: good luck tryin' to take away our guns, champ; might as well be looking to uncarve a credo from stone," the cool collected response not lost on Cleburne. *(Best to not take such respect granted lightly, son.)*

The mediators of dialogue are the bourbon shots they knock back; one every 15 minutes. (You know, pacing. It's everything.) Faithful Howard, like clockwork, sets them up for the knock back. Which is not to insinuate that time is a factor here. The fact that Goodspeed and Cyrus have been at this since *Asa's* opened (it now nearing 1 p.m.) is irrelevant. All that is relevant would be the character flowing out as if an uncapped hydrant.

"Back to the larger surround, if you don't mind: The work of revolution is never done, Cleburne." Their 15 minutes up. Two shots up. Two shots knocked back. "However, the self-proclaimed revolutionary is a fool. Detached, he's just a satellite revolving in a controlled little orbit, divorced of the society he is whippin'—gets up every morning with the aim to fight to the death. You don't win that war, only perpetuate the traits ya hate. Can't label yourself a revolutionary; would be like callin' yourself sir or reverend. It's an earned throne."

Cyrus evades a head-spin as if dodging a boomerang, an occupational hazard having gone straight to his skull. He shakes it off, resolves, steps up to the plate and prods Goodspeed one step further. No free rides. (Give the kid credit, this time he IS working hard here.)

"But you use fiction to dispatch perceived enemies in all you do. And you do it with a revolutionary zeal. A satellite man, wouldn't ya say?"

The composure, the sharp wit under fire? (C'mon, folks: credit where credit is due!)

Goodspeed clucks a half-laugh, pulls a half-folded pack of cigarettes from shirt pocket, leans, drunkenly, to more easily pull out a lighter from pants pocket. He lights up, exhales.

"Like Kerouac said: Fiction is just non-fiction with all the names changed. But that said: tailoring villains from whole bolts of fabricated cloth, if only—or specifically—to aid the selling of books? Just moves the message all the more. Hardly a crime in my book."

"Kinda my point."

The day limps into the afternoon. The marred paneling beginning to dance in a clockwise motion, pennants and posters counter-clockwise. Cyrus shakes his head. How long, really, can his dodging continue? He stands, steadies himself on the bar, throws a twenty atop bar top. The room's floor is a ship deck encountering heavy swells. Light pours through front door. Rays plead for tolerance. *Hoo, lawd!*

"Okay, folks, hate to cut it short; but I gotta run."

"Leaving? Why we're just gettin' started, ain't that right, H?" Goodspeed slurring in his comfortable quarter, his command-and-control centre.

"Muth is just about to serve up some lunchtime stew there, son," adds Howard, Martha peeking over the kitchen's order-counter, her motherly grin creased by the cigarette notched in lip-corner.

"Thanks all, I do, I really do 'presh, appreciate it; but I'm a gotta run," Cyrus giving a wave, the gesture more stand-back demand than cordiality, swaying some.

"Best settle into walkin' there first, champ," Goodspeed laughing as if simply to hear himself laugh, curling back into the routine and not missing a beat.

Cyrus leaves Goodspeed to his work, exits, enters "out here." The sharp mid-day light hits Cyrus as it must have on his birth: confusing, disorienting, welcome in a way not yet obvious. The day, still so young, so much promise, Cyrus tight-roping consciousness. It is hard work, at the moment working hard on one-step-in-front-of-the-other. He aims slurred steps up Washita. Time skips, as if missing every other frame; but seems no less real for the surreal of it. It is a state one could get used to, could get hooked on: painless, free. Why, has time been rendered meaningless? Well, I'll be damned....*it does work.*

Several stagnant hours have passed. Cyrus comes-to from a hazy dream, a fumbling transition to a hazy real. The vitality of Spring is doing its damnedest to drown out the spoil of smog. A traffic-copter whirrs in ever-tightening circles: a buzzard assessing the state of carrion below. The stalled fuming rumble of the parkway connector, the dream-state traipsing off with the helicopter's ascent. He rubs eyes, drags hands down his face, stretching and clenching his face up into plastic mask-like contortions. It is oddly therapeutic, like cracking knuckles.

Cyrus props himself onto elbows. He scans. An afternoon pass-out nap on the stonewall running the length of Highland Avenue: just what the good doctor ordered. A headache looms, as much from the tsunami of exhaust as the sheer volume of liquor he'd consumed before 1 p.m. *(Hoo!)* The age-old catalpa, its branch-ends green, gregarious. One more season yet. Spring-time optimism flings fragrances doing their damnedest to sweeten the smothering emissions of quittin' time. Cyrus swings to a seated position, stretching, shaking off the blur: a little mental smelling salts....*Shake it off, Cleburne! Just had your bell rung! Get back out there!*....He stands, pivots, heads towards *Candler Hills*. He can feel good about the damage done on this day.

For it is in Goodspeed's camp where *promise* has had a rough-go: this creative inferno, so often neutralized by the unconditional defeat of one more day being flushed down the toilet, the cowl of inebriation well advanced. And this would be the correct assessment (for fuck sakes it is the correct assessment, subjective observation noted), but for that peculiar inversion of things, in here. Promise, optimism, potential, these are just words. And we all know by now that words can be strung together to insinuate one thing, while being very much in service to some other thing....

"Forked tongues prostituting the real, the finger-crossers twisting up statements and promises so as to squander your *freedom* for their *profit*."

In short, words—like the reality they are meant to describe—can mean what we'd like them to mean. "In here" could well happen to be one of those places where normal is not so much, where the lie could be anything but. *Real. Myth.* It's all in the interpretation....right? And if so, by his own "yardstick" Goodspeed could right then view this day through a constructive lens: one more in a long line of successes....

Goodspeed shifts his prone position in a back booth of *Asa's* backroom, working hard at drunken slumber after a full day of *freedom* achieved. He will not allow the marrow-sucking parasites an opening for attack, the reward of "convenience" and "financial security" and "social acceptance" for toeing the company line a traitorous act in his book (in all his published books, actually). In fact, by his own metrics he has more reason to feel good about the results of this day than most, having achieved precisely what he set out to do despite the array of duplicitous enemy corps down here and aligned against him. He is showcasing a marathon endurance in the face of overwhelming odds. This here, hard work: to swing up that slope into the point-blank maw, to roll onto inevitable *Victory!*

Actually, this day can go to hell for all he cares; his snoring coarse, nasally.


CINCO DE MAYO often foretells the temper of Summer waiting in the wings. And if this day is any indication, it would hint at a broiler to come. But Goodspeed grants this early bout of humid heat no ill-will.

It is just doing its thing, what it always has—what it must.

The mitre-ing of soffit slats to replace those of a front porch eave having rotted through pools sweat atop his brow. Our man had been working hard for most of the past week hanging sheetrock. He will be hiring a crew to finish it, mud and sand.

"Hell job, go hire up some mariachi band to knock it out; pay 'em with a rock-on tequila bender to get in on the festivities," he mutters while standing in a saw-dusted patch of front yard, chugging his third bottle of Gatorade that afternoon, lofting a shrug at his own latent ability to slum in stereotypes. "Do Mexicans even celebrate Cinco de Mayo?"

Electricians had completed rewiring the house but a few days back, the roofers having finished all but the tricky turret. It was slowly coming together, the *old* standing up to be heard amongst all that is *new* (the *new*, of course, admitting nothing of its instinctual reliance on the *old*). He had been determined to call up general contracting skills of old in order to take care of his old friend, as promised. The results have been varied. Sheetrocking had been put on hold following Goodspeed's spot-on hammer blow to thumb the previous afternoon. He can now sense that the pint of bourbon he had drained for lunch probably hadn't helped. "Focus, Goodspeed, focus," he'd pleaded over the throbbing digit.

He pulls out a half-crushed pack of cigarettes, shakes one loose, notches it in lip-corner, lights it, exhales, scans. A breeze showers the yard with the last of the oak pollen, DNA strands spiraling down. Everywhere the promise of the season reigns. Waxwings cluster in the canopy, glide-diving into a nearby mulberry busting with berries....chatter, emphatic, chatter....Smoking, his sunken gaze is right then cut through by a fire still evident. His squinting hints at it being time to reel things in, get to work. Ideas have been percolating under the gauzy grey of alcoholic tendencies that instinctually sink productivity (if providing grist for fiction and *myth*). And he is, right then, sensing that some of these wayward dogs might just hunt. But he wonders if the time is right to pull the trigger, sobriety—as fleeting as that relationship can be—not for the faint of heart, not for those unwilling to commit fully. "Gotta pick yer battles." He scans the scene, the budding mimosas along property edge to bloom rose-orange flak-puffs by June.

And just at that moment of indecision, all hints of his "correct" course vanish—or more correctly, come into view: Dorothy ambling up from the sidewalk. A wicked smile accentuates her full round visage. She holds a bottle in a paper bag by the neck, that look in her eye. For there is still work to be done. There is the *myth* to nourish, replenish, inebriate. Working her man to optimal effect, doing what is right, for the both of them. A warmth fills Goodspeed, blends with the afternoon heat....

"Quittin' time, soldier!"

Goodspeed takes a final drag, flicks cigarette to sideyard and gathers the buoyant D in his arms. He hoists his trophy for the evening, the duty—the love—evident. There is the get-down-to-business practicality of the whole venture; and then there is the hot love. And though the two run on tracks of varying gauge, they are not mutually exclusive: money and love being partners of an age old vintage. It can be argued over who stands to win or lose the most: its novel set of goals, its debatable technique. But then (as we have been told), labels, standards, moral authority, these are the ravening manipulative tools of the *Gilded* bastards who have only their own freedom and profits in mind. Foes of self-determination, those assholes look to erase the freedom of others to do as they see fit. They are for slave labor, gaming the innocent of their birthright liberties—the enemy.

And these two, knowing it to be so *(oh, and it is so)*, seem ever more committed to the outlier tactics that they employ. In fact, it is no stretch to say that they are at this very moment committing all the more to a *cause* non-committal, their non-participation in "wholesome ways" an act of civil disobedience. It is the one true *out* that this brand of freedom guarantees....*I can neither confirm nor deny the charges*.... the Fifth Amendment to a constitution all newcomers to this universe of regulars must come to respect. For all the greedy "know nothings" will work this society, corrupt it with the numbing rot of hyper-consumption, force-feed it to the brim of a self-pleasuring puritanical superiority. It is a zero-sum tyranny that will not stand....*To prove this, let Facts be submitted to a candid World*.... The unknowing must be learned, post-haste, that the dominant trends of society will find no friends where it runs afoul of those just looking to be left—the—fuck—alone....*Blend with the wall-flowered minions doing what they must, johnny-come-lately, or your latent oppression will be dealt no quarter.*

Sure, the everyday trappings of the regulars' ways have a deliberate effect on....well, do we even need to say it? They tranquilize *progress!* But then, perhaps we have stumbled across its very point. (Perhaps?!)....Still, in the actual pursuit of accomplishing such disobedience, there is at least, in this case, a balance to be struck, a DMZ to be established. We know that the nature of this arrangement will have it occasionally and regularly being overrun by plundering hordes (George Dickel, Evan, Jack?), which makes it all the more imperative to, on occasion, enforce that permeable barrier, attend to the duty-at-hand and all that entails—lest the bastards' boosters swamp your subversive message, cheat you of your life savings.... Still, when one has worked hard, it is only right to play hard, eh? It is the next logical step. It is as nature intended. And if nature has provided us any indication, the next logical step would suggest a bender.

It is an hour later. Goodspeed, the maestro, and D, the maestro's de-facto manager / lover, steer into inebriation via the cold logic of warm liquor. The inconsequence of time—burying that little prick in the blur—is the chief aim, as vital a tool to *the cause* as pencils sharpened to a nub, sweet bud, Goodspeed's verse-smithing honed to mah—sta—piece. A portable stereo belts out new *Dylan*, old *Van Morrison*, *The B-52s*; audio moonshine via mix-tape. D is dancing and whirling, their reveling weaving up their smoking and drinking to slipknot-tight. Worry, pain, the steady disintegration of their tethered subservience to a society used and abused by the monied thieves—economic, political, cultural—all of that dissolves in the music and the booze on a hot Spring afternoon. Here, now, it is all coming clear. The grins pasted to their faces of genuine grade.

And here, now, is where the regular will ratchet-up his or her caustic conviction. What is in plain view deceives.

What may seem reckless alcohol-fueled debauchery to the unobservant (the trowel-less?) is, in fact, a deep devotion to *cause*. Blind faith is the cornerstone of belief, blind drunk to the irritants of this life sacrosanct to this brand of worship. And it is all working beautifully. Time is neither here nor there.... And the believers take their revival on the road.

The couple stumbles down Austin, through the *Druid Heights* and up through *Delta Point Park* into *Springvale's* innards. They fumble through obliviousness arm-in-arm, *free*. Goodspeed grabs a tit, copping a hearty feel. D grabs a handful of assets in response, threatens a twist....

"Best be another masterpiece, lover. Momma wants a new jacuzzi."

"All fer you, babe. All fer you!"

"That's my cowboy," the threat downgraded to encouraging member blood-flow. Priming the pump, she'll have use for it soon enough.

Done molesting each other for the moment, Goodspeed takes a swig from a flask, passes it to his beloved, picks up and hurls a rock through an abandoned car's side-window. Never to be outdone, D's attempt sails over the target and smashes into the windshield of a car parked on the dead-end street beyond the lot. The car's alarm wails. They both run off. *Oh shit!* laughs. Dodging responsibility a natural response, out here...."Damn kids, today."

They duck down Dixie, jogging down the sidewalk. Goodspeed stubs toes, stumbles over an uprooted slab of hexagonal stone. He grimaces, waiting for the pain—then realizes he is pain free.... It works every time, guaranteed.

Even his laughter is slurred, stopping, swaying,

unzipping and pissing into a storm drain. He draws an evil eye from an old man sitting on a front porch rocker. Goodspeed shakes, zips, waves to the old man, who gives him the finger, the Regular trotting off.

D, meanwhile, has liberated the lust of her intentions, having torn off her shirt, laughing and running topless into the heart of Dixie. Goodspeed unbuckles his belt, unfurls it from loops like a whip. He chases her. She comes to an abrupt halt in front of her house, undoes her jeans and lets them drop. She bends over and offers up a shapely target.

"Show mercy!" she taunts, howling laughter.

"Time to teach the wicked the err of their ways!" Goodspeed winding up and delivering a flesh-kissing smack. Dorothy recoils, a scream of approval, kicking off her jeans and striding naked up her front walk. Goodspeed takes a swig, runs up behind her, gathers her in his arms. He hoists his girl and his flask, marching up the front walk with his trophies. They drain the flask and do it on the front porch.

And they will kick back in the afterglow, will light cigarettes, drink domestic lager from cans and nap. The sun will sink heavy and orange. They will bask in the glow, the full glow of what the evidence has led us to believe, as public and known as if bright-hued flyers stapled to telephone poles about town advertising the show we know has been playing for some time: *the love evident*. D's bungalow perched atop a rise, downtown light-points wavering in the Spring breeze. The city, a steaming pit of pulsing embers. They will awake just in time to loft their promise to *The Beacon*, will do so without uttering a word. They will fight for what they love and all that that entails.

THE DAY NOW NIGHT, Cyrus strides within darkened urban hollows skimmed of light pollution. He is heading for *Asa's*: that most haunting of haunts. He is a hundred feet off. A flash and hollow pop-crack recoiling down the valley of avenue. Backlit by front window neon, a ragdoll human shape crumples to hexagonal stone.

Cyrus is frozen in his tracks. His instinct is to make tracks, but his morbid journalistic curiosity defies street smarts. He takes to shadows beyond the intersection as Howard staggers out the front door swearing, his hands outstretched, curled fingers gripping the air. He grabs his head, shakes his head. His arms go limp and drop to his side. It is a defeated reaction. Paul and Omar are next out the door. They act out like displays. Ez, Jude, Tench, Chuck, Sax, Victor, Sang, Martha, they all pour out, craning necks, crying out, turning to exhale repulsion. Victor hits the stations, rubbing a necklace rosary as if his own life depended on it. The rest of the group mills aimlessly as if head-struck geese, as if waiting for further instruction, or an explanation to fill in the inexplicable blank. Neither seem imminent, just blood pooling from exit-wound.

"Ohhhh—god-damn, god-damn! Thought that ol' codger was pullin' our leg; didn't for a second think he actually meant it, that he was actually gonna do it. Damn, damn," Howard the only clear utterance amongst a chorus of low expletives, nervous pacing, heads shaking.

Someone has already radioed in. Distant sirens snake through the neighborhood, gaining volume. Laverne and Trey arrive in separate cruisers, simultaneously. Cruiser lights whirl, sirens go silent—as in requiem to the fallen regular. Zell *Boo* Hadley, a plug of a man who'd found twenty plus years of refuge within *Asa's* all that was required of his devotion, his vigil. The *freedom* to determine his own end having seemed a heartening and logical conclusion. This blackened hollow, drinking lives into submission—having claimed one of its own.

Cyrus is already backtracking, the sight of a man taking his own life having rubbed out any desire for "research" and / or camaraderie. He just can't believe it. But then, he can. A knot in his stomach, walking backwards trance-like, instinct urging him to run. The strange calm seems suspect, eerie, a low-voltage hum. It chills the vertebrae, runs down his spine. Life, death. Having witnessed death. He turns, jogs away from there. That place, so mercurial a temper. It is free in a way most of us can only imagine, free to live and die by its own hand. An ambulance flies down the avenue past him, lights whirling, no siren. It is heading for *The Asa Inman*.

Goodspeed and Dorothy, having night-strolled their way up through *Springvale* and down Elizabeth, arrive to a scene. The bagged body is right then being loaded in through ambulance doors. Rough-hewn neighbors in bathrobes, tank tops, and plaid have formed an outer ring that eddies mulling and muttering about on the sidewalk. A respectful wary distance is given. Even the reclusive cabinetmaker and *busboy* have ventured out to mix with regulars, EMTs, officers. The silent whirl of red and white lights casting a carnival requiem across the intersection.

Goodspeed runs up from the shadows, hands outstretched.

"What the hell—is this!?"

"Shot himself, Marv, right here, right in front of the window," Howard venting off erratically, weeping openly....

"This place was like home for him, I know that, I know that. But right here?! Right in front of us all!? Dammit all!" Howard pulling out a pile of hose from the far side of *Asa's*, turning on the spigot.

"Who—what!?" Goodspeed in blank shock amazement.

"Boo, Marv, Boo," Chuck laying a hand on the Regular's shoulder, wiping away his own tears with the other. "He's like: well, it sure has been nice to have known all yous. No angels in here, no model citizens, but good solid folk, all. I'm proud to have been of ya, but is time to move on—sum'n like that."

Victor lets out a heavy exhale, rubbing holy beads, running his other hand through his black shock of hair striped grey. He hard-swallows the shock of a fallen brother in arms: "I just thought he was drunk rambling like he does and heading for home, when he pulls out that old Ruger he always is showin' off. Ate the God-damned thing—forgive me, Lord, just upset."

"There was a pair of young ones set up at the bar end next to Jude that I never did see before; them there," Saxby pointing out the now stunned set, likely from the hip new apartment buildings having just opened up Highland. "I was thinkin' for some reason he's about to threaten 'em with that gun. He didn't like 'em being around here, all the changes goin' on around here lately."

Goodspeed is staggered as if concussed by the weight of it all, dragging his hands down his face, watching on as

Howard clears the way and begins hosing down the sidewalk. Trey and Jack and Laverne get another call and are moving on, D having bypassed the whole scene and already sequestered inside with Martha. Goodspeed stands silent, staring at the crimson wash rushing down storm-drain. Howard cursing, the crowd dispersing....

"What now? What do we even do now?" Goodspeed, too numb to rationalize, to call up protocol; numb in spirit and mind.

"We go in and we drink to him, seems that's what he wanted; may be why he went out the way he done," the usually silent Jude providing the stoic leadership all the regulars are in need of at that moment, absolving the deed by defining the need to honor a fallen comrade. They all shake their heads in agreement.

Howard has not stopped cursing, looks set to cry or explode in a rage as he continues to hose down the sidewalk. The cabinetmaker and his deadbeat *busboy* son have launched into a heated argument. Goodspeed gripping his forehead, is disbelief-grinning....

"Well, is that it, Boo? Just wanted one final toast before ya up 'n split? Planned it all out, didn't ya? Amongst all of the random, there are still some things we can plot out, can expect."

And an old random Chevy comes tumbling wild and reckless down Austin Avenue from *The Points*. It is completely out of control, firefly headlights. A late '70s Monte Carlo bounding and veering onto and over the flagstone curb, a tire blowing, its steel-rim scraping and throwing sparks. And the vehicle, having obviously survived like events (multi-colored doors, unpainted Bondo), rides the sidewalk as if it were an alternate lane.

It takes out a row of mailboxes, runs through garbage cans and a boxwood hedge and barely misses a century-old water oak before skipping sideways through the intersection. Brakes now screeching, it careens off a telephone pole beyond Euclid, crash-stopping against the brick facade of the cabinetmaker's storefront. A few seconds of singing calm before the storefront plate-glass begins to splinter. The front window, original to the building and proceeding commercial-use of laminated window glass by decades, cracks and splinters and cascades completely onto car hood.

The cabinetmaker, having just re-entered his shop (also his residence) lets fly a profanity string heard over the fading din of glass bits, telephone lines twanging, a hubcap coming to rest. The driver kicks open car door and stumbles out, stunned. He is shit-faced, the cabinetmaker emerging from the dust cloud and stepping through the gaping hole in his storefront red-faced and fuming and rolling up his sleeves as he approaches the drunken perp. The dude snaps to and sprints off into *Springvale*, the cabinetmaker in hot pursuit, their footfall and screaming soon blending with the night. It is just another night: the random violence backdropping planned violence in a way odd, strange, perfect.

Howard has continued hosing the sidewalk through it all, the high-pressure stream of water his attempt to hose clean all things. A police cruiser rolls headlong down Euclid, lights boiling, siren wailing as tires skip-screech in banking down onto Austin. It all disappears into the bowels of *Springvale*. This evening, the routine out here primed to usurp the norm and the expected at every turn— and this despite the dutiful desire of some to clutch hard to things tagged as *immemorial.*

Goodspeed turns toward *Asa's* front entry, shakes his head and enters along with the rest. They will toast the fallen. It is what should be done. It is the only thing that can be done. Howard turns off the spigot and coils up the hose at the far side of the building. A final stream trickles out as he drops the nozzle atop the pile, rubbing away a final tear. He takes one last look at the spot on the sidewalk. He stares up, exhales hard. He closes the door behind him, on all of that.

SOME TIME HAS PASSED. Days, weeks, a month—it hardly seems to matter. For it's been eventful, and for all the wrong reasons.... The bank up in *The Points* had been robbed the morning after Boo's suicide, The General having been shot by a rookie cop who just happened to be parked at *Los Alamos* next door, not knowing the drill with The General: the homeless vet having appeared as he does—from nowhere—at the sound of the bank's alarm going off, wild in brandishing his starter's pistol as he ran into the fray; this all happening within a few yards of the still numb and mourning Goodspeed, the Regular (knowing the drill) having not thought twice about The General and traipsed, unawares, into the line-of-fire, royalty check in hand.

"That's it, god-dammit. Gettin' one of those direct-deposit wire deals set up!" Goodspeed had yelled lying face-down on the asphalt of the bank's parking lot, cruisers screeching in all around him.

Shaken, now even more than he was, Goodspeed had made tracks down Austin only to sight an ominous smoke-plume rising up from down near the intersection. Multiple sets of sirens were converging. He set to a jog and then broke into a run as a fire truck flew past him down the avenue. *Asa's* came into view just as the first-responders were rushing in the front door, hose-in-hand. A grease fire had erupted in the kitchen where Martha had been preparing a heap of ribs, reaching a point of out-of-control while she'd tended to other items of inventory. Howard, with the help of Gid (having luckily tucked in to take a little nip), had brought Martha to safety; some second-degree burns and light smoke inhalation, is all. Goodspeed came running up, sucking air, breathless, as paramedics helped her to an ambulance, Howard and Gid, faces black-smeared. Two days, two ambulances—*fuck all!* With the previous night still fresh, the look roaming about Howard's face veered between shock and cosmically pissed.

"Fuck all! Kitchen's totally destroyed, smoked up everything in there. Should just gut it all and finally fix up this shithole! Shoulda done it years ago, blend in with all the new around here. Hell, d'know why I don't just close it all down, move to Myrtle Beach like we said we would one day—god-dammit all!"

"Now, okay. I know you're hot right now, H. But hey, c'mon, shouldn't just say things," Goodspeed's lump-in-throat shock stunning him into a moment of tunnel vision, all his worst fears, once abstract, inflating to real in an instant.

"Fuck it! Fuck it all!" Howard heavy-foot stalking around the side of the place, getting with a fire chief who just did arrive to assess things.

Goodspeed, who given the back-slide temper of things

could have used his watering hole right then, could only hang his head.

"No worries, Marv. I'll drop by the new house with a little somethin'—check yer mailbox later on. This here? This'll all turn out."

Goodspeed looked at Gid from beneath the immensity of the unknown, the realization of a savage rift in *the status quo*. He turned without a word and walked off, defeated.... Goodspeed knocked about through west *Springvale* and into the once blighted *Old Fifth Ward* where he noticed a marked change in demeanor. Urban pioneers had begun to tempt second-wave urban settlers; even a rough-hewn, if fancy, pub, organic bakery, and some business called *Media Forge* having sprouted up since last he'd made tracks. This did not strike him as threatening, but it was something else. It was not what had been, and hinted at more and more *new* and less and less of the old and familiar, as run-down—or—as fucked-up-and-bullshit as the *old* had been....

Goodspeed stopped into a new clean tidy mart where an old shitty one had been right on the edge of the two 'hoods along Highland. He stepped to the counter and asked for a pack of smokes....

"You bet," the young hip student-age worker (less old-school freak) had said, sliding out the pack. "Hey man, aren't you —

Goodspeed threw down three bucks and left without a word. No, this was all too much. All at once with the non-anonymity, this trending towards *newness* and distinct trending away from the *old predictable-ness*. And here, in a place where popular regional instincts wile their way down worn familiar lanes—mental gullies cut out of predictable wear....

It was all coming with millennial speed, this day—these days. Rattled, devotion and duty were returning question-marks sans the ironclad instinct to fight on in the face of overwhelming odds. Goodspeed made tracks E x NE, a worn familiar route aiming for the library up in *Candler Hills*. A cache of reads in hand, he stopped off at the liquor store in *The Points* and set off to hole himself up within *The Woodruff House*. There, within surroundings requiring no consideration, no projected motivations beyond the salve of routine and the habitual, Goodspeed set up shop with all the Steinbeck the library had available. Best to lay low at so low a point, avoid attracting any more the attention of dark humors. There seemed little within his control but to make a rearguard stand, to plant tarheels firm and wait—wait and see if this fad required but a strong breeze of devotion to carry it away, or if this was a juggernaut of overwhelming newness unto which his only choice would be to go with and carve out his space within.... He read and he drank and he steeled himself for either.

Days fell away inside reclusive shrouds of pot smoke. Goodspeed buzzed through the cache. First up was *Cannery Row*. The novella, so goes the legend, had only taken the author sixty days to write. It took Goodspeed about six hours to devour: the dutiful sentry perched on front porch, face buried in paper-and-ink and half expecting a swarm of interloping Moleskine-scrawling locusts or even some full-on apocalyptic tempest at any moment. But then there was only Lee, Doc, Mack, and a warm westerly breeze.

The vigil continued, all work on the house halted, visits

by D with pre-made dinners and gallon jugs of orange juice the only thing that came between Goodspeed, Steinbeck, and "a few pack-loose dogs hinting that they'd hunt." It all seemed to point towards a brief truce. He had stopped drinking all day and was finding a groove. As bothered and uneasy as it was, his answer seemed to lie where one might expect: to write himself through those things ending, pick up fresh with those things then beginning. His instinctual scribbling (which really never ends) had begun to coalesce: a thin scab over the double-barreled gut shot of all that had come down. And having given time the slip, he was putting pen to paper. He was doing so one night up in the unfinished turret when he looked out to see the neighbor's carriage house going up in flames.

"Fuck all! What kinda god-damned fool was I to think I'd come through the other end of it unscathed. Here it is, the fiery end, right here."

It was not (the hellfire end, that is). But it was an interesting night. According to the neighbors, they'd caught a junkie in the outbuilding the previous week smoking up and had driven him off. Addicts, being creatures of routine, he had returned and inadvertently fired the place, nearly incinerating himself in the process. The previous homeowner, a house-painter, had apparently made the carriage house a turpentine repository, the latest owners having not gotten around to removing the wildly flammable contents in the six-months since they'd moved in to the house and begun the long haul of *renovating and renewing* it to its former (future?) grandeur. Having been the driest Spring most anyone could remember, the fire danced about in funnels and threatened to set the whole damned neighborhood ablaze. Two pines—one dead, one not—had caught in the sideyard as if pitch-soaked kindling. And there was Goodspeed standing picket: a 40 oz bottle of malt liquor in one hand, garden hose in the other. This resolute sentry: defiant, proud, ridiculous, checking the fiery offensive that the fire department soon brought under control.

The following night, a drunk tried to outrun a fleet of cruisers in pursuit, mistook a road-curve, roared down a service-drive and plowed clean through a reinforced chain-link fence into the heart of a municipal substation serving all of *Springvale*. The driver was incinerated, the *grand olde belle* having been without power going on five days. The dark unknown was closing in: an army encircling, slowly strangling and suffocating will, devotion. Goodspeed, sensing the urgency to plumb deep the dry well of resolve, fell to instinct. He put on a days' long bender....*Fight the good fight, soldier! Buck up! For freedom!*....

And that brings us to this: Goodspeed standing on the half-refinished front porch of *The Woodruff House*—his house—a length of 2x2 held as if broadsword in his right hand. He looks past a pulsating twinge in right shoulder, looking on as the young publicist-type stumbles down the front walk and across the sidewalk in removing himself from the property. Goodspeed says not a word. A squint-eye is all....

"You—are—a fucking asshole, just like everyone has said!" Goodspeed having stomped down from the turret to front door, makeshift brickbat in hand, and having clapped the audience seeker on the skull following his unsolicited "invasion," and at such a troubled moment....

"And that there was just a little love tap. Be sure to send my regards to the bastards who sent ya," Goodspeed watching on as the young chump gets in his car, rubbing his forehead and giving Goodspeed the finger as he roars off.... And like that: a snap, a crackle, a buzzing pop runs along powerlines, as electricity surges pole to pole. The sound comes off like the stitch-scratch open of a vinyl record coming to full RPM, filling him with a warm analog nostalgia. A powerful sense of purpose surges through him. He is actually smiling. It is the first time in days, weeks....

> *And though it seemed that challenging and undermining the establishment was his calling in life, he secretly longed to leave things be; let it to its own self-absorbed vice. It would inevitably do itself in, he figured. And who was he to upset the nature of things.*

Marvin Goodspeed  ~ *Within*

Knowing all about the fire at *Asa's* (having naturally been tapped by Lacy to do a write-up for *The Weekly*) and not having seen the *man / myth* since, Cyrus has been mulling over how best to gauge the emotional weather of our good Regular. An unannounced visit would seem likely to end with a head contusion, regardless of recent hospitable treatment. Cyrus glides down from Austin @ Euclid, cutting through side streets and the echoes you can swear still resonate throughout the *grand old 'hood*. The ghosted peals frame the squalls and lingering fragments of history and memory and the way folks once wanted to remember all of that, and still do want to remember all of that. It seems clear as day, out here, kicked up with every footfall, embedded in every view—the mental postcards like animated frames. *And oh, those halcyon frames!* Shining steeds high-stepping under the reins of affluence, life-beaten servants slaving away in the dim background to sustain and maintain gross *Gilded* wealth; the drawn hunch of the millworkers, the trippers and the bootleggers, the slumlords and the pimps and those of red-light intent, the blacks just wanting dignity and equity and for once, just once, to be left—the—fuck—alone, and all of the post-white-flight white artists and hippies, and those immigrants from Cuba and Vietnam and not here. And this here new blood, an amalgam of all of that: the urban pioneers and the settlers in their wake. Each era, each character, burned as time-stamps in tintype. Cyrus can see each day as fresh bait for the future, a looking glass glossing over a past giving the present all it can handle. Every view: the balustrades, the widow's peak, the porticoes of Doric order raining down the passing of eras. Some facades drum up the credo of *renovation, restoration, renewal,* gentrification and a return to some semblance of grandeur—while some stand rotting, fainting within the amnesia of things better left forgotten. You will swear that you can hear the past in conference with itself. So vivid, so proud. So pained, so ashamed....*You cannot question nature, except when you must question nature. You cannot force people to change, except when they must be forced to change....* This here is his test, Cyrus giving it his best.

Now standing before the stone stairs leading down

into *Waverly Park*, our good journalist watches as a car motors up over the hill and past him, the driver fuming and red-faced. The driver looks familiar; from the industry, maybe? Cyrus can't place him, but a certain thought draws up a smirk: "hmmmm, wonder if that dude just earned himself a little love tap?"

Another car pulls up in its wake, stops mid-avenue. Anna, glancing in rear-view, cranks down car window....

"Yo, Anna-bo. What's up?"

"Get my email?"

Cyrus, having not yet ventured into the office, had not, inquires. Anna fills him in: "Grey found it, two poems and a short story in a periodical collection, forget which; mentions her by name: Pauline Goodspeed. The back-cover blurb likened her to Kate Chopin, was published sometime in the '50s. Grey mailed it yesterday."

"Well, I'll be damned."

"Figured you'd be psyched. Check ya later, kid," Anna zooming off.

And Cyrus looks down at the paper bag in his hand containing a fifth of Evan Williams. He rethinks his destination, course corrects and heads for the office. He trips on a corner of a hexagonal stone elevated a micro-degree more than last year by the root of a grand water oak's slow steady progress. It is a progress that rings true, honest, ultimately irresistible. Cyrus moves through under the watchful eye of spindled gables, ocular fanlights. The fortunes have long since moved on (at least for the moment). Only the overindulgences having stuck around. Cyrus crests the rise that separates *Waverly Park* from *The Ashlands*...."Ya, pro'ly need to let our man digest it all. Best to let all this change settle some."

Wise choice, young son.

AND HE IS MOVING, is lighter than air as he clips along, blazing a trail up through *the field parks*. Decisive steps carve through mats of feral vines and the ghosted calls of *Gilded* dreams, steps nearing a sprint as he comes up on the sidewalk with purpose. Side streets pass. He is on a mission, is vaulting through. He is swinging his arms, whistling, giddy. For he is on his way. *It is the day*.... And having arrived, standing tall and proud atop hexagonal stone. Brown paint peels from door and window frame, the buckled siding. The neon of front window signs: *Cold Beer! Pabst Blue Ribbon! Y'all Come!* fighting the mid-day sun. He cups his hands to shield the glare, looks in through the front window. *The Asa Inman Blue Ribbon Buffet*, its blue letters gilded, in an arc. Goodspeed takes a deep breath of *freedom*. A grand re-opening, indeed. The front door opens, as it would in a dream. The bar front vigil, the devotion, a greeting like none other running down the line: *Here Comes A Regular*....

And the honking of horns slice their ticked off call-and-response through the ruptured grey of his coming-to. He sits up with a start, a breath missing its beat. Dorothy inquires silently, groggy half-open eyes, rubs a hand across his back. "I'm alright," he says without saying it, D taking him at his unspoken word, turning over, drifting off.... One could expect a fuming boil-over from our man, ready to take on the heresy out there, the bastards' demand for toil and time interrupting his longing, his pining. But there is only the hard blink of eyelids, a deep slow exhale.

He had been hanging tight with a tepid optimism of late, even establishing a weak-kneed DMZ enough to go to work. But it had not gone well. His resolve seemed to falter. As with so much these days, it was unlike what had been. His pen sat idle, pad unmarked. It had all come so naturally before, as by instinct. And now, coming up empty try after try. And it was not anger that he felt. A couple of well-placed sticks of TNT in order to detonate writer's block would not do it. A few well-engineered brawls with the crony creative industrial complex would not generate fuel enough to burn through this coal-black smog smothering output and gumption. No, this was something else. It was....was it?

"Well, I'll be god-damned. This is fear."

He gets up, puts on what he was wearing the day before, goes into the kitchen and makes coffee. He stares out the window over kitchen sink. D's back yard knoll is overrun by green and a surging seasonal optimism he cannot at that moment share. It is all he can do to make and drink coffee. He does so, pops a few aspirin, heads through dining and living rooms for the front door. D emerges behind him from the side-hall, wearily tying up a bathrobe, one eye still closed, the other half-so....

"Hey, sure you're okay?"

"Ya, up 'n at 'em, y'know?"

"It wouldn't be the end of the world."

"No?"

"There's other ways we could get by."

"What, time murder?"

"Your words on a page don't have to be the be-all 'n end-all."

"Would have to leave a lot behind; would have to let a lot go."

"Ya, you would."

"Not sure I'm ready for that, not just yet."

"If the words don't come back, I got it. We'll make do just fine, hon."

"Ya, okay. Gonna head out for a bit, clear the head," Goodspeed grinning automatically before turning and exiting. He breathes deep, rush-hour fumes on the warm thick morning air. It may even be worse than was let on, as in he hasn't written a fucking word worth saving in two weeks and has been stone-cold sober the whole damned time. He has lately thought that it all may just have run its course, the turbines of this alcohol-induced populist revolt idle, all systems down. Is such a *Victory!* ever possible, all of the duty, the devotion, the zealous conviction just a run of dumb luck? This here is a hypothesis with an inherited precedent, as it has always been for this Scots-Irish clan. But then heritage has a way of running aground of shoals oddly unexpected (odd in that it keeps happening over and over and over). The metaphorical obstacle in this instance is a future that could give a damn about old ways and how *it* has always been. For *it* (as we know by now, dear reader) is open to interpretation. What *it* means is in service to the prevailing trends of the day. And on this day, one could argue that *it* doesn't give a tinker's damn about an underground writing sensation fearing that his luck may have run out.

Goodspeed is kicking about a familiar route, having veered onto Elizabeth and then up Highland and now down Washita. He stops at Austin, a most familiar view, the zone behind his eyeballs lit by a blinding dread of all one's knowledge being distant and alien. He lights a smoke, exhales and breathes deep before turning. He strolls up to the building, if only out of lament—as if visiting an ill-friend in the hospital, the prognosis poor. There is brown paper hung from the inside over all the windows: unlit neon signs crackled grey. The blue gilt-ringed letters run out in an arc that seems flatter than it once did *(though it is the same as it ever was)*. A sign in the front-door reads: *Closed for Renovations*.... It is all he can do to sigh, taking one last smoke, exhaling, and putting out cigarette in the outdoor ashcan still dutifully on the job. He is moving on down past the row of mailboxes at the top of the alleyway when he sights the box beneath it. 2x2 feet square, heavily taped, one corner bent-in but holding. In neat black sharpie print, it reads....*To: Marvin Goodspeed, 420 Austin Avenue / From: Flour City Press, Minneapolis*

"Wait, really?"

He pulls out a set of keys (though he still feels no use for locked doors) and begins rough-slicing at the taped lid. He punctures it enough to begin ripping through, quickly pulling it open. Packing paper and more packing paper and some styro-peanuts, digging down, down to pull out one of the "total contents: 25" (according to the shipping manifest). He turns the sleek-jacketed hardcover over in his hand....

*Within  ~  A Novel by Marvin Goodspeed*

Goodspeed looks up and down the avenue. It is strangely empty, the parkway connector but a distant roaring river. He watches the lights at the intersection run through an entire cycle for no one. It is done dutifully, doing what it must.... And right then he knows it is not over, not by a long shot. And whether this all points at a simple re-up of the dumb luck that may just be juicing the entire enterprise—*or*—something more comprehensive, something more along the lines of hard work paying off, pointing towards something else.... Well, doesn't that all seem beside the point? Regardless of why, he now knows it is on. It is back on. Just when Appomattox seemed imminent, *a lifeline*. Just when the 1896 election was set to deliver its killshot, *a pulse*. But this, this here, it hints at more than just a simple resuscitation. It is not just snatching *Victory!* from the jaws of defeat, but something else entire. This points at a whole other way. This here is a future.

And like that, he is grinning again. It is more sly and more devout than it may have been just a few weeks earlier. It reveals a sense of duty. He is shaking the brand-spanking-new advance copy in his hand, an affirmative head shake. He knows what must be done. He must carry on. He must fuel *the myth* that feeds *the man*. It is on. Oh, it is back on, motherfuckers!


A BLOOD ORANGE BLOOM, dawn's graffiti a gaunt scumbled grey. This bloodshot vernacular, this leaden humidity. The fissile orb pulls itself free, liquid mercurial steps laboring up off the horizon amidst a fume spume. The rush-hour swells in volume, blooming, fuming, laced of particulate metals that crowd out oxygen. It is all an unwelcome guest, coercing its way up nostrils, prying at eyelids. A slit-eye scrutiny of this newest of days. A smear, all a blur. The trials yet to come, all-comers to be met with an anonymous resolve. *Buck up, son! For honor! For country!* Fighting as if in the fighting alone lay the glory, the *Victory!* sought.... And the vialed contradictions, lined up as they are along the rim of a deep-canyoned instinct: the contraband—the controlled-substance—fueling the high that insulates this *myth.*

Prone, his fingers work their way down thrumming temples. Its exploration uncovers a new crevice hung carved and rankled upon a mug struggling under the recent strain of many like discoveries. No worries. Resolve, commitment. "Focus, son, focus." He props himself onto elbows, hard blinks determined in their attempts to flush the view clear. The drear of sobriety authors a menacing nausea, the depth charge *thud-thud-thud* of heartbeats inside a headache otherwise singing as a wall of struck metal. It is a careless pain. He could care less.

A line of traffic jumps a green light, work-a-day responsible-ness motoring up the avenue alongside him. A blast of motor-made wind rolls over him, a styrofoam cup jumping up and over his legs. The spume, the bloom. The wet blanket of air. It already feels like it is 90°. Downtown, the towers of *progress!* standing rigid and virile in the mist, metallic blue hard-ons calling the dutiful legions unto their toil—to ruin and death. This is their aim. It is the end goal of this circus. *He knows it is so.* It is just another morning. He smiles, and we begin again....

"Man, oh' man. Well, up and at 'em." ~

# OUTRO

Much is made of even minor offenses of fictionalizing in memoirs, shading in and around facts and truths in the way of biography. And though those leveling the charge certainly have a point, if the whole point veers towards a strict journalistic interpretation of facts. But what of the fact that such authority itself rests atop a delusion, that being: memory as anything but a self-serving editorial. What are we all if not ourselves—and—*the myth of ourselves*, the person we are and the person we want to think we are? And what of the character who has so fully imbibed the *myth* piece of this equation as to blot out any reckoning with hard fast truths? A character so entirely embedded in their own *myth* as to employ it to justify, if not wholly explain away self-destruction? At what point must the products of this self-fictionalizing instinct of memory be considered a piece of the truth, if the whole-truth-and-nothing-but is to be told?

Yes, much is made of one scarlet dividing line these days: the innocent self-editorializing (as if that itself were ever possible) v. creative fudging designed to sell more books. And perhaps therein lay an ironic (albeit absurd) nugget of nuance: in that it's all in the presentation. Lying, be it innocent or not, and then denying it—well there's your stumble, compadre. Whereas lying, be it white lying or full-on fabrication, and then admitting it with a grin, pleading *nolo contendere* in the court of public opinion? Now, couldn't that just be considered creative hustling?

The long and short is that after months of digging and months more spent evaluating the dig, Cyrus Cleburne had come to the conclusion that the preeminent author of *Springvale* led a life of routine tedium peppered with moments of hermitic literary brilliance that was otherwise drowned in a dreadnought inebriation. Good luck submitting 366 pages of that.... And yet, all of the digging and the troweling and the evaluating of the digging and troweling had uncovered a facet of this dude so third-rail real that it by itself devoured any alternate take on the subject. It spun hermitic into *defiant invective-spitting color-bearer*, his dull (if entertaining) stupors run out as *sleek corvette raiders of the cause*. But the real kicker? That this forge of character, being fired by the white-hot boilers of *myth*, made it no less real—made it, somehow, seem all the more.

So, in the name of selling more books via sly-grin (a squint-eye?) subterfuge, Cyrus had approached our good Regular with what amounted to a plea deal. He had him dead-to-rights and was going to write of the *Springvale bard* whether Goodspeed blessed the effort, or expressed his displeasure via make-shift truncheon. Having put in the requisite legwork and having strop-sharpened an even more requisite objectivity, our good journalist had earned at least that. For he had come to comprehend (if not fully understand) and at least acknowledge (if not in any way understand) the *duty* that prodded this Regular to drag his hungover carcass out into the trenches each and every morning and fight his fight. That, as one fair voice had made clear to him, was *the story*. It was *his story*. Moreover, Cleburne could sense that even if this proved to be a conscious engineered program, it was so intent on transcendent *Victory!* that the hard alcoholism around which the whole thing revolved was not open to critique—

let alone intervention. And it was to this pyrrhic end that facts and truths alone came to seem irrelevant; were, in fact, for shit....

So, a few months back Cleburne had put it to our good Regular: how about pleading this one out? The proposition being this: Instead of producing one more biographical doorstop true to *the puny inadequacies* of fact, why not stand behind the creative act of a documentary true to *man* and *myth?*

"So, yer gonna change up all the names and locations, preserve the integrity of the status quo by takin' some liberties? Instead of a straight-on bio yer gonna square up some home truths with, what did ya call it? A firehose of the imagined real?"

"Trust me, the *myth* is far more interesting."

"That one of yer home truths? Not that you ain't right."

"Even got *your* name picked out: Goodspeed, Marvin."

"Marvin Goodspeed. Hmmmm."

And the Regular had thought on that for a second, scratching at the pepper-grey lining jaw-line. He peeled off a grin: resolute, taut, pulling out a smoke from a pack in front-shirt pocket. He lit it, exhaled.

"Well, I'll be damned; looks like ya got yer Gatsby."

And as you, dear reader, may have already divined from our lengthy study, one Marvin Goodspeed is just not able to pass up a good hustle, the results going something like this....


A NEW DAWN BREAKS. *The haze is fine mesh gauze...*

# ACKNOWLEDGEMENTS

To Nick Courtright, Kyle McCord, and all the fine folk at Atmosphere Press who made this a reality. To Sandra Fluck and *The Write Launch* for instilling the inspiration to give it one last shot. To Stacy Estep for incisive critiques (and our *Giant Head Summits* for the nights of awesomeness that they are). To Jim Threlkeld and Joe Peery for timely necessary suggestions when they mattered. To Floating Coats, my fellow raconteurs, my brothers in arms—*the best damned band in the land*—to us for decades of weekly musical therapy. To Charles McNair who urged me to keep at it, at it, and at it—*no matter what.* To Inman Park and Delta Place, the original spark—*where it all began.* To my family, *of course.* And to Kerri, love of my life, who believed with unwavering faith that I could, that I eventually would, pull this thing off  ~

# ABOUT ATMOSPHERE PRESS

Atmosphere Press is an independent, full-service publisher for excellent books in all genres and for all audiences. Learn more about what we do at atmospherepress.com.

We encourage you to check out some of Atmosphere's latest releases, which are available at Amazon.com and via order from your local bookstore:

*This Side of Babylon,* a novel by James Stoia
*Within the Gray,* a novel by Jenna Ashlyn
*Where No Man Pursueth,* a novel by Micheal E. Jimerson
*Here's Waldo,* a novel by Nick Olson
*Tales of Little Egypt,* a historical novel by James Gilbert
*For a Better Life,* a novel by Julia Reid Galosy
*The Hidden Life,* a novel by Robert Castle
*Big Beasts,* a novel by Patrick Scott
*Alvarado,* a novel by John W. Horton III
*Nothing to Get Nostalgic About,* a novel by Eddie Brophy
*GROW: A Jack and Lake Creek Book,* a novel by Chris S McGee
*Home is Not This Body,* a novel by Karahn Washington
*Whose Mary Kate,* a novel by Jane Leclere Doyle
*Stuck and Drunk in Shadyside,* a novel by M. Byerly
*These Things Happen,* a novel by Chris Caldwell

# ABOUT THE AUTHOR

Dave Buckhout is a writer of short and long fiction, creative non-fiction, history, and verse. Having begun with semi-automatic writings pulled from simply observing the whirling scenes and random scraps of substance to be found in this wonderful mad world of ours, Dave moved through short fiction, travelogues, historical essays / meditations, verse, verse, and more verse, before finally wrapping a full length novel. Published works of all of the above preceded *The Regular*, and non-fiction adventures—*Ghost On The Hill: My Life In The Civil War* and *Through*—will follow. Dave lives with his beautiful wife on the hip east side of Atlanta in a house filled of dogs, cats, guitars, and thousands on thousands of well read books. Stay tuned @ *davebuckhout.com*.

CPSIA information can be obtained
at www.ICGtesting.com
Printed in the USA
LVHW030126090421
683894LV00010B/242